COMMUNITY PROPERTY

IN A NUTSHELL

Second Edition

By

ROBERT L. MENNELL
St. Paul, Minnesota
and

THOMAS M. BOYKOFF
Contributing Editor
Madison, Wisconsin

WEST GROUP

Bancroft-Whitney ● Clark Boardman Callaghan
Lawyers Cooperative Publishing ● WESTLAW ● West Publishing

For Customer Assistance Call 1-800-328-4880

COPYRIGHT © 1982 By WEST PUBLISHING CO.
COPYRIGHT © 1988 By T. ELIZABETH MENNELL & THOMAS M. BOYKOFF

610 Opperman Drive
P.O. Box 64526
St. Paul, MN 55164-0526

Library of Congress Cataloging-in-Publication Data

Mennell, Robert L, 1934–
  Community property in a nutshell.

  (Nutshell series)
  Includes index.
  1. Community property—United States. I. Boykoff, Thomas M.
II. Title. III. Series.

KF526.Z9m46   1988   346.7304'2   87–31819
347.30642

ISBN 0-314-68355-0

Mennell & Boykoff—Comm.Prop. 2nd Ed. N.S.
5th Reprint — 2004

PREFACE

This book attempts to serve three constituencies: The lawyer who is unfamiliar with community property, the law student who has not had the subject in law school, and the law student who has enrolled in a course purporting to teach the subject.

For the lawyer unfamiliar with the outline of community property, the first portion of each chapter presents a broad overview. For the law student facing an examination on the subject, the detail of the law is set forth in the second part of each chapter. For those who are trying to determine the application of the law in a particular state, the third part of each chapter attempts to present the uncommon thread, i.e., how the various individual states differ.

The second edition is occasioned by the enactment by Wisconsin of its version of the Uniform Marital Property Act (UMPA). A possible fourth constituency for this book consists of the lawyer or legislator in a state considering enactment of UMPA. The overview and detail portions of each chapter provide the theory. The UMPA and Wisconsin statutory modifications are described in the last portion of each chapter.

ROBERT L. MENNELL
THOMAS M. BOYKOFF

St. Paul, Minnesota
Madison, Wisconsin
January, 1988

*

ACKNOWLEDGMENTS

Many persons have assisted in the preparation of the manuscript. At the risk of omitting some, we admit the assistance of the following:

Assistance on the first edition was rendered by Professors Harry M. Cross of the University of Washington and Max Goodman of Southwestern University School of Law and Dean W.J. Williamson of South Texas College of Law. Assistance with the second edition was rendered by Professor Paul J. Goda, S.J., of Santa Clara University. Invaluable proofreading assistance was given by Antoinette Y. Mennell and Charlotte Bunzey.

The addition of material on Wisconsin and the Uniform Marital Property Act (UMPA) was facilitated by Donald J. Dyke, John E. Knight and Michael Wilcox of Madison, Wisconsin. Professor June Miller Weisberger of the University of Wisconsin Law School provided thoughtful suggestions on Wisconsin's, UMPA's and other community property systems.

*

OUTLINE

PART IV. TERMINATION OF THE COMMUNITY

PART V. SPECIAL PROBLEMS

*

TABLE OF CASES

References are to Pages

XIX

TABLE OF CASES

TABLE OF CASES

COMMUNITY PROPERTY

IN A NUTSHELL

Second Edition

•

PART I

PRELIMINARY MATTERS

CHAPTER 1

OVERVIEW AND HISTORY

A. OVERVIEW

The community property system exists in nine states of the United States: Arizona, California, Idaho, Louisiana, Nevada, New Mexico, Texas, Washington and Wisconsin. The nine states have common patterns for property acquired by a married couple, but each state has developed its own variations.

1. Definitions (Characterization)

The term "characterization" is used in this nutshell to describe the process by which separate property is distinguished from community property. The "character" of property may be separate, community or partly each. (California has added another type of character, "quasi-community", by statute.)

The community property system is derived from the "civil law" (as opposed to "common law") system. The civil law system is at full strength in the United States only in the state of Louisiana. Else-

THE COMMUNITY PROPERTY STATES
Arizona, California, Idaho, Louisiana, Nevada, New Mexico, Texas, Washington and Wisconsin (UMPA)

where, community property is engrafted upon a common law system.

Terminology also varies from state to state. Although the more popular term of "community property" is used in this nutshell, the Texas and Wisconsin term "marital property" more accurately describes property owned by a married couple, as opposed to a larger community, such as the entire family. Similarly, "separate property" is used in this book although Wisconsin uses the term "individual property" derived from the Uniform Marital Property Act (UMPA).

A working definition of community property is as follows:

Community property is property acquired onerously by a married couple domiciled in a community property state.

This definition is so broad and so subject to exceptions that it serves only as a guide. Five of the key words—"property", "acquired", "onerously", "married" and "domiciled"—require pages of explanation. A summary of these major considerations is as follows:

●**Property:** Whether tangible or intangible, real or personal, the community property item must be one which is capable of being owned. While a certificate of stock, a bank account, a parcel of land, a real Ota or a toy Ota may be owned, the marriage itself is not community property.

●**Acquired:** Original acquisition is the key to this term. If an item is purchased, it generally takes the character of the funds which were used to purchase it. Thus a lawnmower purchased during marriage with funds acquired prior to marriage is separate property. The funds to purchase the lawnmower were acquired prior to marriage and are therefore separate property; the lawnmower retains the characterization of the funds with which it was purchased. This concept of original acquisition requires tracing the funds back to some original source such as earnings, gifts, property owned prior to marriage or property acquired during marriage while domiciled in a non-community property jurisdiction.

• **Onerously:** Onerously means through the efforts and labor, either physical or intellectual, of one or both spouses. The opposite of "onerous" is "gratuitous". Gratuitous transfers include lifetime gifts and devises, bequests and inheritances.

• **Married:** Alternatives to marriage, including the "putative" and the "meretricious" spouse, are more fully treated in Chapter 11. For the purposes of this chapter, the term "married" has its traditional or common meaning.

• **Domiciled:** Domicile (often confused with or substituted for "residence") is a conclusion of law based upon presence and intention. Further details are presented in Chapter 12.

"Separate" property is that which is not community. Generally one must be married in order to have community property, but not all property of married persons is community. If the property of a married couple is owned by only one of them, it is her or his separate property. If the property of a married couple is owned by both of them, it can be either community or some form of separate property in concurrent ownership.

2. Implications of Characterization

The major legal problems of community property systems center around two issues:

1. What is "community property"? and

2. What legal difference does it make?

Community property systems treat each item of property which either member of the couple acquires while married and domiciled in a community property state as acquired by them as equal owners of one half each. The implications of this treatment arise both during and at the end of the marriage.

Issues regarding the treatment of property during marriage commonly include the following:

- Management and control of the property,

- The rights of creditors,

- Tort liability or

- Tax implications.

The most common problems of termination of a marriage arise upon death of a spouse or divorce. Death and divorce not only prevent the further creation of community property, they also terminate the community status of accumulations.

- Death triggers the transfer of property from its owner to either heirs or will beneficiaries. Since one does not have the right to devise property belonging to another, only one half of the community property can be devised by the first spouse to die. There is no community property upon the death of the second to die except in the case of simultaneous deaths. (If you do not understand why this last statement is true, reread the last sentence of the preceding paragraph.)

•Divorce judgments make either an "equal" or an "equitable" division of property. In the "equal" division jurisdictions and in all jurisdictions before the divorce, each spouse is entitled to all of that spouse's separate property and one half of the community property.

In addition to the major problems which occur during and after the marriage, issues may arise under particular state law provisions, federal constitutional or statutory requirements or conflict of laws areas. These issues are explored in Chapter 12.

3. Rationale for the System

At ancient civil and common law, a wife not only did not have a share of her husband's earnings, her very identity was considered merged into that of her husband. When a husband died, his wife was not an "heir" under the common law primogeniture system of inheritance. The common law widow did receive dower, the right (after the husband's death) to occupy for her life one third of the realty of which the husband was seised during the marriage. Under traditional common law (i.e., before the "Married Women's Acts" of the 19th century), the husband was the owner of all property acquired during marriage and of the wife's premarital personal property. The civil law system had a similar beginning: The husband had a complete, despotic control over the property and person of the children, and the wife was sometimes treated as if she were one of his children.

Community property evolved as a series of modifications to the absolute marital rights of the husband. The first step in the process was protection of the wife's "share of the community" to which she was entitled at the dissolution of the marriage. This protection is similar to the modern concept of the "augmented estate" as embodied in the Uniform Probate Code. The modifications were subsequently rhetorically raised in dignity by statements that the wife was a co-owner. In some respects, she was more like an heir or a creditor.

The differences are symbolized by the choice of the pronoun which describes a married couple's property: Under traditional common law it was "his". After the passage of Married Women's Acts, it is generally "his" but sometimes "hers". In the community property system, it is now "theirs". The difficulty in determining whether a married couple is "he", "she", "it" or "they" is also found in the federal income tax provisions for individual taxpayers: Differing statutory answers are given to the question of whether a married couple is treated as one "individual" or two.

Community property systems recognize (and, in some cases, invent) the contribution of both spouses to the acquisitions during marriage. The theory presumes equal contribution by husband and wife to the family wealth. The presumption of equal contribution is irrebuttable. It reigns de-

spite clear evidence to the contrary, such as cases
where a spouse detracts from, rather than contributes to, wealth accumulation. There are types of
onerously acquired community property where the
onus may be slight (unearned income, windfalls) or
entirely borne by one spouse (some recoveries for
personal injuries).

The language of equality in the community property statutes preceded actual equality in many
cases. For example, it was not until 1927 that
California fully acknowledged that the interest of
the wife was present and equal. In California, the
wife's interest was said to mature only upon the
husband's death, thus making the California form
of community property acquired before 1927 very
similar to a dower interest at common law. Additionally, the management and control of community property was generally given to the husband
under all community regimes until the 1970's.

4. Types of Community Property Systems

There is no single community property system.
Rather, a number of different approaches to community property exist. Some of the major differences among the systems are as follows:

• Present, vested and equal rights of the wife in
community property, although universal in the
United States today, were not the original form of
community property. Originally, the systems
tended to give complete control of the community
to the husband during the marriage, that control

being limited only by a few provisions which protected the right of the wife to have an equal share upon the dissolution of the community. France added in the 14th century the device of offering the wife, on the dissolution of the marriage, one half of the community property on the condition that she accept a personal liability for one half of the community debts. The wife was kept out of the community until it was known whether the community was solvent or insolvent; this determination was made when the community was to be dissolved (typically by death or divorce); she could then accept or reject the community. In that system, the community rights began when the marriage ended. That community property system existed in the civil law of France and Spain while the community system was being adopted in the United States.

• Community "regime", as opposed to community "property", indicates that the system deals with both assets and liabilities. The regime approach is historically accurate and has been maintained in Louisiana. Some states, such as Washington, may be reviving the regime attitude because of new legislation and a willingness to classify debts as "community debts". The common law states have treated community property as a form of tenure, a method of holding title to assets, without regard to corresponding liabilities. California, for example, has long resisted the concept of a community debt while admitting that there are debts which are payable out of the community assets.

• Universal, ganancial and middle approaches exist in deciding which assets of the married couple will be shared under the community property system. The focus is upon what, if any, parts of the premarital property should be converted into community property by virtue of the marriage:

The universal, or Roman-Dutch, form of community property changed all premarital property into community property. This form was carried to the Dutch colonies in southern Africa, the East Indies and the West Indies. It remains today in the Netherlands.

The Spanish form of community property, called the "ganancial" system, is found today in the nine states of the United States, the Spanish-American republics of Central and South America, the Commonwealth of Puerto Rico and the Philippine Republic. The ganancial form of community property does not change the ownership of property owned prior to marriage; premarital property remains the separate property of its individual owner. Thus, marrying a millionaire who is domiciled in California or Nevada will not make one wealthier; further generous acts of the millionaire are required. The states differ as to whether income received during marriage from separate property is separate or community property, but the basic asset retains its separate character despite marriage of the owner.

Among middle approaches between including and excluding all premarital property from the community was that found in France between 1804 and 1965: The community included all immovables acquired during marriage (similar to the ganancial system) and all movables, whenever acquired (similar to the universal system). Modifications were also made for dowry and for gifts to the married couple. In 1965, France adopted a ganancial system.

B. HISTORY: ORIGINS OF COMMUNITY PROPERTY

The first written recognition of community property was in the Fuero Juzgo of Visigothic Spain in 693 A.D. The Visigoths are also credited with administering the only defeat suffered by Attila the Hun. The reader is left to draw any conclusions about links between the two events.

The Visigoths claimed a Nordic origin and had been driven across the Danube River into the Roman Empire in 376 A.D. by the Huns. In their travels first south and then west from Scandinavia, the Visigoths left a heritage of the community property system in areas which they visited directly and in lands colonized by the inhabitants of lands the Visigoths visited.

Various forms of community property systems exist today in countries of Western Europe and in their former colonies.

There have been few instances of intentional adoption of a community property system without invasion or colonization. Only the country of Scotland and some of the states of the United States have applied this form of Gothic humor. Prior to 1948, acquirers and possessors of community property had federal income, estate and gift tax advantages which did not exist for domiciliaries of separate property states. In order to gain those advantages, the states of Michigan, Nebraska, Oklahoma, Oregon and Pennsylvania and the (then) Territory of Hawaii adopted community property systems. In Pennsylvania, the community property statute was declared unconstitutional; in the other states and in Hawaii the community property system was repealed shortly after the 1948 amendments to the Internal Revenue Code eliminated the tax advantages. These 1948 amendments permitted joint income tax returns, a marital deduction for both gift and estate taxes and the gift-splitting provisions of the gift tax.

Currently, proposals for adoption of a community property system in the Uniform Marital Property Act (UMPA) form have been made in state legislatures in an effort to obtain greater equality between the marital partners. Additionally, individual state modifications of the Uniform Marriage and Divorce Act, as in Kentucky, create results similar to community property states at divorce.

C. INDIVIDUAL COMMUNITY PROPERTY STATES

1. Common and Uncommon Threads

The common threads of the community property system unravel when an examination is made of the law of any particular state. We have seen instances of what would be called local peculiarities were it not for the fact that the entire system is one of local peculiarities:

• Texas, Wisconsin and UMPA usage prefer the term "marital" to "community".

• California was slow to clarify the fact that, although the husband had management and control of the community property, the wife's interest is "present, existing and equal". The 1927 predecessor of Calif.Civ.Code § 5105 finally brought California into line with the other states but the prospective-only operation of the section created two classes of community property in California: Pre-1927 and Post-1927.

• Wisconsin created "deferred" marital (community) property to apply community property concepts to property acquired during marriage, but before the 1986 effective date of the Wisconsin community property system.

We will see a number of other instances of subdivisions of community property within the states, especially California and Wisconsin. Legislatures are reluctant to state that legislation which

changes community property interests shall operate retroactively because of constitutional and
practical problems. Thus each change in the definition of community property is likely to create a
new category of community property which is added to those which existed before.

2. Historical Differences Among the States

The history of statehood and adoption of the
community property system in each of the states
also has both common threads and individual variations:

Arizona, California, Nevada and part of New
Mexico were acquired by the United States in 1848
by the Treaty of Guadalupe Hidalgo which official-
ly terminated the Mexican-American War. The
same treaty also gave to the United States the
territory now comprising the state of Utah and
parts of Colorado and Wyoming, but the community property system was not adopted in those states.
The practical difficulty of adopting community
property in pre-statehood polygamous Utah can be
readily seen.

Arizona was originally a part of New Mexico; at
least since 1865, the community property system
was recognized by the Arizona Territory. Since
statehood, Arizona has tended to follow decisions of
the states of California and Texas, with some early
leanings towards the laws of Washington.

California has maintained the community property system by state constitutional provisions and

many legislative tinkerings. It is unique in many of its decisions and trends, but serves as the experimental workshop for the western community property states.

Idaho was originally included in the Oregon Territory and was added to the Washington Territory in two parts in 1853 and 1859. Idaho existed from 1863 until 1867 as a territory without the community property system. The community property system was added in 1867 to the Idaho Territory and has continued from that date to and through statehood in 1890 to the present.

Louisiana has the oldest and historically purest form of community property in the United States. It is also recognized as the only state with the legal traditions of the civil law system which nurtured the community property system. The present state of Louisiana bears only a slight resemblance to the vast territory which was named after Louis XIV of France. The shifting ownership of the mouth of the Mississippi River during the 17th and 18th centuries is a history in miniature of Spanish and French influence. When Napoleon terminated the alternating ownerships by selling the Louisiana Territory to the United States in 1803, the community property system had already been well established. The Custom of Paris prevailed in Louisiana until 1769; after that date the Spanish ganancial scheme has been in effect. Of all the territory acquired in that vast purchase only the land south of the 33d parallel (called by Congress

the Territory of Orleans and now the state of
Louisiana) retained the community property system. The balance of the states which were formed
from this purchased land (like the territory of East
and West Florida) did not continue the community
property system which was part of their history.

Nevada, acquired from Mexico along with California, was originally part of the Utah Territory.
Since admission as a state in 1864, Nevada has had
a state constitutional provision recognizing community property.

New Mexico, consisting partly of land from the
Republic of Texas and partly of land acquired by
the Treaty of Guadalupe Hidalgo, included the
present state of Arizona until 1863. New Mexico's
borders between Texas and California were—similar to Poland's borders between Germany and Rus-
sia—subject to change from time to time. Histori-
ans may differ as to whether Mexican community
property rules continued in an unbroken chain, but
it is clear that the community property system
predated statehood in 1912 and has existed ever
since.

Texas, an independent republic from 1836, joined
the union in 1845. Its Spanish-Mexican heritage
of community property was carried over to the
republic and the state. Part of the legal history of
that state is the low regard in which decisions of
the post-Civil War Reconstruction period courts are
held.

Washington, part of the Oregon Territory until 1853, did not have a strong French, Spanish or Mexican tradition as the other states did. Like Idaho, Washington borrowed the community property system for its territorial government from California. The system has been in force before and after statehood in 1889.

Wisconsin attained statehood in 1848 and had a common law regime through 1985. Wisconsin, effective January 1, 1986, was the first state to enact any form of the Uniform Marital Property Act (UMPA).

PART II

CHARACTERIZATION

CHAPTER 2

TRANSMUTATIONS

A. OVERVIEW

Transmutation is the trump card in the bridge game of community property. A valid transmutation prevails over all other provisions.

Except in Louisiana and Texas, the marriage partners have complete power to agree upon the characterization of their property as community or separate. A voluntary change of the character of property (which can be from separate to community or community to separate) is called a "transmutation" by lawyers because the synonym, "change", is not sophisticated enough.

The transmutation may be either bilateral (by contract) or unilateral (by gift usually, but also under certain relatively rare statutory provisions such as the "sole trader" and "unilateral statement" statutes). The gift (as well as the contract) may relate to property which is not yet in existence (such as future earnings), despite traditional property law requiring that the subject of a gift be in existence.

Federal law prohibits or restricts transmutation of federal obligations from separate property into community property; see Chapter 12.

Efforts to transmute property sometimes are effective between the spouses, but ineffective against third parties, especially creditors and tax collectors. See, for example, Lucas v. Earl, 281 U.S. 111, 50 S.Ct. 241, 74 L.Ed. 731 (1930) in which a transmutation agreement was valid between the spouses under state law but ineffective to shift the federal income tax burden.

B. TYPES OF TRANSMUTATIONS

1. Agreements Between the Spouses

The community property system provides a framework which all married couples are deemed to accept unless they manifest an intention to change it. Generally, the community property system is viewed as being voluntary rather than mandatory. Therefore the presumption of community is subject to contrary agreement by the spouses.

Although spouses could agree to maintain exactly the same character of property as would have existed without the agreement, usually the contract between the spouses concerning their property assumes importance because it changes the character of the property. Thus, the parties can agree either that property owned prior to marriage (or property received gratuitously) will be community rather than separate or that property acquired onerously during marriage will be separate property of one or both spouses instead of the community property of both. Texas and Louisiana do not permit all types of transmutations. Separation agreements generally transmute the community property into the separate property of one or both spouses.

Generally legal and equitable rules for the validity and construction of contracts apply to contracts concerning marital property. Contract law issues which commonly appear in connection with marital agreements include the following:

a. Formalities required,

b. Consideration,

c. Undue influence, and

d. Public policy.

a. Formalities Required: All of the community property states permit premarital agreements; the authorizing statutes generally impose requirements as to the formality of the contracts. During the marriage, the parties are still able to contract with one another concerning marital property; in Louisiana the contract must be a "matrimonial agreement" in order to alter the rules of the regime.

Statutes authorizing spousal marital or premarital agreements usually require "a writing signed by both spouses" as in Wisconsin. Many statutes impose the additional restriction that the writing be "acknowledged and recorded". This additional restriction, while providing excellent evidence of the agreement, does so at a cost of invalidating many otherwise valid, nonfraudulent mutual agreements. The additional formalities of acknowledgement and recording are seldom accomplished without the advice of counsel.

The jurisdictions vary greatly as to whether the statute authorizing property agreements which are "in writing, acknowledged and recorded" is exclusive. Should other, less formal, agreements also be permitted? The extreme example is an agreement which is not reduced to writing which purports to change the separate property realty of the wife to the community property of both. California apparently would validate a pre-1985 agreement, having more trouble with the fact that it is the wife's property being transmuted than with the fact that realty is involved. On the other hand, New Mexico, Washington and Wisconsin (and UMPA) would not give effect to the oral agreement, even if it involved only separate property personalty of the husband being converted into community property.

b. **Consideration:** Consideration is necessary to support a contract, but marriage or the promise to marry is generally considered sufficient to support a premarital contract. The acceptance of marriage or the promise of marriage as consideration is weakened or eliminated when the marriage was already promised or performed. In a community property state, the reciprocal waiving of community property rights by both spouses gives the appearance of reciprocal consideration. Wisconsin (and UMPA) do not require consideration for marital agreements.

Often only one member of the married couple will benefit from an agreement that future earnings will not be community property. For example, if Husband and Wife agree that all future earnings will be separate but only Husband receives compensation for labor performed, did Wife receive consideration for her agreement that his earnings would be his separate, rather than their community, property? The question is whether the appearance, but not actuality, of consideration is sufficient.

c. **Undue Influence:** A confidential relationship is said to exist between husband and wife by reason of the intimacy and the need for trust. Often courts will find that this confidential relationship arises prior to the marriage. This confidential relationship requires a high degree of fairness and good faith.

Premarital agreements are generally validated if they either were arrived at after a full disclosure or were "fair" at the time when made (which is determined by the court on a retroactive basis).

Agreements made during a marriage are often subjected to fewer formalities but greater scrutiny because of the confidential relationship between husband and wife. Additionally, when the rights of third party creditors are involved, the possibility of collusion between the spouses suggests that their agreements be examined closely.

d. Public Policy: The marital contract executed in contemplation of divorce may offend public policy for any one or more of the following reasons: 1) attempting to eliminate support obligations of one or both of the parties, 2) attempting to oust the court of jurisdiction over a vital state interest or 3) facilitating divorce.

Divorce judgments deal with both property (division of existing and future property, support obligations for spouse and children) and person (termination of the marriage, restoration of birth name, custody of the children). Only the property aspects of division of existing and future property appear to be a proper subject for a separation agreement. Agreements which attempt to eliminate or limit the support obligation without judicial supervision are frequently held to be violative of public policy. Less frequent in modern times is the rejection of a premarital agreement because it contemplated (i.e., facilitated) a divorce.

2. Gifts Between Spouses

Transmutations can also be effected without consideration. One spouse makes a gift to the other. Different rules are involved when the character of the donated and recipient property varies:

A gift *from* the *separate* property of one spouse *to* the *separate* property of the other is possible in all community property states.

A gift could be made *from* the *separate* property of one spouse *into community* property in most community property states. The conceptual difficulty is that the property is received gratuitously (rather than onerously) by the recipient spouse. Conceptually, the transmutation is accomplished by considering the "acceptance of the gift" to be the acceptance of an offer to contract to change the character of the property. (This rationale also supports the community property character of wedding gifts received by the spouses despite the gratuitous—and possibly premarital—receipt.)

The concept of a gift *from* the *community to* the *separate* property of one of the spouses is linked with the "management and control" concept, which is more fully explained in Chapter 7. Until the 1970's, management and control of the community property was vested in the husband (with a few statutory exceptions for wife-generated income). Under that system, if the husband transferred community property to the wife alone (or, in some cases, when she acquired it by a written document of title naming her alone) the property was (or was presumed to be) the wife's separate property. During the 1970's a trend arose in which the equal status of the wife as owner was made even more equal by vesting equal (or separate) management and control in her. The change in management and control was made by statute; the presumption of a gift by the manager-husband to the nonmanager-wife was judicially created.

The interaction of the statutory change and the judicial rule has not yet been fully perfected. Should the presumption of gift be maintained? Can it be maintained constitutionally on a sexual basis? Is the individual agreement of the various married couples as to the management and control to be the new controlling factor?

C. INDIVIDUAL STATES

CALIFORNIA

California, historically very liberal in permitting transmutations, tightened its requirements by recent legislation.

Numerous California cases permitted oral (as well as written) transmutations of character of property. The nonretroactive provisions of Calif.Civ.Code §§ 5110.710 through 5110.740 require a writing signed by the spouse whose interest is adversely affected in order to have a transmutation.

California enacted the Uniform Premarital Agreement Act as Calif.Civ.Code §§ 5200 through 5317. Those provisions govern both premarital and marital agreements. Additionally, Calif.Prob.Code §§ 140 through 147 govern contractual arrangements relating to rights at death.

IDAHO

Idaho spouses may agree at any time to transmute separate property to community and vice versa, Suchan v. Suchan, 106 Idaho 654, 682 P.2d 607 (1984).

LOUISIANA

La.Stat.Ann.—Civ.Code art. 2338 specifically provides that "property donated to the spouses jointly" is community property.

Louisiana restricted dealings between husband and wife except in very limited circumstances until recently. At one time, gifts between spouses were prohibited by statute. A restriction on contracts between spouses was repealed in 1978. Modification of the regime is now permitted only by a "marriage agreement" which usually requires court authorization. Thus, much of the law of postmarital contracts in Louisiana is yet to be developed. See La.Stat.Ann.—Civ.Code art. 2325, 2326 and 2343.

NEVADA

Nev.Rev.Stat. 123.220 expressly permits an "agreement in writing between the spouses, which is effective only as between them" to change the character of property.

NEW MEXICO

New Mexico permits transmutations of the character of property, but has different tests as to the quantum of proof required to demonstrate the transmutation. See Chapter 5 at pages 126 to 127.

TEXAS

Texas has been the slowest of the community property states to allow the spouse to transmute separate property into community property and vice versa. Amendments to the Texas Constitution in 1948 and 1980, were necessary to reach the present permissiveness. Prior to those amendments, the Texas Supreme Court in Kellett v. Trice, 95 Tex. 160, 66 S.W. 51 (1902) held that there could not be a gift into community property because "the law declares that property so acquired shall be the separate property of the donee". Texas amended its constitution in 1948 to permit partition or exchange of community to separate property. The reverse situation, transmutation of separate into community is not permitted. The 1980 amendment to the Texas Constitution Article XVI, § 15, permits the spouses to agree that future income from separate property (but not the property itself or past income) received during marriage shall be separate (rather than community as would otherwise be the rule in Texas).

The Texas constitutional definition of separate property is usually considered to be exclusive. One application of that approach is that a transmutation by gift from separate property into community property is considered impossible because the constitution provides that all property received after marriage by gift is separate property of that spouse.

In Texas, separation agreements are of no effect until approved by the divorce court. In the other community property states, transmutation by separation agreement may occur without court approval.

WASHINGTON

Washington occupies a "middle" position concerning transmutation of the character of marital property: It permits such transmutations of realty or personalty, but requires formalities greater than an oral agreement as to realty. Change from separate to community is more likely to be recognized without clear proof than the reverse.

WISCONSIN (and UMPA)

Wisconsin follows UMPA in providing almost unlimited contractual freedom for persons who want to adopt, amend or avoid the marital property rules. Among the methods of transmutation (called classification or reclassification in Wisconsin and UMPA) are gifts, bilateral written marital property agreements and written consents regarding life insurance premiums and proceeds.

Two distinctive Wisconsin provisions exist:

(1) A spouse may prevent unearned income from his or her nonmarital property from becoming community (marital) property by a unilateral statement. The provisions apply prospectively only.

(2) A transition rule, effective only in 1986, permitted married persons to utilize a statutory individual property classification agreement to classify pre-1987 property as individual property of either husband or wife. The agreement is treated as a marital property agreement as to third parties and does not affect the rights of the spouses at death or divorce.

CHAPTER 3

SEPARATE PROPERTY

A. OVERVIEW: WHEN AND HOW ACQUIRED

1. Emphasis Upon "Acquired" in Theories

"Acquired" has a precise meaning in both the classic civil law definition and in the statutory formula definition of community property. In either usage, it is necessary to be able to identify the act which is the acquisition. Although both use the term "acquired", they differ in the usage as follows:

• The statutory forms of characterizing property as community or separate focus upon *when* the property was acquired. The types of separate property are specifically enumerated; all other property acquired by a couple domiciled in a community property state during marriage is community.

• Classic civil law definitions of community focus upon *how* property was acquired during marriage; it was either "onerous" or "gratuitous". ("Lucrative" is commonly substituted for "gratuitous".)

The "when" and "how" analysis is only a rough guide for distinguishing separate from community property. It is capable of manipulation. For exam-

ple, a major split exists among community property states as to the community or separate character of rents, issues and profits of separate property
which occur during marriage. An emphasis upon
the "when" acquired may either tend toward community by stressing that the income occurred "during marriage" or may tend toward separate by
stressing that the acquisition date of the income
relates back to the premarital acquisition date of
the property. An emphasis upon the "how" acquired could result in the property being characterized either as community because not acquired
gratuitously or separate because acquired onerously, i.e., in exchange for the use of separate
property. The latter theory recognizes that rent is
a sale of the property for a period of time and that
interest is merely the rental paid for the use of
money for a period of time.

2. When: Before Marriage

An inherent element of the Spanish "ganancial"
system of community property is that property
owned prior to the time of the marriage is the
separate property of the owner. Although the
Roman-Dutch system would convert such property
into community property, premarital property remains separate property in the United States.

In all of the community property states, statutes
(and, in some cases, state constitutional provisions)
specifically dictate that property acquired prior to
marriage is, and therefore remains, separate prop-

erty of the person acquiring it. The statutes are
phrased in absolute terms ("Property owned before
marriage *is* separate property."), but interpreted as
being presumptions.

Generally, premarital property will remain separate property of the person owning it before marriage. The two most common exceptions are transmutation and commingling:

• Transmutation of premarital property occurs
when its owner gives it to the other spouse or to
the community or when the spouses agree to
change the character.

• Commingling of separate property by its owner
with community property results in community
property if the separate element cannot be identified by tracing.

3. When: During Separation and After Di-
vorce

Although there is no statutory authority for the
proposition, it is universally agreed that community property is not created after the formal termination (i.e., by divorce) of a marriage.

But, what of marriages which have terminated
in fact, but not in law? Divorce and separate
maintenance decrees terminate the marital relationship in law; yet, many couples no longer consider themselves to be a "couple" before or without
going through the legal formalities.

In addition to formal separations, there are separations in fact, some of which will be deemed to

prevent the creation of any further community property. Property acquired by a married woman (but not a married man) while "separate and apart" from her husband was separate property of the wife in six community property states at one time. It has always been community property in Louisiana and Texas, but is under the sole management and control of the earning spouse in Texas. Attempts to equalize the rights of husbands and wives resulted in statutory changes so that today only California and Washington retain valid statutory provisions that the earnings of either spouse while they are living separate and apart are separate property. The other states and UMPA do not recognize this exception to the general rule that all earned income of married persons is community property.

4. How: Gratuitously

Property which is received gratuitously by either or both of the spouses, whether before, during or after the marriage, is the separate property of the spouse receiving it. Louisiana modifies this rule as to gifts to both spouses.

Gratuitous receipts are either by gift from a living person (including the other spouse) or by will or intestacy from a dead person.

Community property jurisdictions have generally declined to follow the rigid property law definition of a gift as being totally without consideration and a sale as being for any consideration. A transaction can be partly a sale (in which it generally takes the character of the property for which it was exchanged) and partly a gift (thereby creating separate property).

Community property states examine not only the nature and amount of the consideration in relation to the value of the property acquired, they also consider the relationships of the parties involved. A purchase for less than full market value may be a bargain between strangers, but partly a gift when the parties are related by blood. "Business" gifts, i.e., gifts received in a business context, often are treated as earned income. In this regard, some analogies are possible to federal income tax cases such as Commissioner v. Duberstein, 363 U.S. 278, 80 S.Ct. 1190, 4 L.Ed.2d 1218 (1960) which treated the "business" gift as onerous rather than gratuitous.

Inter-spousal gifts are generally treated in the same manner as if the gift were from a third party.

Wedding gifts to the married couple are often received prior to the marriage and are gratuitous receipts in any case. It is possible to hold that wedding gifts are community property by finding or inferring a transmutation agreement between the spouses. In Louisiana, a gift to a couple who intend to marry can be treated as community property upon the marriage of the couple, even though the present is received gratuitously and before the wedding ceremony. Additionally, Louisiana specifically provides that a gift made to both spouses is community property rather than the separate property of each. In Texas, gifts (including wedding gifts) are declared to be separate property by constitutional provision; therefore, Texas law does not permit transmutation of such gifts into community property. Wisconsin (and UMPA) provide that a gift to both spouses after the marriage ceremony becomes marital (community) property unless the donor expresses a contrary intent.

5. How: Rents, Issues and Profits (Fruits)

The methods of acquiring property have been divided into onerous and gratuitous. Onerous acquisition has two major producers of new wealth: labor and capital. Earnings from labor of the spouses during the marriage are almost always community property, but the community property states have a clear division concerning the character of the income from separate property capital during marriage. These earnings are commonly known as the "rents, issues and profits". The rents, issues and profits derived during the marriage from separate property are generally considered to be community property in Idaho, Louisiana, Texas and Wisconsin. In the other five community property states, the rents, issues and profits of separate property are separate property.

The problems which arise when separate wealth and community labor are commingled in the same asset are dealt with in Chapter 6.

**CHARACTER OF RENTS, ISSUES AND PROFITS RECEIVED
DURING MARRIAGE FROM SEPARATE PROPERTY**

Separate: Arizona, California, Nevada,
New Mexico and Washington

Community: Idaho, Louisiana, Texas
and Wisconsin (UMPA)

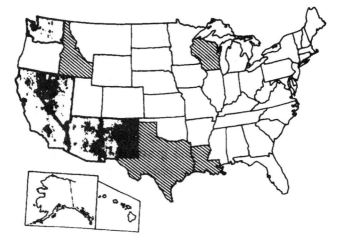

6. How: Personal Injury Recoveries

Ordinarily, the distinction between separate and community property is relevant for the purpose of determining who is entitled to the property at the dissolution of the marriage by divorce or death. The character of personal injury recoveries, however, is relevant for litigation issues such as the proper party to initiate the lawsuit, inter-spousal immunity, and the community property defense (a form of imputed negligence which is interwoven with contributory and comparative negligence).

The community property states have had difficulty in characterizing recoveries for personal injuries. Although such recoveries seemed to fit within the general presumption that property acquired during marriage is community, a trend developed in the opposite direction. Today no state continues to classify all such recoveries as community property.

Louisiana by statute and Nevada by judicial decision led the way in declaring that at least part of the personal injury recovery was separate property. Initially, the rule was applied for wives only; Louisiana in 1980 became the last community property state to apply the rule to both husband and wife. Most community property states characterize part of the recovery as community and part as separate property of the injured spouse.

When a personal injury recovery is characterized partly as community and partly as separate, the division is made on the basis of the nature of the interest for which the compensation is paid:

• Compensation for **future earnings** during the marriage is community.

• Reimbursement for actual **medical expenses** (which are normally paid from the community) is community.

• Payment for **pain and suffering,** however, is generally regarded as a separate asset of the injured spouse.

• Payments for **loss of body parts** (which are separate property because received prior to marriage as a birthday gift from one's parents) are separate property.

7. Historic and Unique Separate Property

Because of constitutional problems, most statutory changes in the character of property operate prospectively only. Thus, in each state historic forms of separate and community property exist. Indeed, each change by statute (and many of the decisional changes) creates another class of historic property which maintains its now-outdated character. On the other hand, statutes which create presumptions for the proof of community or separate property character appear to be applied retroactively with few constitutional objections.

Historic forms of separate property include the variations of earnings of one or the other of the spouses when they were living separately from each other and personal injury recoveries, among others.

Conflict of laws and enactment provisions also create special categories. Separate property often exists when acquired by a married couple domiciled in a non-community property state and sometimes when domiciled in another community property state. Wisconsin places property acquired prior to adoption of the community property system in an entirely different category called either "predetermination date" or "unclassified" property.

Under the supremacy clause of the federal constitution, the federal government can declare the separate property nature of a grant to married persons domiciled in a community property state. See Chapter 12.

The greatest category of separate property is one which is ignored by statutory schemes (except in Louisiana and Wisconsin), yet is completely recognized by decisions: Property received in exchange for separate property is also separate property (unless the spouses agree otherwise).

Accessions and accretions to separate property are also separate property, even in the four states (Idaho, Louisiana, Texas and Wisconsin) which deem the income from separate property to be community property when acquired during marriage.

B. DETAIL

1. Acquisition

The precise term, "acquired", is used here to describe the *original* acquisition, as opposed to an exchange. We are concerned here with property at its wellspring, the point where it becomes property. Examples include salaries for labor exerted and earnings produced by writings, inventions or artistic endeavors.

If property is received in exchange for other property, it generally takes the character of the property for which it was exchanged. If property is the product ("rents, issues or profits") of other property, it will take the character of the property from which it is derived, although Idaho, Louisiana, Texas and Wisconsin (UMPA) declare the rents, issues and profits received during marriage from separate property to be community property.

The acquisition of property is usually the net effect of a series of acts over a period of time. For example, an inventor may have an idea, research existing inventions, work upon and perfect the invention, seek a lawyer and apply for and receive a patent. Clearly the patent is property, but was there a property interest prior to the formal granting of the patent? If so, when is the property "acquired" ?

By a legal fiction, all of the various acts and ceremonies necessary to complete a purchase, gift, conveyance or title are generally deemed to be taken together as of the time of some substantial part. It is usually the earliest significant act which is deemed to be the substantial part. The later acts are said to "relate back" to the earlier acquisition. Thus, the task often is to determine what is the substantial part which will be the flagship for the fleet of acts which make up the "acquisition".

In the case of the inventor, it is probable that the time of acquisition will precede the grant of, and even the application for, the patent. Somewhere around the time that a working model is made appears to be the most likely time for the "acquisition". We then focus upon the marital status of the inventor at the time of the significant act which is determined to be the substantial part in order to determine whether the invention is separate or community property.

Recall that we are dealing with original acquisition (rather than exchanges) at this point and that we are further examining only onerous title because gratuitous title, whenever acquired, is separate property (except a gift in Louisiana or Wisconsin to both husband and wife).

Among the ways that property could be acquired onerously are labor and industry (whether for another or self-employed), theft, discovery, invention and finding, land grants, adverse possession and prescription, occupancy of unowned goods, recoveries for causes of action and strike and governmental benefits.

The various approaches taken by community property jurisdictions under the "Inception of Title" theory are described more fully in Chapter 6.

2. During Separation and After Divorce

The existence of a valid marriage is required for the creation and continuation of community property. At divorce the existing community is usually divided ("equitably" or "equally") by the divorce court. Any portion not so divided is generally deemed to be held by the former spouses as tenants in common rather than as community property.

Divorces generally pose no problem except when there is a delay in the granting of the decree of the divorce. The individual statutory schemes for divorce generally dictate whether the division of the community is made at the time of the filing of the initiating or concluding divorce papers (i.e., the bill/petition on the one hand or the decree of divorce on the other) or some other time (e.g., upon the expiration of an "interlocutory" or decree nisi period).

The statutory scheme for divorce within a state usually includes an alternative form of ending the marital relationship without ending the marriage itself. This divorce-substitute (usually called a legal separation) prevents the remarriage of either party.

Earnings while living separate and apart: At one time, five of the community property states had statutory provisions which provided that the earnings of a "wife living separate and apart" from her husband were her separate property. A corresponding provision did not exist for the husband. Initially judicial inquiries sought a definition of what was "separate and apart" and then tried to integrate the provision with the concepts of the husband's management and control of the community property and the "fault" divorce (i.e., that divorce was the result of a tort-like fault of one of the parties rather than a mutual problem). Arizona did not have such a statute, but reached similar results by case law.

During the 1970's as equality between the sexes became a more articulated goal, all five of the statutes were changed in one way or another. Four were changed by the legislature: California and Washington changed the "wife" to "either spouse", thus retaining this category of separate property. Louisiana and Nevada eliminated the statutory provision, thus making property acquired by either spouse while living separate into community property. Idaho's statute (which stated that the earnings of the wife while living separate were separate property) was declared unconstitutional as a denial of the equal protection of the laws as guaranteed in the 14th Amendment of the Constitution of the United States because the statute created an unconstitutional distinction upon the division of marital property upon divorce. There has been little case law as to the retroactive effect of the statutory changes, but issues remain as to whether it was unconstitutional to declare the wife's earnings while living separate to be separate property and whether it is now unconstitutional to make such amounts earned before the modification of the statute into community property.

A related issue concerning a married couple who are separated in fact, but not in law, is the right to management and control of the community (and sometimes certain types of the separate property such as the homestead declared out of separate property). In Texas, the statutes and decisional law (which interpret the constitutional definition of separate property) do not reach the characterization issue of whether the property was separate instead of community because of the separation of the parties, but instead have concerned themselves more with the management and control of the property when the parties were living separate.

3. Rents, Issues and Profits (Usufruct)

Under the Spanish law approach to community property, *all* rents, issues and profits accrued during the marriage were community property. Thus, although the ganancial system of community property did not convert premarital property into community property, the income from that property did fall into the community.

An early California case started a contrary trend which is now the law in all community property states except for Idaho, Louisiana, Texas and Wisconsin. In George v. Ransom, 15 Cal. 322 (1860), the California Supreme Court interpreted a provision of the California Constitution that all property owned by the wife prior to marriage shall be her separate property, as requiring that the rents, issues and profits of that property also be her separate property. California then equalized the situation by providing by statute that the rents, issues and profits of the *husband's* separate property would be his separate property. Other states followed the California lead in interpretation and application of the constitutional provisions. The five states which follow the "California" or "American" rule as to the separate property character of the rents, issues and profits of separate property have enacted statutes expressly so providing. The New Mexico statute uses the broader terminology that "property includes rents, issues and profits" while Arizona, California, Nevada and Washington provide in their statutes that the rents, issues and profits of separate property are separate property.

The California Supreme Court in *George v. Ransom* is generally considered to have misapplied common law principles of property ownership to a civil law entity. The Texas court, construing an identical clause in the Texas Constitution in Arnold v. Leonard, 114 Tex. 535, 273 S.W. 799 (1925), reached an exactly opposite conclusion: The Texas legislature was constitutionally prohibited from making the rents, issues and profits earned during marriage by the wife's separate property into separate property. Regardless of the historically inaccurate basis of the California rule, it is so embodied into the community property systems of the five states that it is not likely to be changed.

As a matter of first instance, the doctrinal choice for characterization of the rents, issues and profits of separate property earned during marriage seems to be the civil law system used by Idaho, Louisiana, Texas and Wisconsin. In the states which adopted

community property systems for tax advantages
prior to 1948 (and then eliminated the systems), all
provided that the rents, issues and profits of separate property during marriage were community.
Of course, this choice produced the best income tax
results by dividing the income between two taxpayers.

The doctrinal disagreement concerning the character of rents, issues and profits of separate property earned during the marriage deals only with that
certain area. The jurisdictions are in agreement
as to the character of the following rents, issues
and profits:

1. Rents, issues and profits from separate property earned prior to marriage or after divorce are
separate property in all jurisdictions. Thus the
doctrinal dispute concerns only the amounts
earned during the marriage.

2. Rents, issues and profits from community
property are community property. Thus, the doctrinal dispute concerns only the amounts earned
from separate property during marriage.

While the state-by-state division is clear as to the
separate or community nature of the marital income of separate property, it is not always clear
what constitutes "rents, issues and profits".

• Rental and interest for use of property or money and other items which are renewable, recurrent
and non-consuming are definitely classified as
"rents, issues and profits".

• Community property labor, when added to separate property capital, produces profits which are difficult to classify in the five "separate property" states; these items include increase in livestock, profits from supervised investments and cultivated crops. Generally, these have been held to be separate property but apportionment or reimbursement is required in some cases for the community contributions. Wisconsin (UMPA) has codified a special rule on "active" participation: If one spouse applies substantial labor, effort, inventiveness, physical or intellectual skill, creativity or managerial activity to either spouse's non-community property, a portion of that property becomes community property if reasonable compensation is not received and substantial appreciation of the property results from the application.

• Depreciating or depleting items produce receipts which are often, but not always, classified as being rents, issues or profits. Among these items are timber, coal, stone and mineral extraction. Three of the major oil and gas producing states, California, Louisiana and Texas, are community property states.

• Complete consumption of the item which produced receipts, such as a legal or equitable life estate or an annuity, poses problems in the states which follow the civil law rule that rents, issues and profits realized from separate property during marriage are community property. If such receipts are deemed to be rents, issues or profits, a total conversion of separate property into community property could result. Conversely, if those receipts were not characterized as being similar to rents, issues and profits, there would be no allocation to the community of the income produced by holding wealth for a period of time and the civil law rule would be circumvented. While a proportionate allocation between separate and community is possible, it is common in the civil law states to treat the receipts of such assets as being similar to a liquidating dividend from a corporation, i.e., as a receipt of capital as opposed to a rent, issue or profit.

Community property states generally decline to apply many common accounting and economic concepts of income. Thus, adjustments are seldom made for depletion, depreciation or the diminished purchasing power of the dollar.

Dividing rents, issues and profits from other property raises problems in all jurisdictions:

• In Idaho, Louisiana, Texas and Wisconsin, the dividing line is between rents, issues and profits (which are community in most instances in those states) on the one hand and "natural increases" in property on the other hand. Increase in the size, bulk or value is not a distinct interest and therefore retains the separate property character of the original property. Increases in value due to market conditions or increases in dollar amount due to inflation should not change the character of property. Accessions and accretions normally have the same character as the original property.

• In the other five states which follow the "California" or "American" rule that the rents, issues and profits of separate property are separate property, the dividing line is between the separate rents, issues and profits on the one hand and the community increase in value due to community property labor (as opposed to capital) on the other hand. The commingling of separate premarital property (typically a business) and community labor is more fully explored in Chapter 6.

4. Personal Injury Recoveries

a. **Litigation Issues:** Litigation issues which arose in connection with the determination of the character of personal injury recoveries included the following:

(i) **Proper party to bring the action:** The husband or wife to whom separate property belongs is the proper party to maintain an action at law concerning that asset. Prior to the changes made in management and control in the 1970's, the husband was the proper party to bring most actions concerning community property. The revision of management and control provisions, explained more fully in Chapter 7, requires reconsideration of the necessary party issue. When a jurisdiction recognizes that some of the elements of the recovery are community (and that portion of the community is under either joint management and control or the management and control of the non-injured spouse) and other elements of the recovery are separate, it is possible that both spouses will be necessary parties to an action. Separate lawsuits are seldom, if ever, permitted by the pleading rules of the jurisdiction.

(ii) **Interspousal immunity:** This ancient doctrine which forbade certain (or all) types of law suits between the members of a marriage was justified on the basis of the hoary "unity of husband and wife", public policy of preserving peace and tranquility in the home, supposed adequacy of criminal and divorce law, fear of a flood of trivial matrimonial disputes and fear of collusion and fraud of insurers. The trend has been to discount all of these fears and abolish the doctrine, as was done in Washington by Freehe v. Freehe, 81 Wash.2d 183, 500 P.2d 771 (1972) and has been more recently done in Nevada and New Mexico. In Wisconsin (and under UMPA), interspousal immunity is explicitly eliminated in several situations. To allow spouses to protect their vested property rights in marital property, several new actions between spouses are expressly permitted. These new actions include an action for damages for breach of the mutual duty of good faith, for an accounting of the property and obligations of the spouses and for adding one spouse's name to the title of certain marital property. Often the abolition of interspousal immunity is the first step in

declaring the recovery of the injured spouse to be
his or her separate property.

(iii) **The community property defense:** A variation of the theme of imputed negligence is the
"community property defense" in a personal injury
action. It is a defense (as opposed to a reduction of
damages) in jurisdictions which recognize the doctrine of contributory (as opposed to comparative)
negligence. Thus, if the wife is injured in an
accident in which the husband is contributorily
negligent, a recovery would be denied to the community on the basis that the husband would otherwise benefit from his own wrong.

In the case of unmarried persons of the opposite
sex who are living together, there is no community
property and thus no community property defense.
Putative marriages sometimes produce community
property or community property analogies; therefore, they could also produce an analogy to the
community property defense. Thus an ironic twist
is presented: The more formal the marriage, the
more the community property defense applies. The
couple living together without benefit of clergy
avoids the defense to which a putatively married
couple is perhaps subject and to which a validly
married couple is subject.

It is possible that these practical problems of
litigation were more responsible for the trend toward characterization of personal injury recoveries
as separate property than was a conceptual recognition of the non-community character of such

recoveries. In the typical automobile accident case, the defense was invoked by and for the benefit of a casualty insurance company to avoid liability, rather than being invoked by and for a spouse personally.

b. Conceptual Support: Commentators have been remarkably uniform in suggesting that at least part of a recovery during marriage for personal injuries should be the separate property of the injured spouse. Emphasis is placed by various writers on at least three bases:

(i) **Not property:** A cause of action for personal injury was not an assignable property right at common law. This historical explanation is not satisfactory because such rights are now assignable. The explanation sometimes indulges in circuity by saying that the cause of action is not "property" because the cause of action is not assignable.

(ii) **Onerous-gratuitous distinction:** Emphasis upon the onerous or gratuitous nature of the acquisition of the cause of action can be combined with a characterization technique by which all property received during marriage is characterized as community unless it was received gratuitously. Under this logical progression, the cause of action and all recoveries received are community property. However, the opposite technique is equally available (though applied less frequently): All that is acquired onerously during the marriage is community property; since the personal injury recovery was not the product of the work, efforts or labor of the

spouses (or their capital), it is not acquired onerously. Therefore, the personal injury recovery is
separate property. The problem with this analysis
is that "onerous" and "gratuitous", although oppo-
sites, are not truly all-encompassing. An intermediate ground exists for certain types of rights such
as personal injury recoveries. Not all acquisitions
fit the "acquired during marriage, but not gratuitous" mold. For example, property received during marriage in exchange for separate property is
usually characterized as separate. Other acquisitions which are difficult to characterize include
welfare payments, disability payments and worker's compensation.

(iii) **Exchange for private right:** This begs the
question of whether the right to personal health
and wholeness is truly separate property. Disability payments by an employer and worker's compensation are often classified as being derived from
the employment (which sounds in community) even
though measured by the type of injury (which is
said to be personal) and is designed to replace
future loss of income (which could be community
or separate depending upon the continuance of the
marital relationship).

Scholars have reasoned that the body which the
injured spouse brought into the marriage was peculiarly his or her own and that if any property was
involved in a personal injury to a spouse, it was
peculiarly his or hers. The reasoning is that the
recovery is a replacement, in so far as practicable,

and not the "acquisition" of an asset by the community estate. This approach avoids analysis of the fact that the "right" for which the recovery is exchanged was not a separable and assignable property interest.

Although the position urged by the commentators has been gradually adopted, it does not acknowledge the theory that pain and suffering could be considered to be a form of labor by the injured party for the benefit of the community. The mental and physical wear and tear on the human body is an incident of labor which produces community property. If a married person sold (replaceable) blood, it appears that the price received would be community. Should payment for spilled blood have a different character?

One problem with the system of characterizing the personal injury recovery by the nature of the right which has been injured is that there is no certainty that the jury which allocates to various elements the total recovery is being accurate in the allocation. For example, juries which are aware that a plaintiff's fee for his lawyer will not be paid by direct court award might increase the amount of the recovery for "pain and suffering" (a separate property item) in order to reimburse amounts paid from the community to lawyers.

Apportionment problems arise in connection with the expenses and fees paid to attorneys in order to collect amounts for personal injuries. If the attorney's fee is deducted from the recovery, should it be allocated to one item or borne proportionately by all items? If the attorney's fee is deducted proportionately from a recovery in which the jury increased the "pain and suffering" portion in contemplation of the fee, the medical expense reimbursement to the community will not recover 100 cents on each dollar which the community paid while the separate property will receive slightly larger payments for pain and suffering.

Regardless of the conceptual support for such a decision, personal injury recoveries can constitutionally be declared by statute to be separate property, in whole or in part.

c. **Elements of a Personal Injury Recovery:** Most jurisdictions have not mentioned the fees and expenses of attorneys, but have viewed a recovery for personal injury as containing the following elements:

•Compensation for future earnings during the marriage are deemed to be community. Divorce could make a portion of the future earnings postmarital and therefore separate. The courts have not been uniform in either considering the possibility of a divorce or allocating a portion to earnings while married and the balance to earnings after divorce.

•Reimbursement for medical expenses is often given to the community on the premise that the medical expenses have been paid from community property. The better rule appears to require an examination of the character of the funds actually used to pay the medical expenses and to direct that the recovery shall be of that character to the extent necessary to effect a complete reimbursement. The jurisdictions vary in presumptions as to the character of funds used to pay medical expenses. What presumption should apply when the expenses have not yet been paid?

•Compensation for pain, suffering and disfigurement are generally regarded as separate property of the injured spouse. The conceptual support for this decision is not clear.

•Payments for loss of body parts are also generally treated as separate property, especially when the injury is not related to a job. If the injury is job-related and is measured by the injury to the worker, some states hold the award to be community, rather than separate, property.

Disability payments pose special problems when combined or taken in lieu of retirement benefits. The courts have difficulty in characterizing (and ensuring collection from) retirement benefits; see Chapter 6. In some cases, a worker has been entitled to either retirement or disability payments, but not both. The election to take the disability payments should not impair the spouse's right to one half of community funds in the retirement account. Typically, the courts will decide that the vested retirement fund is the first item paid and that the balance of the payments received are disability payments.

C. INDIVIDUAL STATES

ARIZONA

Ariz.Rev.Stat. § 25–213 provides:

All property, real and personal, of each spouse, owned by such spouse before marriage, and that acquired afterward by gift, devise or descent, and also the increase, rents, issues and profits thereof, is the separate property of such spouse.

Until 1970, Arizona case law characterized recoveries for **personal injuries** as community property. In Jurek v. Jurek, 124 Ariz. 596, 606 P.2d 812 (1980), the Arizona Supreme Court followed the lead and logic of commentators and the courts of Nevada and New Mexico in stating that compensation for injuries to the personal well-being of a spouse is separate property of the injured spouse while expenses incurred by the community for medical care and treatment and any loss of wages resulting from the personal injury should be considered community.

CALIFORNIA

California Constitution, Article 1, § 21 provides: "Property owned before marriage or acquired during marriage by gift, will, or inheritance is separate property." Statutory provisions which amplify the state constitution include **Calif.Civ.Code §§ 5107** and **5108**:

§ 5107: All property of the wife, owned by her before marriage, and that acquired afterwards by gift, bequest, devise, or descent, with the rents, issues, and profits thereof, is her separate property.. . .

§ 5108: All property owned by the husband before marriage, and that acquired afterwards by gift, bequest, devise, or descent, with the rents, issues, and profits thereof, is his separate property. . . .

During Separation: Calif.Civ.Code § 5118 presently provides that the earnings of either spouse while "living separate and apart" are separate property. The predecessor section (which applied to wives only) was interpreted in Makeig v. United Security Bank & Trust Co., 112 Cal.App. 138, 296 P. 673 (1931) to mean that the parties were estranged rather than simply geographically apart.

Section 5118 also provides that the earnings and accumulations of the minor children living with or in the custody of one spouse separate and apart from the other spouse are the separate property of the spouse having custody. This unusual provision reflects an engrafting upon the community property law of a common law concept that the parents are entitled to the earnings of unemancipated minor children. Modernly, it appears that such earnings should be given to the minor child. It is difficult to reconcile community property status of such earnings of the children to the classic community property concept that community property is

that which is acquired as the result of the labor of
the members of the marriage or their capital.
Nevertheless, the merger of common law parental
right and community property concepts of acquisition during marriage results in the earnings of
minor children being treated as community property.   The California statute then proceeds to the
next logical step.   If the child is in the custody of a
parent who is living separate and apart from his or
her spouse, the earnings of the child should be
separate property of the custodial parent rather
than community property of the married couple.

Personal injury recoveries have swung from
one character to the other because of attempts to
avoid imputation of negligence to the injured
spouse.   Except for the period from 1957 to 1968,
personal injury recoveries have been characterized
as community when the cause of action arose during marriage.

The conceptual problem was the potential "bene-
fitting from one's own wrong" when a community
half of the property was received by a non-injured
spouse who contributed to the compensated injury.
The overly broad original "solution" was to characterize all personal injury recoveries (whether or
not the negligence of the spouse was involved) as
separate property.   The better solution, adopted in
1968, restored the community property character
of the recovery and attempted to eliminate the
imputed contributory negligence.

Currently, Calif.Civ.Code § 5126 declares that in certain limited situations (e.g., reimbursement of separate property disbursements, actions against the spouse or when the couple is separated or divorced) the recovery is separate property.

California has also enacted legislation to deal with specific problems of personal injury recoveries, including Calif.Civ.Code § 5112 which eliminates the defense of negligence of a spouse where the actions would not have constituted a defense if the parties were not married. Although the intention of the statute seems clear and the language is inclusive, there is a possibility that the statute will be interpreted not to bar a reduction in damages because of the comparative negligence of the spouse of the injured person. In Li v. Yellow Cab Co., 13 Cal.3d 804, 119 Cal.Rptr. 858, 532 P.2d 1226 (1975), the contributory negligence defense was eliminated in favor of comparative negligence which is a "reduction of damages" rather than a "defense".

IDAHO

Idaho Code § 32-906 provides, among other things:

The income of all property, separate or community, is community property unless the conveyance by which it is acquired provides or both spouses, by written agreement specifically so providing, declare that . . . the income from all or specifically designated separate

**property be the separate property of the
spouse to whom the property belongs.**   . . .

The provision for the mutual agreement of the
spouses adds little, except recognition, to the general concept of transmutation. The reservation of
separate property income as separate property
would be unusual in property acquired prior to
marriage; it suggests that a conveyance to an
intermediary with reconveyance (containing the
reservation of separate property character) to the
spouse might be a means of preserving the separate character of future income from the property.

Idaho abandoned the use of the term "rents,
issues and profits" to adopt the word "income".
The substitute term, "income", is probably even
less precise but has an extensive body of legislation
and litigation in the fields of both federal income
taxation and trust accounting. It was this word
which prompted Justice Holmes in Towne v. Eis-
ner, 245 U.S. 418, 425, 38 S.Ct. 158, 159, 62 L.Ed.
372, 376 (1918) to stress the ambiguity of words
generally and the word "income" specifically by
saying that "a word is not a crystal, transparent
and unchanged, it is the skin of a living thought
and may vary greatly in color and content according to the circumstances and the time in which it
is used."

During Separation: Idaho Code § 32–909 is
still "on the books" as a statute, but has been held
to be an unconstitutional distinction based upon
sex because it applied only to wives. That statute

states that the earnings of the wife (but not the husband) while she is living separate from her husband are her separate property. Suter v. Suter, 97 Idaho 461, 546 P.2d 1169 (1976) declares that such earnings are the community property of the spouses.

Personal Injury Recoveries: Idaho case law initially classified personal injury recoveries as entirely community property, but Rogers v. Yellowstone Park Co., 97 Idaho 14, 539 P.2d 566 (1974) allowed an Idaho wife to recover damages for her pain and suffering as her separate property, basing its characterization upon the nature of the right violated and the interest damaged (medical expenses paid, future earnings lost, pain and suffering). In the same decision, the Idaho Supreme Court abolished the doctrine of interspousal immunity. (The plaintiff was married to an employee of the defendant, not the defendant itself.)

LOUISIANA

In Louisiana, the **natural and civil fruits** (roughly equivalent to "rents, issues and profits") of separate property earned during marriage are community property, but the spouse owning the separate property may unilaterally exclude himself or herself from that rule. Thus, the conversion of such natural and civil fruits could be considered consensual, at least by default.

La.Stat.Ann.—Civ.Code art. 2339, provides, in part:

The natural and civil fruits of the separate property of a spouse, minerals produced from or attributable to a separate asset, and the bonuses, delay rentals, royalties, and shut-in payments arising from mineral leases are community property. Nevertheless, a spouse may reserve them as his separate property by a declaration made in an authentic act or in an act under private signature duly acknowledged.

Formerly, La.Stat.Ann.—Civ.Code art. 2386, repealed effective January 1, 1980, extended only to the wife the right to withhold from the community the fruits of her separate property.

During Separation: Former La.Stat.Ann.—Civ.Code art. 2334, repealed effective January 1, 1980, stated (similar to California, Idaho, Nevada and Washington provisions) "The earnings of the wife when living separate and apart from her husband . . . are her separate property." The statute was clear that the situation was one in which the parties were *not* separated by judgment of court. It also provided that earnings of the wife when living separate and apart and "carrying on a business, trade, occupation or industry separate from her husband" were her separate property. The Marital Regimes Act of 1979 which repealed the former Article 2334 did not replace that language. Additionally, La.Stat.Ann.—Civ.Code art. 2329 limits modifications of the marital regime. Thus, Louisiana presently has no provision making the earnings of non-judicially separated married persons into the separate property of the earner. Indeed, not even the management and control of that property is given to the earner, as is done in Texas.

When property is received by one or both of the spouses from a third party, the characterization as community or separate property is made according to the intention of the donor.   La.Stat.Ann.— Civ.Code art. 2341 follows the general rule of other community property states that donated property is separate property of the donee spouse, but only "property acquired by a spouse by inheritance or donation to him individually". On the other hand, La.Stat.Ann.—Civ.Code art. 2338 provides that if the property is donated to the spouses jointly, it is community property. The drafter's comments indicate that if the spouses "do not live in community", i.e., if they have agreed upon a (conventional) non-community arrangement in lieu of the (legal) community regime, "the donor may not create a community regime for the spouses. In such a case, the property given to them is separate property held in indivision."

Louisiana has the most extensive statutory pattern outside of the uniform principal and income acts for defining what other jurisdictions call the "rents, issues and profits".   La.Stat.Ann.— Civ.Code art. 535 through 629 deal with the "usufruct", a right of limited duration on the property of a second person who is called the "naked owner", possibly due to the fact that with the usufruct being in another, the naked owner has only (own-ly?) a bare title. Leaving that behind us, the usufructuary (possessor of the usufruct) is entitled to the "fruits" which are defined as things that are produced by or derived from another thing without diminution of its substance.

Fruits are divided into two kinds for which the ownership is decided at different points in time: Natural fruits are the product of earth or of animals and belong to the person entitled to the usufruct at the moment of severance. Thus a hay crop growing on the wife's separate property is her separate property until severed and, after being severed, the crop is community property. Civil fruits, on the other hand, are apportioned. Civil fruits are revenues derived from a thing by operation of law or by reason of a juridical act, such as rentals, interest and certain corporate distributions. They are accrued and apportioned without regard to the actual date of receipt. This is similar to the common law rule concerning interest, but unlike the common law treatment of rent.

La.Stat.Ann.—Civ.Code art. 551, enacted in 1976, excluded from the definition of "fruits" receipts which cause a "diminution of its substance"; but La.Stat.Ann.—Civ.Code art. 2339, quoted above, stresses that certain payments from mineral leases are community property even though not encompassed within the statutory definition of "fruits".

Louisiana has abandoned the term "profits", previously found in the English-language version of its civil code as an erroneous translation of the French-language word for "fruits".

Personal Injury Recoveries: Louisiana was the first community property state to characterize by statute recoveries for personal injuries. Case law based on the omnibus clause of former Article 2334 initially classified all such recoveries as community property. The first specific statute, in 1902, made the damages resulting from personal injury to the wife her separate property. In 1912, this statute was expanded to classify as the wife's separate property all actions for damages from "offenses and quasi-offenses". The court interpretation of these statutes limited the separate portion of the wife to the damages for her pain, suffering and disfigurement. The recoveries for loss of earnings and reimbursement for medical expenses paid from community funds were community. Thus, Louisiana was a pioneer in recognizing the distinctive elements of a personal injury action and being willing to characterize each part in accordance with the right violated. The recognition was maintained and extended to the husband in **La.Stat.Ann.—Civ.Code art. 2344**, effective January 1, 1980:

Damages due to personal injuries sustained during the existence of the community by a spouse are separate property.

Nevertheless, the portion of the damages attributable to expenses incurred by the community as a result of the injury, or in compensation of the loss of community earnings, is community property. If the community regime is terminated otherwise than by the death of the injured spouse, the portion of the damages attributable to the loss of earnings that would have accrued after termination of the community property regime is the separate property of the injured spouse.

NEVADA

Nevada Constitution Article 4, § 31 provides, in part:

All property, both real and personal, of a married person owned or claimed by such person before marriage, and that acquired afterward by gift, devise or descent, shall be the separate property of such person.   .   .   .

The constitutional provision is amplified by Nev.Rev.Stat. 123.130:

1. All property of the wife owned by her before marriage, and that acquired by her afterwards by gift, bequest, devise, descent or by an award for personal injury damages, with the rents, issues and profits thereof, is her separate property.

2. All property of the husband owned by him before marriage, and that acquired by him

afterwards by gift, bequest, devise, descent or by an award for personal injury damages, with the rents, issues and profits thereof, is his separate property.

During Separation: Formerly Nev.Rev.Stat. 123.180 provided that the earnings of a wife living separate from her husband were her separate property. This provision was eliminated, apparently making the earnings of both members of the couple into community property whether they are separated or not.

Personal Injury Recoveries: Nevada's court was the first to classify judicially any part of a personal injury recovery as separate property and among the first to divide judicially the recovery between separate and community in accordance with the right violated and damage suffered. By stressing the onerous acquisition of property received during marriage and using a strict definition of "acquired", the court concluded that personal injury recoveries were not necessarily community and proceeded to classify the recovery for injury to personal security as a replacement or exchange of an existing separate property asset rather than a new asset. The courts and the statutes concede that medical expenses and loss of earnings during the marriage are community. In addition to Nev.Rev.Stat. 123.130, quoted above, **Nev.Rev.Stat. 123.121** provides:

When a husband and wife sue jointly, any damages awarded shall be segregated as follows:

1. If the action is for personal injuries, damages assessed for:

(a) Personal injuries and pain and suffering, to the injured spouse as his separate property.

(b) Loss of comfort and society, to the spouse who suffers such loss.

(c) Loss of services and hospital and medical expenses, to the spouses as community property.

2. If the action is for injury to property, damages shall be awarded according to the character of the injured property. Damages to separate property shall be awarded to the spouse owning such property, and damages to community property shall be awarded to the spouses as community property.

NEW MEXICO

N.Mex.Stat.1978 § 40–3–8 provides:

A. "Separate property" means:

(1) property acquired by either spouse before marriage or after entry of a decree of dissolution of marriage;

(2) property acquired after entry of a decree entered pursuant to Section 40–4–3

NMSA 1978 [which deals with judicial separation] unless the decree provides otherwise;

(3) property designated as separate property by a judgment or decree of any court having jurisdiction;

(4) property acquired by either spouse by gift, bequest, devise or descent;

(5) property designated as separate property by a written agreement between the spouses including a deed or other written agreement concerning property held by the spouses as joint tenants or tenants in common in which the property is designated as separate property.

* * *

C. "Property" includes the rents, issues and profits thereof. . . .

During Separation: Although New Mexico specifically provides that the earnings of either member of the couple are separate property after a *decree* of separation, New Mexico did not have a provision for the estranged, but not legally separated couple. Thus, such earnings will be community property under general principles.

Additionally, management and control by one spouse rather than both (under court supervision) is provided in situations when "a spouse disappears and his location is unknown", N.Mex.1953 Comp.Laws § 57–4A–8 (added in 1973). The former provision (N.Mex.1953 Comp.Laws § 57–4–5, repealed in 1973) listed a number of situations in which the wife could avoid the then-usual rule of husbandly management and control of the community property.   In addition to changes to satisfy the Equal Rights Amendment to the state constitution (New Mexico Constitution, Article II, § 18), the 1973 change modified the former terminology concerning a husband who "abandoned" his wife. The change of language from "abandons" to "disappears" eliminated some of the problems of proving intention of a person who has departed, but did not encompass all situations in which the spouses are living separate and apart.

Personal Injury Recoveries: New Mexico has a relatively uncluttered treatment of the character of personal injury recoveries.   In Soto v. Vandeventer, 56 N.M. 483, 245 P.2d 826 (1952), the court characterized the claim for compensation for pain and suffering as the wife's separate property and the claims for compensation for medical expenses, earnings and loss of service to the community as community property. Subsequent cases extended the rule to recoveries by the husband and to worker's compensation benefits.

TEXAS

The **Texas Constitution, Article XVI, § 15,** as amended in 1980, begins with a definition of separate property:

All property, both real and personal, of a spouse owned or claimed before marriage, and

that acquired afterward by gift, devise or descent, shall be the separate property of that spouse; . . .

Vernon's Ann.Tex.Stat.Family Code § 5.01 provides:

(a) A spouse's separate property consists of:

(1) the property owned or claimed by the spouse before marriage;

(2) the property acquired by the spouse during marriage by gift, devise, or descent; and

(3) the recovery for personal injuries sustained by the spouse during marriage, except any recovery for loss of earning capacity during marriage.

(b) Community property consists of the property, other than separate property, acquired by either spouse during marriage.

Since Texas follows the civil law system of declaring all **rents, issues and** profits from separate property earned during marriage to be community property, the key is the *absence* of the phrase "rents, issues and profits from separate property" in the constitutional provision and its supporting statute defining separate property. There is no statutory provision which states that the rents, issues and profits of separate property earned during marriage are either separate or community property, but case law has consistently interpreted the state constitution to hold such income to be community property.

Texas has made various short-lived and unsuccessful efforts to change the civil law rule that the rents, issues and profits of separate property earned during marriage are community property. Arnold v. Leonard, 114 Tex. 535, 273 S.W. 799 (1925) held unconstitutional two Texas statutes which attempted to provide that the rents and revenues of the wife's separate property would be her separate property although received during the marriage. The court ruled that the Texas constitutional provisions describing the extent of the wife's separate property contained an implied prohibition against legislative power to change the specified circumstances in which property would be separate property. Subsequently, other statutes were enacted seeking the same objective, but those statutes have been repealed. There does not appear to have been much of an effort to scrape away at the civil law rule by tightening the interpretation of "rents, issues and profits" ; one federal case interpreting the term "increase" to include rents (thereby making the rents received during marriage from separate property into separate property in Texas) has not been cited in other cases and the term "increase" was deleted from the statute defining separate property.

Personal Injury Recovery: Although Vernon's Ann.Tex.Stat.Family Code § 5.01(a)(3), quoted above, resolves the split character of two elements of a personal injury action, it does not mention medical expense reimbursement. Moreover, the statutory pattern of saying that "the recovery for personal injuries" is separate "except any recovery for loss of earning capacity during marriage" suggests that medical reimbursement would fall under the general rule and therefore be the separate property of the injured spouse regardless of the source of payment.

In Graham v. Franco, 488 S.W.2d 390 (Tex.1972), the Texas Supreme Court upheld the constitutionality of the statute while declining to define a cause of action as "property". The court also indicated that even without the statute, the pain, suffering and disfigurement elements of the recovery are the separate property of the injured spouse. The court held that the medical reimbursement element of the recovery was community, but did not face the issue of the statutory language which seems to demand the opposite result.

WASHINGTON

Washington's statutes are distinctive in that they do not describe or declare the property to be separate property, but rather describe the incidents of separateness. **Rev.Code Wash.Ann.** has separate provisions for husband and wife:

26.16.010 Separate property of husband

Property and pecuniary rights owned by the husband before marriage and that acquired by him afterwards by gift, bequest, devise or de-

scent, with the rents, issues and profits thereof, shall not be subject to the debts or contracts of his wife, and he may manage, lease, sell, convey, encumber or devise by will such property without the wife joining in such management, alienation or encumbrance, as fully and to the same effect as though he were unmarried.

26.16.020   Separate property of wife

The property and pecuniary rights of every married woman at the time of her marriage or afterwards acquired by gift, devise or inheritance, with the rents, issues and profits thereof, shall not be subject to the debts or contracts of her husband, and she may manage, lease, sell, convey, encumber or devise by will such property to the same extent and in the same manner that her husband can, property belonging to him.

During Separation: Rev.Code Wash.Ann. 26.16.140 was amended in 1972 to change "wife" to "either spouse" so that earnings and accumulations while they are living separate from each other are separate property rather than community property.

Personal Injury Recovery: Washington shifted from a community property characterization of the total recovery to a characterization of the elements of the recovery in Freehe v. Freehe, 81 Wash.2d 183, 500 P.2d 771 (1972). That case classified the injured spouse's recovery for pain and suffering as

separate property and abrogated the doctrine of
spousal immunity as to interspousal torts.

Washington changed from contributory negligence to comparative negligence and abolished the
community property defense by statutes effective
in 1974, Rev.Code Wash.Ann. 4.22.010 and
4.22.020.

WISCONSIN (and UMPA)

Wis.Stat.1985–86, § 766.31, titled "Classification
of Property of Spouses", provides, in part, as follows:

**(6) Property owned at a marriage which oc-
curs after 12:01 a.m. on January 1, 1986, is
individual property of the owning spouse if, at
the marriage, the spouse has a marital domicile in this state.**

**(7) Property acquired by a spouse during
marriage and after the determination date is
individual property if acquired by any of the
following means:**

**(a) By gift during lifetime or by a disposi-
tion at death by a 3rd person to that spouse
and not to both spouses. A distribution of
principal or income from a trust created by a
3rd person to one spouse is the individual
property of that spouse unless the trust provides otherwise.**

**(b) In exchange for or with the proceeds
of other individual property of the spouse.**

(c) From appreciation of the spouse's individual property except to the extent that the appreciation is classified as marital property under s. 766.63.

(d) By a decree, marital property agreement or reclassification under sub. (10) designating it as the individual property of the spouse.

(e) As a recovery for damage to property under s. 766.70, except as specifically provided otherwise in a decree or marital property agreement.

(f) As a recovery for personal injury except for the amount of that recovery attributable to expenses paid or otherwise satisfied from marital property and except for the amount attributable to loss of income during marriage.

*   *   *

(9) Except as provided otherwise in this chapter and except to the extent that it would affect the spouse's ownership rights in the property existing before the determination date, during marriage the interest of a spouse in property owned immediately before the determination date is treated as if it were individual property.

(10) Spouses may reclassify their property by gift, marital property agreement, written consent under s. 766.61(3)(e) or unilateral statement under s. 766.59. If a spouse gives proper-

ty to the other spouse and intends at the time
the gift is made that the property be the individual property of the donee spouse, the income from the property is the individual property of the donee spouse unless a contrary
intent of the donor spouse regarding the classification of income is established.

Wisconsin and UMPA create three basic property classifications; Marital property (equivalent to
community property), individual property (equivalent to separate property) and "predetermination
date property" (also called "unclassified property").
All property of spouses is presumed to be marital
unless classified otherwise by the spouses or by
statute.

A Wisconsin married couple's "determination
date" is the last date to occur of the following:

1.   Marriage;

2.   Establishment of a marital domicile in Wisconsin; or

3.   January 1, 1986.

"Predetermination date property" is property acquired by one or both spouses prior to their determination date (i.e., prior to the date on which the
marital property law first applies to them). Wisconsin (and UMPA) subdivide predetermination
date property by the event which is the determination date: Property owned at the determination
date either "is" individual property or "is treated
as if it were" individual property, respectively,

dependent upon whether the marriage or one of the other two events is the last to occur.

Wisconsin differences from UMPA: Wis.Stat.1985–86, § 766.31, parallels UMPA in its basic classification statute but has the following differences:

1. Trusts: Wisconsin's statute specifies that a distribution of principal or income from a trust created by a third person to one spouse is the individual property of that spouse unless the trust provides otherwise.

2. Personal Injury Recoveries: Both Wisconsin and UMPA provide that a recovery for personal injury is generally individual property except amounts recovered which are reimbursements of expenses satisfied from marital property. Wisconsin also treats as marital property any amount attributable to the loss of income during marriage.

3. Written Consents: Wisconsin sharply reduced the circumstances under which a "written consent" (a document signed by a person against whose interests it is sought to be enforced) may be used to reclassify marital property into individual property. Such a consent may be used only in relation to life insurance policies, but remains a valuable planning device for them. Wisconsin does authorize a "marital property agreement".

4. Unilateral Statement: Wisconsin authorizes a legal document analogous to the Louisiana "fruits" concept. A spouse may unilaterally create (or amend or revoke) a document which changes the character of income attributable to individual property. Ordinarily, post-determination date income from either predetermination date property or individual property is characterized as marital property in Wisconsin. Individual property characterization can be preserved by observing the statutory formalities for the unilateral statement which include signing, acknowledging before a notary public and service by delivery or certified mail to the other spouse.

5. **Income from Inter-Spousal Gifts:** Wisconsin, but not UMPA, provides that when one spouse makes a gift intending the property to be the individual property of the other spouse, then the income from the donated property shall also be the individual property of the donee spouse. Without this provision, the commingling of the marital property income with the donated property principal could result in reclassification as community. The statutory provision is intended to avoid adverse death tax results while expressing the intent of the donor spouse that the income from the gift also be individual property of the donee spouse. The donor spouse may negate the statutory provision by establishing a contrary intent.

EXERCISE

Assume that W owned all 100 shares of Corp, of which she was also an employee, prior to marriage. After her marriage, W received 100 shares of Corp in a 2-for-1 split. The next year, W received 10

additional shares as a 5% stock dividend. The
value of the business rose due to two factors: The
intrinsic value of the business and inflation.   The
corporation declared cash dividends of $5,000 each
in years 3, 4 and 5, i.e., in years in which there
were no stock splits or dividends. W received as
salary for her services the amount of $10,000 for
each of years 1 through 5. Which of these six
elements are separate property and which are community property in which jurisdictions? General
community property principles apply; assume that
there are no marital agreements nor (where permitted) unilateral statements.

WHICH ELEMENTS ARE COMMUNITY ?

Premarital stock   has six forms of

Growth, Increase, Profit or Product

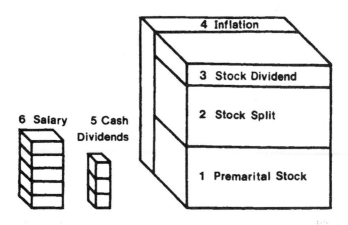

ANSWER

1.   The premarital stock remains separate property in all jurisdictions.

2.   The 2-for-1 stock split is a "mere" change in form.   Although the additional 100 shares are received during marriage, they are separate property.

3.   The stock dividend looks more like an income item, especially when cash dividends alternate with it, but tends to be classified as a change in form rather than rents, issues or profits.

4.   The increase due to inflation is not a change in the original items; a "mere" change in value does not change the character of the property.

5.   In Idaho, Louisiana, Texas and Wisconsin, the cash dividends are community; in the other five states these "rents, issues and profits" are characterized as separate because derived from separate property.

6.   In all the community property states, the income from salary will be community property if earned during the marriage.

CHAPTER 4

COMMUNITY PROPERTY

A. OVERVIEW

1. The Basic Statute

Most of the community property states have a basic community property statute which defines community property by stating that it is property (other than separate property) which was acquired by a couple while married. The statute has the following characteristics:

a. The statute uses absolute terms. Despite this uniformity and certainty of the language, the statutes only reflect a general *presumption* (rather than a certainty) that such property is community.

b. The basic statute provides that community property is "all property except" that which is specifically stated to be separate (usually in accompanying statutes). The statutes use all-inclusive language which specifically excludes that which is defined as separate property. Except in Louisiana, all definitions of community property say what community property is not, rather than what it is. This method of definition tends to include in the community items which are not produced by the labor or property of either spouse. Theorists disagree with the use of the broad statutory definitions in a literal manner. Certain newer types of property acquisitions (such as welfare benefits or strike benefits paid to non-union members) and items which are grounded in common law (such as the right of the parent to the income of an unemancipated minor) do not fit within the classic definition of community property (which includes the element of onerous acquisition) even though they fit within the statutory definitions.

c. The basic statute is the most-often cited statute of each community property system. Thus, methods of legal research (such as Shepardizing or the use of annotated codes) which focus upon citations to specific statutory sections contain more entries for the basic statute than any other community property statute.

2. Statutory and Decisional Presumptions

Presumptions are important in determining whether property is separate or community. The most important, universal and pervasive of the presumptions is the "general presumption" that all property acquired during the marriage is community property. Additional presumptions have been created by statute or decision.

The presumptions, including the general presumption, can be rebutted, although jurisdictions vary as to the amount and type of evidence which is necessary to rebut the various presumptions.

The most common method of rebutting the general presumption is to trace the property by showing that, although acquired during marriage, it was acquired in exchange for separate property without an intention to transmute the property.

If community and separate property are so commingled that each element cannot be traced, the combined product is presumed to be community property. This frequently-invoked presumption is not applied when the relative amount of community is extremely small. This presumption is generally used against the spouse, who having the management and control of the community, commingled it with his or her separate property.

The presumption that property to which the title is recorded or registered (such as automobiles, real estate, stock certificates and so forth) belongs to the person in whose name it is registered is especially important to protect third parties who deal with a married person concerning property held in his or her name.

A number of other presumptions are created by statute in the various community property states.

B. DETAIL

1. The General Presumption

Many questions of whether the character of property is separate or community are resolved by the "general presumption" that property *owned* during (or, in some states, at the end of) marriage is community property. This presumption sometimes applies to property which is *acquired* during marriage, but that usage of "acquired" is not the same as the original acquisition by the couple of new wealth. Rather, all property which the couple receives during marriage is presumed to be community property by the general presumption. If the property was not new wealth, e.g., if it is shown that the item in question was received in exchange for separate property without an intention to change its character, then the general presumption is rebutted. On the other hand, if the property was new wealth, then the property is both presumed to be and is community property. In summary, the presumption is raised by the acquisition of property during marriage. The property is community if the acquisition was of new wealth or an exchange for community property or the presumption of community is not rebutted.

The general presumption can be rebutted by evidence which traces the separate property nature of property used to acquire the item in question, e.g., a gift or by tracing the acquisition back to its separate property origin. Most jurisdictions have additional presumptions by decisional law or by statute which provide that property shall be presumed to be separate property under certain circumstances. Statutes may provide the means of rebutting; in a few instances, statutes provide that the general presumption shall not apply to certain circumstances or for certain purposes. For example, Calif.Civ.Code § 5111 provides that the presumption shall not apply for the purposes of distribution upon the death of one who was divorced more than four years before his or her death.

Although all jurisdictions apply the general presumption that property acquired during marriage is community property unless evidence is presented to rebut the presumption, there is some disagreement as to whether there is, or should be, a presumption as to *when* property is acquired if it is owned at the end of a marriage. On the one hand, Texas specifically provides by statute that property possessed by either spouse on the dissolution of marriage is presumed to be community property. On the other hand, in Fidelity & Casualty Co. v. Mahoney, 71 Cal.App.2d 65, 161 P.2d 944 (1945) California declined to find that a dollar bill which was used to purchase flight insurance on the life of a husband of two months had been acquired during marriage.

The force and impact of the general presumption must be reckoned with: Any property which is acquired during marriage is presumed to be community property unless the party opposing such finding rebuts the presumption with sufficient evidence.

2. Presumptions Arising from Record Title

Certain assets such as realty, stock certificates, automobiles and boats, have documents of title. What effect should be given to a recitation in the document that the property is (or is not) community property?

Recitals in a deed (e.g., as to the character of the property) are prima facie and not conclusive evidence that the couple intended the property to be separate or community. Regardless of the form of title, property may be of different form or character than that which is shown by the certificate of title because of the agreement of the parties or because of the intent with which the deed was made.

A presumption arose at common law (as opposed to the civil law community property system) that a husband who purchased property and took title in the name of his wife intended a gift to the wife. The civil law had no comparable presumption. The amalgamation of the common law and the civil law system produced uneven results: Texas and Wisconsin (UMPA) declined to adopt the common law presumption while California and New Mexico enacted statutes (repealed prospectively in the late 1970's) by which all property in the name of the wife (and not merely that for which the husband furnished consideration) was the separate property of the wife.

Except in Wisconsin (UMPA), the most commonly encountered problem of the form of title arises in the attempt by married couples to obtain the benefits of both the community property system and the survivorship feature of joint tenancy. See the separate analysis of this problem in Chapter 5.

The trust, another product of the common law system, also had difficulty in being adapted to the

community property system.   California, Idaho
and Wisconsin (UMPA) have passed specific statutes which preserve the community property character of property which is held in a revocable trust.
These statutes assist in preserving the "stepped-up
basis" for the survivor's half of community property provided by Internal Revenue Code § 1014(b)(6).

3. Statutes Protecting Third Parties

Many statutes protect third parties who deal
with a married individual, but who do not obtain
the signatures or approval by spouses to each individual transaction.   The statutory protections oft-
en were based upon the model of male management of the community property; changes in the
management and control provisions complicate the
picture.

Some statutes are designed to protect banks and
other financial institutions by permitting them to
transact business with either spouse.   Although
these statutes validate certain transactions between a spouse and a third party or specify that
such property is to be presumed to be separate
property, they do not necessarily govern the community or separate status of the property or the
right of management and control between the
spouses.

Some protection statutes retain former statutory
rights or methods of characterizing property. The
constitutional necessity for the retention of such
rights is seldom tested because of the practical

need to preserve the stability of record title, especially in realty transactions.

The rights of bona fide purchasers without notice from a married person are protected by Vernon's Ann.Tex.Stat. Family Code § 5.24(b) if the property is presumed to be subject to the sole management, control and disposition of that spouse.

Washington and Wisconsin similarly provide that a bona fide purchaser takes realty clear of the community property claim of any spouse whose name does not appear of record and who does not protect his or her interest.

4. Miscellaneous Statutory Presumptions

Other than the general presumption, there is no uniformity among statutory community property presumptions. The most common provision is authority for the recording of an inventory of the premarital separate property, as described below.

Among the various other statutory provisions which create presumptions are the following:

• California provides that the general presumption (that property acquired during marriage is community property) does not apply to property acquired during a marriage terminated by divorce more than four years prior to the death of the former spouse in whose estate the question arises, Calif.Civ.Code § 5111.

• California and New Mexico have retained provisions which created the presumption that property acquired by a married woman by an instrument in writing was her separate property, but only for property interests created before a certain cut-off date (January 1, 1975, in California and July 1, 1973, in New Mexico). These provisions applied to title acquired by the wife alone or with another person, but had been modified to exclude title acquired by her with her husband (thus eliminating the problem of one half of the property being the wife's separate property under this presumption and the other half being the community property—of which the wife was entitled to one half—under the general presumption). Both of the statutes also protected persons who dealt in good faith and for a valuable consideration with the married woman or her legal representative or successor in interest.

• Washington and Wisconsin permit either spouse to convey the community property to the other as the other's separate property.

• Nevada "deems" the written permission of one spouse to the other spouse to use his or her own earnings to be a gift to the earning spouse, Nev.Rev.Stat. 123.190.

• Louisiana and Wisconsin (UMPA) have presumptions of community property debts.

5. Recording Inventory of Separate Property

Recording an inventory of the separate property owned at the time of the marriage was known to the Spanish law as a means to avoid confusion and facilitate proof of separate property character.

California, Idaho, Nevada and Texas have statutory provisions which permit a married person to create evidence of the separate character of his or her premarital property by filing in the county records an inventory of the property owned at the time of the marriage. The recorded inventory serves as evidence of the ownership of the listed items, but is not immune to transmutation or to problems of ambiguity, fungibility, change of form or commingling.

California, Nevada and Texas extend the protection to both spouses while Idaho mentions an inventory of only the wife's property; the extension of equal rights regardless of sex, as in Suter v. Suter, 97 Idaho 461, 546 P.2d 1169 (1976), may require a change in the Idaho approach.

The technique of creating an inventory and establishing its authenticity as to specified assets is, of course, available informally in all states and is very useful in segregating separate property from community property.

The Nevada statute has the strongest application. In effect, property of a married person is presumed to be community unless an inventory of separate property is recorded. Nev.Rev.Stat. 123.160 provides that the failure to record an inventory is prima facie evidence that the property is not the separate property of such person.

Louisiana does not have a provision for the recording of an "inventory" of the separate property, as such, but formerly required preservation of the separate property character of individual assets by the "double declaration" (that the husband acquired an immovable with separate funds and that he intends to acquire the property for the benefit of his separate estate). Currently, La.Stat.Ann.— Civ.Code art. 2342 permits a "declaration in an act of acquisition that things are acquired with separate funds", which declaration can be "controverted" by the other spouse, the forced heirs or the creditors, but not when the item has been alienated, encumbered or leased for consideration.

The Louisiana provision is similar to an inventory in its unilateral creation, but different because it is done on an asset-by-asset basis and at the time of the acquisition of the asset. The other statutory provisions do not specify a time for the recording of the inventory, but appear to contemplate a recording close to the time of marriage. Nevada also provides for recording supplemental inventories at later times.

C. INDIVIDUAL STATES

ARIZONA

The basic statute is **Ariz.Rev.Stat. § 25–211** which provides:

All property acquired by either husband or wife during the marriage, except that which is acquired by gift, devise or descent, is the community property of the husband and wife.

CALIFORNIA

Calif.Civ.Code § 5110 is the basic statute. It provides, in part:

Except as provided in Sections 5107, 5108, . . . all real property situated in this state and all personal property wherever situated acquired during the marriage by a married person while domiciled in this state . . . is community property. . . .

The basic statute differs from those in most of the other community property states in two ways:

1. The statute contains exceptions which deal with presumptions such as acquisition of title by a married woman by an instrument in writing prior to January 1, 1975 and the infrequently-invoked provision concerning conveyances by a married woman who acquired title prior to May 19, 1889.

2. California has the only basic statute which expresses the conflict of laws rules and limits itself to the traditional areas where a statute applies— "all real property situated in this state and all personal property wherever situated acquired during the marriage by a married person while domiciled in this state". The statute is backed up by two other statutes which divide "quasi-community property", i.e., property which would have been community if acquired while the parties were domiciled in California, but actually acquired while they were domiciled in another state. Calif.Prob.Code § 66 and Calif.Civ.Code § 4803 deal,

respectively, with the division of such property upon death and divorce.

The California restriction upon the general presumption, imposed by **Calif.Civ.Code § 5111**, is unique among community property states:

The presumption that property acquired during marriage is community property does not apply to any property to which legal or equitable title is held by a person at the time of his death if the marriage during which the property was acquired was terminated by dissolution of marriage more than four years prior to such death.

California and New Mexico had detailed provisions concerning a married woman's acquisition of title by written instrument. In both cases, the statutes were repealed prospectively, but still apply to prior acquisitions. A portion of **Calif.Civ.Code § 5110**, excluded above, is as follows:

whenever any real or personal property, or any interest therein or encumbrance thereon, is acquired prior to January 1, 1975, by a married woman by an instrument in writing, the presumption is that the same is her separate property, and if so acquired by the married woman and any other person the presumption is that she takes the part acquired by her, as tenant in common, unless a different intention is expressed in the instrument; except, that when any of the property is acquired by husband and wife by an instrument in which they

are described as husband and wife, unless a different intention is expressed in the instrument, the presumption is that the property is the community property of the husband and wife.

IDAHO

Idaho Code § 32–906 is the basic statute. It provides, in part:

All other property acquired after marriage by either husband or wife is community property. . . .

The statute merely implies, rather than directly stating, that property acquired after marriage by *both* spouses is also community property.

The reference to "all other property" points to Idaho Code § 32–903 which provides as follows:

All property of either the husband or the wife owned by him or her before marriage, and that acquired afterward by either by gift, bequest, devise or descent, or that which either he or she shall acquire with the proceeds of his or her separate property, by way of moneys or other property, shall remain his or her sole and separate property.

Idaho's provision for the recording of an inventory in Idaho Code §§ 32–907 and 32–908 is phrased in terms of the "wife" only and is probably subject to attack similar to that in Suter v. Suter, 97 Idaho 461, 546 P.2d 1169 (1976).

Idaho, like California, has enacted a detailed statute to preserve the community property character of property held by a revocable trust, Idaho Code § 32–906A.

LOUISIANA

Louisiana's basic community property statute, **La.Stat.Ann.—Civ.Code art. 2338,** contains a definition of community property in addition to a final sentence which is similar to the all-inclusive approach of the basic statutes of the other community property jurisdictions:

The community property comprises: property acquired during the existence of the legal regime through the effort, skill, or industry of either spouse; property acquired with community things or with community and separate things, unless classified as separate property under Article 2341; property donated to the spouses jointly; natural and civil fruits of community property; damages awarded for loss or injury to a thing belonging to the community; and all other property not classified by law as separate property.

A separate provision (La.Stat.Ann.—Civ.Code art. 2339, set forth on page 63, above) provides that the fruits and revenues of separate property of a spouse (and additional forms of revenue, as described in Chapter 3) are community property unless such receipts are reserved as separate property.

Louisiana also has a statutory form of the general presumption set out in **La.Stat.Ann.—Civ.Code art. 2340:**

Things in the possession of a spouse during the existence of a regime of community of acquets and gains are presumed to be community, but either spouse may prove that they are separate property.

Louisiana creates an unusual presumption of a community property debt in **La.Stat.Ann.—Civ.Code art. 2361:**

Except as provided in Article 2363 [dealing with premarital and postmarital debts, debts not for the common interest or the interest of the other spouse or for the separate property of a spouse to the extent it does not benefit the community, the family or the other spouse and obligations resulting from intentional wrongs not perpetrated for the benefit of the community], all obligations incurred by a spouse during the existence of a community property regime are presumed to be community obligations.

Another distinctive Louisiana statute is La.Stat.Ann.—Civ.Code art. 2342:

A declaration in an act of acquisition that things are acquired with separate funds as the separate property of a spouse may be controverted by the other spouse unless he concurred in the act. It may also be controverted by the forced heirs and the creditors of the

spouses, despite the concurrence by the other spouse.

Nevertheless, when there has been such a declaration, an alienation, encumbrance, or lease of the thing by onerous title may not be set aside on the grounds of the falsity of the declaration.

NEVADA

Nev.Rev.Stat. 123.220 is the basic statute:

All property, other than that stated in NRS 123.130, acquired after marriage by either husband or wife, or both, is community property unless otherwise provided by:

1. An agreement in writing between the spouses, which is effective only as between them.

2. A decree of separate maintenance issued by a court of competent jurisdiction.

3. NRS 123.190.

Nev.Rev.Stat. 123.190 "deems" the written permission by one spouse to the other spouse to use his or her own earnings to be a gift. This unusual statute crosses the line from management and control to ownership; it is the reverse of a trend in Texas to allow management and control to one spouse in a situation where other states classify the property as separate, e.g., where the spouses are living separate and apart.

Nevada has the most extensive legislation concerning the procedure for and effect of recording of an inventory of the separate property of a married person. The applicable statutes include Nev.Rev.Stat. 123.140, 123.150 and the following language of **Nev.Rev.Stat. 123.160:**

the failure to file for record an inventory of [the] . . . separate property [of a married person resident in Nevada] . . . or the omission from the inventory . . . of any part of such property . . . is prima facie evidence, as between such married person and purchasers in good faith and for a valuable consideration from the other spouse, that the property of which no inventory has been so filed, or which has been omitted from the inventory, is not the separate property of such person. . . .

Nev.Rev.Stat. 123.140, subsection 3, specifically permits the recording of "a further and supplemental inventory".

NEW MEXICO

N.Mex.Stat.1978 § 40–3–8 states its definition of separate property in part "A." of the statute (set forth on pages 69–70, above) and then provides:

B. "Community property" means property acquired by either or both spouses during marriage which is not separate property. . . .

Additionally, New Mexico has codified both the general presumption and special presumptions taken from California but modified to comply with the equal rights provision of New Mexico Constitution Article II, § 18. **N.Mex.Stat.1978 § 40–3–12** provides as follows:

A. Property acquired during marriage by either husband or wife, or both, is presumed to be community property.

B. Property or any interest therein acquired during marriage by a woman by an instrument in writing, in her name alone, or in her name and the name of another person not her husband, is presumed to be the separate property of the married woman if the instrument in writing was delivered and accepted prior to July 1, 1973. The date of execution or, in the absence of a date of execution, the date of acknowledgment, is presumed to be the date upon which delivery and acceptance occurred.

C. The presumptions contained in Subsection B of this section are conclusive in favor of any person dealing in good faith and for valuable consideration with a married woman or her legal representative or successor in interest.

TEXAS

The basic community property statute in Texas is **Vernon's Ann.Tex.Stat. Family Code § 5.01** (set forth on page 72, above) which defines separate property in part "(a)" and then provides:

(b) Community property consists of the property, other than separate property, acquired by either spouse during marriage.

Texas also has codified the general presumption and expressly made it applicable at the time of the dissolution of the marriage in **Vernon's Ann.Tex.Stat. Family Code § 5.02:**

Property possessed by either spouse during or on dissolution of marriage is presumed to be community property.

Texas has one of the broadest statutory authorizations designed to protect third persons. Vernon's Ann.Tex.Stat. Family Code § 5.24(b) provides, among other things, that a third person dealing with a married person is entitled to rely on the authority of the spouse to deal with the community property if such third person is not a party to a fraud and does not have actual or constructive knowledge of the spouse's lack of authority.

Recording of an inventory of the separate property of a married person is permitted by Vernon's Ann.Tex.Stat. Family Code § 5.03, but is not required (as in Nevada) in order to preserve and prove the separate property character.

The 1980 amendment to **Article XVI, § 15,** of the Texas Constitution provides, in part:

if one spouse makes a gift of property to the other that gift is presumed to include all the

income or property which might arise from that gift of property.

The last clause creates a new presumption in Texas (which, being a "civil rule" state would otherwise deem the income from separate property to be community property if received during marriage): The gift of the item to separate property is presumed also to be a gift of the future income from community to separate. This provision was probably aimed at federal estate tax questions raised by Estate of Castleberry, 68 T.C. 682 (1977).

WASHINGTON

Washington's basic community property statute, **Rev.Code Wash.Ann. 26.16.030,** describes attributes of the community property as well as giving the following definition of community property:

Property not acquired or owned, as prescribed in RCW 26.16.010 and 26.16.020, acquired after marriage by either husband or wife or both, is community property. . . .

Rev.Code Wash.Ann. 26.16.050, deals with conveyances between spouses, and Rev.Code Wash.Ann. 26.16.095 gives some protection to third parties. Additionally, Rev.Code Wash.Ann. 26.16.100 permits a spouse to protect his or her interest in real estate by recording an instrument in writing setting forth the nature of the claim; failure to record such a statement of claim theoretically permits a bona fide purchaser of the realty to receive full legal and equitable title from the spouse who, having record title, conveyed to the bona fide purchaser for value. The protection afforded the bona fide purchaser by that statute has been substantially reduced by cases which require the bona fide purchaser to exercise reasonable diligence to obtain knowledge of the existence of a marital relationship within the state of Washington rather than merely accepting a recitation in the deed or the representation of the party with whom the purchaser is dealing. See Campbell v. Sandy, 190 Wash. 528, 69 P.2d 808 (1937).

WISCONSIN (and UMPA)

Wis.Stat.1985–86 § 766.31 is the basic statute:

(1) All property of spouses is marital property except that which is classified otherwise by this chapter.

(2) All property of spouses is presumed to be marital property.

The basic statute also specifies the marital character of passive and active income earned or accrued during marriage as follows in **Wis.Stat.1985–86 § 766.31(4):**

(4) Except as provided [for certain gifts or under a "unilateral statement", "written consent" document or a marital property agreement] **income earned or accrued by a spouse or attributable to property of a spouse during marriage and after the determination date is marital property**.

In Wisconsin, an obligation incurred by a spouse during marriage is presumed to be incurred in the interest of the marriage or family. The presumption can be made conclusive by a statement that the obligation is or will be incurred in the interest of the marriage or the family, separately signed by the obligated or incurring spouse at or before the time the obligation is incurred, **Wis.Stat.1985–86 § 766.55(1)**. When so characterized, the obligation may be satisfied from the couple's marital property and all other property of the incurring spouse, **Wis.Stat.1985–86 § 766.55(2)(b)**. See Chapter 9, Liabilities, for further detail.

CHAPTER 5

JOINT TENANCY MEETS COMMUNITY PROPERTY

A. OVERVIEW

Joint tenancy with right of survivorship (where permitted by state law) is usually the most popular form of holding title in the names of both the husband and wife.

An astonishingly unknown point about **community property** is that except in Wisconsin (UMPA) it **cannot also be joint tenancy.**

The most commonly encountered problem of the form of title arises in the attempt by married couples to obtain the benefits of both the community property system and the survivorship feature of joint tenancy. Although some community property states create a right of survivorship in the homestead, only Idaho, Nevada, Washington and Wisconsin (UMPA) allow further merger of the survivorship incident with community property.

Generally, the intention to create a right of survivorship must be expressly stated in the instrument creating the interest. This requirement is satisfied frequently and casually.

Most major assets such as realty, stock certificates, automobiles and boats, have documents of

title. The character of the asset may be different
from that which is shown by the certificate of title
because of the intent with which the deed was
made. Recitals in the deed (e.g., as to the joint
tenancy character of the property) are prima facie
and not conclusive evidence that the couple intended the property to be separate or community. Oft-
en couples explain an undesirable nominal joint
tenancy designation as having been made "for convenience".

The joint bank account, while not a true joint
tenancy, creates additional problems because so
much of the community wealth flows through such
accounts and therefore risks transmutation into
separate property.

Joint safe deposit boxes may raise the question
whether the form of rental agreement of the box
has converted the character of the contents to joint
tenancy.

B. DETAIL

1. Prevalence of Joint Tenancy Form

The desire to avoid the cost, delay, publicity and
inconvenience of probate administration when the
property passes on the death of one spouse to the
other spouse can be satisfied by complicated and
expensive trust provisions or by the relatively common provisions of a joint tenancy.

Non-lawyers use the joint tenancy form of ownership extensively. Thus, it is quite common for

real estate agents, stockbrokers and financial institution managers of new accounts to suggest the
"joint tenancy" form with the question, "If one of
you dies, do you want the other person to have the
whole [house, stock holding or savings account]?"
or the less-informative "You want joint tenancy,
don't you?" Affirmative response by the property
owners may, and often does, result in transmutation of community property into the separate property form of a joint tenancy. Normally, the need
for choice between joint tenancy or community
property is not brought home to the parties at the
time of the transaction, but rather at a substantially later time.

In the typical situation of a newly married couple, the family home (the largest single asset) is
purchased on a time-payment method. Usually
the main, if not the only, source of funds used for
those payments is the earnings during marriage of
the spouses. Thus, the usual situation involves the
holding of the major community property asset in
joint tenancy form of title.

2. Mutually Exclusive Nature

Joint tenancy is a form of separate property
ownership and is not also community property
except in Wisconsin (UMPA). Statutes in California, Nevada and New Mexico reinforce this conclusion by stating that the husband and wife "may
hold property as joint tenants, tenants in common
or as community property". However, an identical

Washington statute is modified by a more specific statutory provision. Property acquired as "joint tenants with right of survivorship" in exchange for community property must be either joint tenancy or community property, but not both.

The tenancy by the entirety, with a comparable survivorship provision, does not exist in any of the community property states.

Only Idaho, Nevada, Washington and Wisconsin (UMPA) permit married couples to splice the survivorship feature of joint tenancy upon community property. The survivorship feature of joint tenancy causes the entire property interest to vest in the survivor of the joint tenants; this occurs by operation of law and without need for (and risk of claims by creditors in) probate administration. There is no survivorship feature in traditional community property which is comparable to that feature of the joint tenancy even though it is quite common in community property states to provide by intestacy statute for the surviving spouse to inherit (subject to contrary will provisions) all community property.

3. Significance of the Meeting

Often the question arises whether certain property owned by spouses is community property or joint tenancy. Among the contexts in which the question may arise are the following:

• Succession upon death: Joint tenancy property is owned by the surviving spouse without being subject to probate administration. Community property is subject to probate administration, claims by creditors of the decedent, the will (if any) of the decedent and the laws of intestacy.

• Divorce law interaction: If state law allows a court to award the separate property of one party to the other or if state law provides that the division of community property upon divorce shall be "equal" as opposed to being "equitable" or if fault has been eliminated as a basis for the apportionment or division of spouses' property, the question of whether a particular item is joint tenancy or community is less pressing. If, however, the court does not have jurisdiction over joint tenancy, or if the court may divide the community property equitably or if the court is using concepts of fault, the distinction between community property and joint tenancy may be crucial.

• Increased basis for income tax: Property of a deceased joint tenant obtains a new basis for income tax purposes to the extent that the property was included in the gross estate for federal estate tax purposes of the deceased joint tenant. The new basis is generally higher because of inflation and other factors; a higher basis which does not cost more is always advantageous to the surviving taxpayer. Only one half of the value of a joint tenancy between spouses is included in the gross estate for federal estate tax purposes of the deceased joint tenant. On the other hand, the entire community property is entitled to a new basis under Internal Revenue Code § 1014(b)(6), yet the amount included in the taxable estate is the same one half. Therefore, there may be a desire to establish the community property character of otherwise joint tenancy property even though the same party ultimately receives the property.

•Gifts: A joint tenant can give or convey gratuitously his or her proportionate part of the joint tenancy and thereby terminate the joint tenancy. The joint tenant cannot give more than his or her portion, but the gift of that portion cannot be set aside. The manager of the community property, on the other hand, may have the power, but not the right, to give away all of the community property. The purported conveyance can be set aside in many instances; see Chapter 7.

4. Homesteads

In Idaho, Nevada and Wisconsin, a statutory form of survivorship is created for the homestead. A homestead created between husband and wife from community property (or separate property in Nevada) vests absolutely in the survivor. Texas, by state constitutional provision, gives the surviving spouse the right to use the homestead for life.

5. Express Statement to Create Joint Tenancy

Some community property states (including California, Nevada and Washington) require that the intention to create a joint tenancy be expressly stated in the conveyance by which the title is taken.

What is an express statement that property be held in joint tenancy?

•**"Joint"**: The word "joint" is technically insufficient since tenancy in common is also a form of "joint ownership" even though not a "joint tenancy". Occasionally, courts will accept the word "joint" when used by a non-lawyer, but some supportive evidence of intention to have a joint tenancy (or at least no contradictory evidence) may be required.

•**"Joint tenancy"**: Seemingly, the clearest minimum is the term "joint tenancy".

•**"Joint tenancy with right of survivorship"**: Texas requires that the right of survivorship (which is an incident of joint tenancy) also be spelled out. The demand for certainty is met by the redundant "as joint tenants with right of survivorship and not as tenants in common". It is rare to see the addition of "and not as community property".

6. Form of Title v. Intention

Common law analysis looks to the form of title more than the ownership. The document of title must expressly state that the property is joint tenancy (and, in Texas, specify that there is a right of survivorship). Thus, if the property is registered in joint tenancy form, it is stated that there is a presumption that the property is joint tenancy or that a prima facie showing of joint tenancy has been established. The civil law, on the other hand, looks more to the ownership than to the form of title. Property registered in the name of the husband or the wife or in both names (including "as joint tenants") could be community property. Thus, it is possible to rebut the common law presumption of joint tenancy by proving the parties exchanged community property for the acquisitions and did not intend to change the form of ownership.

In efforts to do justice in individual cases, the courts have complicated the rules: The intention of the parties to convert property into joint tenancy (when accompanied by legally sufficient acts) effects a transmutation of community property into joint tenancy, but if the parties did not intend to transmute the property, no transmutation occurs regardless of the actions taken.

The burden of proof is generally upon the person who alleges that the actual title is not in the form it is stated to be. Therefore, if property is stated in a deed or stock certificate or bank account agreement to be joint tenancy, the burden of proof is upon the party who alleges that the ownership is otherwise, e.g., community property except in Wisconsin.

Oral evidence concerning intention to create a joint tenancy (or to preserve community property status) generally can be presented; it is not certain that such evidence is admissible in Texas to show that the community property form of ownership was intended to be retained despite the joint tenancy form of the title.

The owner of property must intend to change its character. In the case of the separate property of either husband or wife, only one owner's intention is necessary in order to convert the property into community property or the separate property of the other. In the case of transmutations from community property into joint tenancy (or vice versa), the intention of both parties to make the conversion is required. Thus, when community property funds are used to acquire property, the title to which is taken as joint tenants, an expression of intention appears to have been made. It is possible that the parties did not intend such a transmutation, but the burden is upon them to show their true intent. The secret understanding, misunderstanding or belief of one spouse as to the effect of the conveyance to the two of them does not affect the estate taken.

7. Nominal Title, "For Convenience"

Why would a couple specify "joint tenancy" if they did not intend to transmute their community property into joint tenancy separate property?

Popular explanations of the nature of "joint-tenancy-in-form-which-isn't-really-joint-tenancy" include statements that the form of title was "nominal", i.e., in name only. The parties did not intend anything by the form of title in which they took the property (including the form of title which they signed a card saying that they did intend). The adhesion character of financial institution

forms and practices makes such explanations reasonable.

Another exposition is that the names of both parties were put on the account "for convenience only",
i.e., so that each party could have access to all of the
funds, but both parties were to have access for the
benefit of only one of them. This argument, too, has
a reasonable ring and is often accepted by the courts.
Naturally, the trier of fact should have the last word
in making such determinations. The trier is called
upon to make a determination based upon the often
self-serving oral testimony of the parties (or one of
them) that they intended exactly the opposite of
what they previously signed a formal document saying they intended. The "convenience" explanation is
often used with non-spousal joint tenancies to indicate that the original depositor of the funds in a joint
bank account did not intend to create a form of co-
ownership, but only intended to create an agency so
that the second person could have access to the funds
to use them for the first person. This is similar to
the difference between joint holding of a safe deposit
box or a bank account on the one hand and the
"deputy" or "signature" authorization to have access
to the box or account on the other hand.

8. Joint Bank Accounts

Special statutory rules exist in most jurisdictions
for deposits of money in financial institutions. Although the term "bank account" is used in this
book, each jurisdiction has a number of differing
financial devices and institutions, e.g., "accounts",

"shares", "certificates of deposit" and "money market certificates" in savings banks, thrift corporations, savings and loan associations and credit unions. Precision is required in practice to determine which type of device in which type of institution is dealt with by a particular statute; often a state will have two or more statutes dealing with "joint" bank accounts, as that term is used here.

Joint bank accounts do not fall within traditional definitions of joint tenancy because of the statutory abrogation of the requirement of the four unities of time, title, vesting and possession. Either party to the banking agreement may withdraw all of the funds, which is contrary to the usual joint tenancy rule that a joint tenant can sever and take only his or her proportionate share of the total, i.e., one half if there are only two joint tenants.

Joint accounts are present in one form or another in every community property state. For example, the "or" form of registration of United States Series E and EE savings bonds is deemed to create a joint tenancy; this interpretation prevails as a matter of federal supremacy over state, e.g., Louisiana, law which does not otherwise permit joint tenancies.

Financial institutions generally have detailed provisions on preprinted cards which the parties sign to open new accounts. Therefore, the parties are very specific in their "agreement" that the property is joint tenancy with the right of survivorship and the financial institution may pay the proceeds of the account in full to either signatory regardless of the death of the other signatory.

The exact terms of the statutes need to be consulted in each case. Often the statute is very specific that the deposits "shall be conclusively deemed to be the separate property of the depositors". The court approach to such statutes is to consider the statute conclusive between the financial institution and the depositors, but not conclusive between the depositors themselves, i.e., the possibility of the money being community property is not foreclosed by the form of title, the specific agreement found in the printed form and the statutory language.

The importance of the joint bank account becomes obvious when one considers the methods of tracing the character of property and rebutting the general presumption: If it can be shown that property acquired during marriage was received in exchange for separate property without intent (or ability) to transmute the property into community property, the new property is separate property. Joint tenancy property is separate property except in Wisconsin (UMPA). Bank accounts may be (and usually are, if both names are on the account) joint. Most acquisitions are paid for (ultimately) by checks or with funds withdrawn from a bank account. Thus, most acquisitions can be traced to or through a joint bank account. Of course, this problem does not arise if the account is in the name of only one of the members of the married couple or if they should seek some special form of holding the account.

9. Joint Safe Deposit Boxes

Safe deposit box agreements sometimes provide that the contents of the safe deposit box shall be joint tenancy between the co-tenants of the box. This agreement, if intended, can be binding upon the parties in the absence of restrictive statute (such as exists in California). The rule is more difficult to apply in the case of documents in the safe deposit box which are registered in the name of one of the spouses or in both their names in a form of ownership other than joint tenancy, e.g., community property. Should the box agreement prevail over the express registration?

If a deed or stock certificate is not registered in joint tenancy form but is located within a safe deposit box which is evidenced by an agreement that the contents shall be joint tenancy, the battle of paperwork probably should be resolved in favor of the express statement of title that is more specific, i.e., the certificates rather than the safe deposit box agreement. Another method of resolving the conflicting paper titles is to give effect to the later in time. Thus, if the boxholder agreement was signed last, it would control; if the certificate was issued later, it would control. A complication under this system would occur if 100 shares of a corporation were owned as community property and placed in a newly-opened safe deposit box which had an agreement that the contents would be joint tenancy (thus converting the joint tenancy under the "later document" theory) and then the stock had a 100% stock dividend which would be issued in the same form as the original certificate, i.e., as community property.

10. Summary

The network of presumptions concerning joint tenancy as separate property is more developed in California than in the other community property states. The approach (which may serve as a guide for arriving at equitable decisions in differing cases) is as follows:

1. Property acquired during marriage is presumed to be community property. This is the general presumption.

2. The general presumption yields to a different intention expressed in the instrument by which title is taken.

3. California holds that a statement of joint tenancy is an expression of intention that the property not be held as community property; Arizona and New Mexico hold that a joint tenancy deed is not sufficient by its form alone to show an intention that the property be transmuted from community property.

4. In order to be joint tenancy (with right of survivorship), it is necessary for the instrument to

state that title shall be held as joint tenants (with right of survivorship). As a practical matter, most deeds to husband and wife do so indicate.

5. An express statement that the title is taken as joint tenants is presumptively correct. It must be rebutted by those who claim that the ownership is different from the form of title. In the case of bona fide purchasers for value, the presumption is conclusive in order to allow purchasers to rely upon that cornerstone of the common law title system, the record title.

6. The intention that the property be (or not be) joint tenancy cannot be unilateral. The secret intention of one party that the property remain (or not remain) community property will not be given effect. The manager of the community cannot transmute it into joint tenancy without the consent of the non-managing spouse.

7. In California (when oral transmutations of the character of realty were permitted), the evidence that the parties did not intend to create a joint tenancy—even though the instrument expressly states that they did so intend—could be oral.

C. INDIVIDUAL STATES

ARIZONA

Arizona permits "express words [which] vest the estate in the survivor upon the death of a grantee or devisee" by Ariz.Rev.Stat. § 33–431.

In re Baldwin's Estate, 50 Ariz. 265, 71 P.2d 791
(1937) is the foundation for distinguishing joint
tenancy from community property in Arizona.
While validating the possibility that community
property could be transmuted into joint tenancy,
the Arizona Supreme Court held in that case that
a deed clause (which is prepared by the grantor
and seldom seen by the grantees) reciting "joint
tenancy" is not enough, alone, to effect a transmutation. The spouse against whom the property is
claimed must know that the deed provided for a
joint tenancy. The burden of proof is upon the
party claiming the effectiveness of the joint tenancy clause in the deed. The knowledge could be
shown, for example, by acceptance of the terms
written by the grantee or a notation by the recorder that the deed was placed of record at the request
of that spouse.

The importance of the distinction between community property and joint tenancy is diminished in
Arizona by the adoption of the following statutes:

● **Ariz.Rev.Stat.** § **25–318** allows the divorce
court to divide equitably the joint tenancy "and
other property held in common" as well as the
community property, even though the separate
property of each spouse is assigned to him or her:

**A. In a proceeding for dissolution of the
marriage, or for legal separation . . . the
court shall assign each spouse's sole and separate property to such spouse. It shall also
divide the community, joint tenancy and other**

property held in common equitably, though not necessarily in kind, without regard to marital misconduct.

• Ariz.Rev.Stat. § 14–2102 (which is similar to Uniform Probate Code § 2–102) gives by intestacy all community property and all separate property to the surviving spouse unless there are issue of the deceased spouse who are not issue of the surviving spouse (i.e., step-issue). Unless there are such step-issue or there is a will which does not leave the potentially joint tenancy property outright to the surviving spouse, the ultimate disposition of the property to the surviving spouse is the same.

Therefore, the only major differences between community property and joint tenancy between spouses in Arizona center upon the rights of creditors, the procedure for clearing title of the deceased person's interest and the income tax basis of inherited property in the hands of the successor in interest.

CALIFORNIA

California permits the creation of joint tenancy "when expressly declared in the transfer to be a joint tenancy", Calif.Civ.Code § 683, but §§ 683.1 and 683.2 impose unique limitations. Calif.Civ.Code § 683.1 states that safe deposit box rental agreements shall not create a joint tenancy in the contents of the box. Calif.Civ.Code § 683.2 restricts the effect of an unrecorded unilateral termination of a joint tenancy.

The difficulty of reconciling joint tenancy form and community property substance in California is spelled out in both Marriage of Lucas, 27 Cal.3d 808, 166 Cal.Rptr. 853, 614 P.2d 285 (1980) and Calif.Civ.Code § 4800.1.

Calif.Civ.Code § 4800.1(b) states: **For the purpose of division of property upon dissolution of marriage or legal separation, property acquired by the parties during marriage in joint form, including property held in tenancy in common, joint tenancy, tenancy by the entirety, or as community property is presumed to be community property. . . .**

Retroactive application of the statutes has been attempted by the legislature, as in Calif.Civ.Code § 4800.1(a)(3), but has repeatedly been rejected by the California Supreme Court.

IDAHO

Idaho Code Section 15–6–201(d) enlarges the Uniform Probate Code by adding material (similar to Washington's provision) permitting a community property agreement which controls the passage of property upon the death of either spouse:

In the case of agreements to pass property at death to the surviving spouse, such agreements shall be executed in writing, acknowledged or proved in the same manner as deeds to real property, contain a description of all real property, be altered or amended in the same way, and shall be revoked in the event husband and wife are subsequently divorced. The existence

of such an agreement shall not affect the rights of creditors. . . .

Idaho also permits the survivorship characteristic of joint tenancy to exist in the case of a homestead declared from community property, **Idaho Code § 55–1206:**

If the selection [of a homestead] was made by a married person from the community property, the land, on the death of either of the spouses, vests in the survivor. . . .

LOUISIANA

Louisiana avoids much of the litigation concerning the transmutation of community property into joint tenancy by the non-existence of joint tenancy. Additionally, see Chapter 2 concerning Louisiana restrictions upon transmutation.

NEVADA

The distinction between community property and joint tenancy is highlighted by **Nev.Rev.Stat. 123.030** which provides as follows:

A husband and wife may hold real or personal property as joint tenants, tenants in common, or as community property.

The transmutation of community property into joint tenancy is expressly permitted by Nev.Rev.Stat. 111.065 which requires a writing. The specificity of this section seems to have avoided much of the litigation concerning the joint tenancy or community property nature of property which plagues the courts of Arizona, California, New Mexico and Washington.

Nev.Rev.Stat. 111.064(2) shows the ease with which a right of survivorship can be attached to community property:

A right of survivorship does not arise when an estate in community property is created in a husband and wife, as such, unless the instrument creating the estate expressly declares that the husband and wife take the property as community property with a right of survivorship. This right of survivorship is extinguished whenever either spouse, during the marriage, transfers his interest in the community property.

Additionally, a homestead (defined in Nev.Rev.Stat. 115.010) when declared upon community property is deemed to be held as community property with right of survivorship, Nev.Rev.Stat. 115.060.

NEW MEXICO

N.Mex.Stat.1978 § 40–3–2 states that:

Husband and wife may hold property as joint tenants, tenants in common or as community property.

N.M.Stat.1978 § 40–3–8 B provides, in part:

Property acquired by a husband and wife by an instrument in writing whether as tenants in common or as joint tenants or otherwise will be presumed to be held as community property unless such property is separate property. . .

Despite the two statutes which seem to state that property cannot be both joint tenancy and community property, the survivorship incident of joint tenancy is seemingly combined at death with community property by **N.M.Stat.1978 § 45–2–804 A.**, added in 1984: . . .**except that community property that is joint tenancy property under Subsection B of Section 40–3–8 NMSA 1978 shall not be subject to the testamentary disposition of the decedent.**

Transmutation of community funds or property into joint tenancy has been permitted since the decision in Chavez v. Chavez, 56 N.M. 393, 244 P.2d 781 (1952), but the quantum of proof necessary has had varying interpretations.

Initially, In re Trimble's Estate, 57 N.M. 51, 253 P.2d 805 (1953) stated that the transmutation must be established by clear, strong and convincing proof—more than a mere preponderance of evidence. Shortly afterwards, **N.Mex.Stat.1978 § 47–1–16** was enacted:

An instrument conveying or transferring title to real or personal property to two or more persons as joint tenants, to two or more persons and to the survivors of them and the heirs and assigns of the survivor, or to two or more persons with right of survivorship, shall be prima facie evidence that such property is held in a joint tenancy and shall be conclusive as to purchasers or encumbrancers for value. In any litigation involving the issue of such ten-

ancy a preponderance of the evidence shall be sufficient to establish the same.

Estate of Fletcher, 94 N.M. 572, 613 P.2d 714 (1980) seemed to state that the statute applies only to the initial character of the property and that clear, strong and convincing evidence would be required to prove a transmutation. Blake v. Blake, 102 N.M. 354, 695 P.2d 838 (App. 1985) held that the quantum of proof to rebut or sustain prima facie evidence of joint tenancy is the preponderance of the evidence and not clear, strong and convincing proof.

TEXAS

Holding title in the form of "joint tenancy with right of survivorship" does not appear to be as commonly used in Texas as in other community property states (except Louisiana, which does not permit joint tenancies).

Texas, the birthplace of the concept of the "Homestead", has the following state constitutional provision in the **Texas Constitution Article XVI, § 52:**

On the death of the husband or wife, or both, the homestead shall descend and vest in like manner as other real property of the deceased, and shall be governed by the same laws of descent and distribution, but it shall not be partitioned among the heirs of the deceased during the lifetime of the surviving husband or wife, or so long as the survivor may elect to

use or occupy the same as a homestead, or so long as the guardian of the minor children of the deceased may be permitted, under the order of the proper court having the jurisdiction, to use and occupy the same.

Texas has had a checkered pattern in forbidding the creation of joint tenancies with right of survivorship from community property:

1. Ricks v. Smith, 159 Tex. 280, 318 S.W.2d 439 (1958), allowed the creation of a joint tenancy with right of survivorship from community property. This case, however, was specifically overruled by the next case:

2. Hilley v. Hilley, 161 Tex. 569, 342 S.W.2d 565 (1961), reasoned that joint tenancy with right of survivorship could not be created from community property because the acquisition during marriage was not by gift, but by exchange (of the community property). Thus, the separate property joint tenancy with right of survivorship could not be created. This rule was modified, in turn, as to federal obligations by the next case:

3. Free v. Bland, 369 U.S. 663, 82 S.Ct. 1089, 8 L.Ed.2d 180 (1962) held that, as a matter of federal supremacy, Texas was not free to deny the joint tenancy status or survivorship characteristic to United States government bonds issued in "or" form (which was given the survivorship characteristic by federal regulation).

4.　The Texas legislature amended the predecessor of Vernon's Ann.Tex.Stat.Probate Code § 46 by adding a final sentence which read "It is specifically provided that any husband and his wife may, by written agreement, create a joint estate out of their community property, with rights of survivorship."

5.　The Texas Supreme Court declared the quoted portion of the probate code to be unconstitutional in Williams v. McKnight, 402 S.W.2d 505 (Tex.1966) for the same reasons as were given in *Hilley v. Hilley*, cited above.　The Texas legislature subsequently deleted that sentence from the probate code section.

6.　A Texas spouse may utilize community property to create a valid joint tenancy with right of survivorship between that spouse and a third party.　If the spouses first partition community property, thus creating the separate property of each, the separate property so created may be used to create a joint tenancy with right of survivorship between the spouses.　Thus, it is possible to create a joint tenancy from community property in Texas, provided the proper steps are taken.

7.　In 1980, the Texas Constitution Article XVI, § 15 was amended to permit more liberal transmutations.　It is possible, though not absolutely certain, that the right to create joint tenancies with rights of survivorship directly from community property therefore presently exists and is constitutional in Texas.

In the same vein of consistency, Vernon's Ann.Tex.Stat.Probate Code § 46 is captioned "Joint Tenancies Abolished" yet it specifically permits joint ownership; it then states that the right of survivorship does not exist, but may be made to exist. In summary, **Vernon's Ann.Tex.Stat.Probate Code § 46** requires that the right of survivorship be expressly stated:

Where two (2) or more persons hold an estate, real, personal, or mixed, jointly, and one (1) joint owner dies before severance, his interest in said joint estate shall not survive to the remaining joint owner or joint owners, but shall descend to, and be vested in, the heirs or legal representatives of such deceased joint owner in the same manner as if his interest had been severed and ascertained. Provided, however, that by an agreement in writing of joint owners of property the interest of any joint owner who dies may be made to survive to the surviving joint owner or joint owners, but no such agreement shall be inferred from the mere fact that the property is held in joint ownership.

The 1980 amendment to **Texas Constitution Article XVI, § 15** provides, in part:

the spouses may from time to time, by written instrument, agree between themselves that the income or property from all or part of the separate property then owned by one of them,

**or which thereafter might be acquired, shall be
the separate property of that spouse. . . .**

WASHINGTON

Rev.Code Wash.Ann. 64.28.010 sets out the
right of survivorship in joint tenancy:

**A joint tenancy shall have the incidents of
survivorship and severability as at common
law. Joint tenancy shall be created only by
written instrument, which instrument shall expressly declare the interest created to be a
joint tenancy. . . .**

Cases have extended the express written requirement for the creation of a joint tenancy to require
additional affirmative evidence of the intent of
both spouses to convert community property into
joint tenancy:

Estate of Olson, 87 Wash.2d 855, 557 P.2d 302
(1976) held that a promissory note and mortgage,
both of which recited that they were to the spouses
as joint tenants, were insufficient to create a joint
tenancy because there was no "clear indication by
the marital community that the property subject to
joint tenancy is intended by them to be held as
such." The court did not consider the doctrine of
law by which the recipient of title by a deed poll is
bound by conditions and covenants in the deed.

In Lambert v. Peoples National Bank of Washington, 89 Wash.2d 646, 574 P.2d 738 (1978), mutual fund
certificates of beneficial interest issued to a husband

and wife as joint tenants at the request of the wife who managed the community funds (the husband being an illiterate immigrant from Belgium) were held to be community property and not joint tenancy despite the joint tenancy form of the certificates. In that case the court affirmed a trial court holding that a presumption of joint tenancy arose from the form in which the securities were registered, but that that presumption was conclusively rebutted when it was shown that the securities had been purchased with community funds. The court quoted with approval the language in the *Olson* case that "The creation of a joint tenancy could not be accomplished by [the debtor's] unilateral act of executing the promissory note and real estate mortgage. In substance there was no writing *by the marital community* expressly declaring the interest created to be a joint tenancy." [Emphasis added.] Written evidence of the request by both spouses for the joint tenancy form is often difficult to locate. Although banks retain signature cards and vehicle registration records are centrally located, brokerage account records may be incomplete or prospective only and the background papers for deeds and promissory notes are often difficult to locate.

The mutual exclusivity of joint tenancy and community property, found in other community property states, seems to be implied by **Rev.Code Wash.Ann. 64.28.020:**

Every interest created in favor of two or more persons in their own right is an interest in common, unless acquired by them in partnership, for partnership purposes, or unless

declared in its creation to be a joint tenancy, as provided in RCW 64.28.010, or unless acquired as community property.   . . .

Nevertheless, Washington serves as a model to the other community property states in its solution to the problem of choosing between community property and joint tenancy: Washington permits a recorded formal "community property agreement" which may create a right of survivorship between the spouses. **Rev.Code Wash.Ann 26.16.120** provides as follows:

Nothing . . . in any law of this state, shall prevent the husband and wife from jointly entering into any agreement concerning the status or disposition of the whole or any portion of the community property, then owned by them or afterwards to be acquired, to take effect upon the death of either. But such agreement may be made at any time by the husband and wife by the execution of an instrument in writing under their hands and seals, and to be witnessed, acknowledged and certified in the same manner as deeds to real estate are required to be, under the laws of the state, and the same may at any time thereafter be altered or amended in the same manner: *Provided, however,* That such agreement shall not derogate from the right of creditors, nor be construed to curtail the powers of the superior court to set aside or cancel such agreement for fraud or under some other recognized head of equity jurisdiction, at the suit of either party.

It is interesting to note that joint tenancy had a difficult struggle for existence in Washington; the present statute permitting joint tenancy with the right of survivorship for persons who are not husband and wife, Rev.Code Wash.Ann. 64.28.010, traces to a 1960 initiative.

One problem that remains with the Washington system is that the emphasis upon the formality of the agreement by which survivorship is affixed to community property (sealed, witnessed, acknowledged and certified documents) may impose too high a standard for the average layperson. On the other hand, similar formalities for deeds (and the requirements for wills) have served the function of impressing the parties with the importance of the act while providing excellent evidence of the intention of the parties.

Although Holohan v. Melville, 41 Wash.2d 380, 249 P.2d 777 (1952) is obsolete because of subsequent changes in the law, it contains an excellent history of the law's attitude toward joint tenancies, overview of the types of statutes by which either that type of tenancy or its incident of survivorship or both were attempted to be abolished and insight into methods used by lawyers to create the same result when joint tenancy with right of survivorship is not permitted by local law.

WISCONSIN (and UMPA)

Wisconsin and UMPA blast through the traditional concept that joint tenancy cannot be community property.

Wis.Stat.1985–86 § **766.60(4)** authorizes the holding of marital property in joint tenancy form:

(4)(a) Spouses may hold property in any other form permitted by law, including but not limited to a concurrent form or a form that provides survivorship ownership. . . . [T]o the extent the incidents of the . . . joint tenancy conflict with or differ from the incidents of [marital] property classification. . ., the incidents of the . . . joint tenancy, including the incident of survivorship, control. . . .

Wis.Stat.1985–86 § **766.60(5):** authorizes a special form of marital property called "survivorship marital property":

(5)(a) If the words "survivorship marital property" are used. . ., the marital property so held is survivorship marital property. On the death of a spouse, the ownership rights of that spouse in the property vest solely in the surviving spouse by nontestamentary disposition at death. . . .

The Legislative Council notes to these statutes point out that the most significant differences between joint tenancy and survivorship marital property are the income tax treatment of basis at the death of a spouse and the right of a joint tenant to destroy unilaterally the right of survivorship. The ability to destroy the right of survivorship in survivorship marital property depends upon both the form in which the property is held and whether the entire ownership interest or only a portion of it is transferred.

Wis.Stat.1985–86 § 766.605 contains a special rule (for which there is no UMPA equivalent) covering some homesteads:

A homestead acquired after the determination date exclusively between spouses with no 3d party is survivorship marital property if no intent to the contrary is expressed on the instrument of transfer.

Under this statute, unless a contrary intent is shown, a deed of realty to a husband and wife (and no other person) as grantees creates survivorship marital property if the realty is in fact a homestead. If the deeded realty is not a homestead, the property is marital property, without a right of survivorship.

Wis.Stat.1985–86 § 766.60(4)(b)1 states that if "a document of title, instrument of transfer or bill of sale" after the determination date expresses an intention to establish (a) a joint tenancy or (b) a tenancy in common, the property is, respectively, (a) survivorship marital property or (b) marital property. Similarly **Wis.Stat.1985–86 § 766.60(4)(b)2** states:

A joint tenancy or tenancy in common exclusively between spouses which is given by a 3rd party after the determination date is survivorship marital property or marital property, respectively, unless the donor provides otherwise.

CHAPTER 6

CHARACTERIZATION PROBLEMS

A. OVERVIEW

1. Approach

Preliminary steps have been taken before the material in this chapter applies:

1. If the husband and wife transmute or otherwise agree concerning the character of the property, the valid transmutation or agreement will prevail over the rules in this chapter.

2. If one spouse makes a gift to the other, the gift rules will prevail over the rules in this chapter. Note that some of the rules concerning the commingling of community and separate property infer a gift from the husband when he is manager of the community.

3. The form of title could be considered by the court in determining whether the rules in this chapter apply to certain transactions.

After deciding that there is no overriding transmutation, agreement nor gift and that the form of title is not determinative, we continue with the following steps:

4. Property generally takes the character of the property used to acquire it. The process of deter-

mining the character of the property by identifying the source from which it is derived is called "tracing". If the property in question was obtained in exchange for entirely separate property, it will be separate property. If the property in question was obtained in exchange for entirely community property, it is community property. These rules apply regardless of the time of acquisition. For example, property acquired during marriage is presumed to be community property, but upon demonstration that the property was acquired in exchange for separate property, the general presumption is rebutted and the separate property character of the property is established.

5. If property's source cannot be traced, then its time of acquisition is material. Property acquired when one is unmarried is separate property. Property acquired during marriage is presumed to be community. If the property cannot be traced, the presumption is unrebutted and prevails. If the property is traced to a separate property origin, then the presumption is overcome. A typical tracing to a separate property origin is a demonstration that the property was acquired gratuitously or in exchange for separate property. Untraceable property acquired by one who is unmarried is not presumed to be community property.

The subject matter of this chapter continues with problems which are more complex:

6. Some problems arise in determining when an asset is "acquired" when the process of acquisition

overlaps both married and unmarried periods in the acquirer's life. What is the exact point at which an asset is "acquired" when there are a series of steps (other than payments) in the acquisition?

7. When we deal with a number of payments, new problems arise: If the wealth used to acquire an asset can be traced, but is traced to both community and separate property, then we are dealing with problems of "commingling". If the proportions of each can be determined, different jurisdictions use different approaches for different assets, but the choice is usually between co-ownership or creditor status for one of the characters of property:

Are the separate and community characters of property co-owners in proportion to their contributions or is one character of property treated as the owner of the property which borrowed from (as opposed to becoming a partner with) the other character of property?

8. If the two characters are so intermixed that they cannot be separated (i.e., the characters are "confused"), courts usually apply the presumption that the "confused" property is community unless the amount of community in the mixture was negligible.

9. In many cases, the property has not been paid for at the time that a determination of its character is made (or was used entirely to pay for itself, as the rent from commercial property being

used to pay off the purchase price). Separate rules have evolved for credit acquisitions.

10. One of the most difficult areas of commingling and confusion involves the premarital (and therefore separate property) business of one spouse (usually the husband) to which community property efforts have been added.

11. Additional complications arise in jurisdictions which recognize (a) different types of community property or (b) characters of property in addition to separate and community. California has both forms in (a) pre-1923 (v. post-1923) community property and (b) "quasi-community" property (property acquired while the spouses were not domiciled in California which would have been community property if the spouses had then been domiciled in California). Wisconsin uses the category of "predetermination date property" to describe property owned by a married couple before the later of 1986 or the establishment of their Wisconsin domicile. This category probably encompasses the largest number and value of marital assets in Wisconsin at present.

2. Commingling

Commingling involves the mixing together of property of different characters: Community and separate of either or both husband and wife.

What status should be given to the separate property interest which is mixed into the same asset as admittedly community property? There are **four major possibilities**:

1. **Complete domination**: The separate property interest could be, but seldom is, treated as the dominant characteristic of the entire asset. This result occurs typically when a minimal amount of community property is involved. If the owner of a separate property house marries and performs services (which would ordinarily be community property) in maintaining the house, the character of the house remains separate and no debt is owed to the non-owning spouse. On the other hand, if substantial community property funds are used to make major improvements in the separate property house, the non-owning spouse has a claim for reimbursement (as a creditor) but still has no ownership in the house.

2. **Co-ownership**: Often the owner of separate property interest is treated as a co-owner of mixed property. For example, if a wife purchases a house and uses 20% separate property of her own and 80% community property in the acquisition, the co-ownership will be in the same percentages as the contribution. This "proportionate" ownership is not fully recognized in all jurisdictions; Louisiana has been the state least willing to proportion the ownership in accordance with the contribution.

Most states apportion by percentage of contribution of the two (or three if both spouses' separate property are involved) characters of property for some types of assets (for example, securities) but not for other types of assets (for example, property acquired by adverse possession).

3. **Creditor**: If untransmuted separate property can be traced but the separate property is not recognized as a component of the asset acquired, it is possible that reimbursement will be permitted. Louisiana again follows the classic Spanish model more accurately by allowing reimbursement to the owner of separate property of the dollar amount which came from the separate property. Assuming an inflationary growth in the number of dollars which an item is worth, the "lending" separate property loses both purchasing power and possible income by the interest-free loan which is deemed to have been made.

4. **Contributor**: The mixing of community property with the separate property of the person having management and control of the community property may result in a "gift". This rule has traditionally been applied only to the husband since he had the management and control. Changes in the management and control theoretically should result in gender-neutral application of this rule. Additionally, if the separate and community are so intermixed that the separate cannot be identified, the mixture will be deemed to be entirely community. Thus, the burden of tracing the separate property is upon the party who intermixed it (or theoretically was in the best position to keep records or to avoid intermixing); if he or

she cannot or does not trace, he or she becomes a contributor of his or her separate property.

3. Tracing

Tracing applies both to the determination by historical research of the uncombined character of property and to reseparating property of mixed characters. The uncombined character of property is determined by tracing it to the character of the property used to acquire it. The characterization of the mixture of separate and community properties depends, in part, upon whether the formerly separate elements can be reseparated. The process of uncommingling is another application of "tracing".

Except in Wisconsin (and UMPA), tracing is a process originated and authorized by decisions, as opposed to statutes. The application of the technique is universal despite the literal wording of statutes dealing with the definition of community property or the general presumption that property acquired during marriage is community property. The existence of the concept of tracing requires a tortured definition of "acquired" as "original acquisition" or requires the modification of the means of acquisition to include "exchange" as well as "onerously or gratuitously".

Not all community property states permit tracing in all circumstances. In the cases where tracing is not allowed or cannot be achieved, commingled separate and community property is deemed to be community unless the amount of community involved in the commingling was negligible. Having classified the property as community, a few of the states follow the lead of Louisiana in allowing a right of reimbursement to the separate property owner.

4. Inception of Title and Apportionment

In all jurisdictions the character of property is fixed at the time that the property is acquired, and that acquisition is achieved at the "inception of title" (or "right"). The jurisdictions differ, however, as to whether the original character continues unchanged when labor or capital of another character is subsequently added to the property. The classic theory (followed in Louisiana, New Mexico and Texas) treats the acquisition character as fixed while the remaining jurisdictions sometimes give a proportionate share of the asset to each character of the property.

The inception of title theory fixes the character of property at the time that the property is acquired. Rigidity occurs, not from the initial characterization, but from inability to change character, regardless of improvements which merge into the basic asset or payments from property of another character.

The characteristic of the inception of title theory which separates it from the proportionate theory is inertia. The character of property remains that which it was at the inception of title, unless positively changed by operation of law or act of the parties (such as transmutation agreement or gift).

The inception of title doctrine is based upon a stereotype of a purchase in which all, or a large part, of the purchase price is paid at one time. The theory accommodates situations in which the purchase price is fully paid and title is delivered at a later time. This stereotype of large initial payment is not met in life insurance and pension fund cases; it has become less frequent in real estate and other major purchases.

A second method of characterizing property with both community and separate property elements is to apportion the character of the acquisition pro rata as the two (or three, if both husband's and wife's separate properties have been contributed) characters of property have contributed to it. This method is used without question as to original acquisitions financed by contributions of the separate properties of each of the two spouses and is generally used as to original acquisitions financed partly by separate property and partly by community property. At this point, the apportionment formula produces the same results as the inception of title theory. It is the effect of subsequent contributions to the purchase price that shows the differences in the two theories:

Under the inception of title theory, the separate or community character (or proportion of each, if permitted) of the property is fixed at the inception of title and does not change to accommodate the

different character of subsequent improvements or
contributions to the acquisition cost. Thus, the
post-inception character is reduced to a role of
contributor or creditor and cannot be a co-owner.
The apportionment theory, however, would allow a
constant process of adjustment of the total character. The apportionment rule is demonstrated in
the following example:

EXAMPLE: Husband paid ten annual payments
for an insurance policy on his life, five prior to
marriage and five after his marriage. H died; his
wife was not the beneficiary designated in the
policy. Under the proportionate or the inception
of right test, the policy was separate property upon
its purchase, through the first five payments and
until the first payment after the marriage. The
theories then go their separate ways. Upon the
sixth payment (presumably from community
funds), the inception of title theory would entitle
the community property to reimbursement, but the
policy and its proceeds would remain entirely separate property. Under the proportionate test, the
sixth payment (which is the first payment from
community property) would result in the policy
and its proceeds being five-sixths separate and one-
sixth community. The ratio of separate and community would change with each subsequent payment under the proportionate test. Ultimately,
half of the policy (and its proceeds) would be community because the half of the payments made
during marriage were presumably from communi-

ty property. Note that the adjustment is only roughly fair; no interest is computed upon the earlier payments. Often jurisdictions do not differentiate between term insurance policies in which the major amount of the proceeds is directly traceable to the last payment (the prior payments having obtained expired insurance coverage and the right to renew) and ordinary or endowment policies in which the past premiums build up a cash surrender value so that the amount of insurance is only a small increment of the total proceeds paid.

To illustrate some typical problems in this area, consider the following examples. In each of the examples, if Time 1 is prior to marriage, is the property separate property? Different results are reached in different states and sometimes within the same state.

TIME PURCHASE: H enters into a contract to purchase (in Louisiana, "bond for deed" for) Blackacre at Time 1, pays the consideration from his separate property at Time 2, and receives title at Time 3.

MORTGAGE FORECLOSURE: W sells Blackacre, taking back a mortgage at Time 1; the buyer defaults and W takes a deed in lieu of foreclosure at Time 2.

LAND PATENT: H enters into federal land for land grant purposes at Time 1; a patent is issued at Time 2.

ADVERSE POSSESSION WITHOUT COLOR OF TITLE: W enters into adverse possession (or prescription) without color of title at Time 1; the time for action is barred by the statute of limitations at Time 2; W perfects her record title by legal action at Time 3.

ADVERSE POSSESSION WITH COLOR OF TITLE: H purchases a colorable, but imperfect title at Time 1 and enters into adverse possession (or prescription) with color of title at Time 2; the time for action is barred by the statute of limitations at Time 3; H perfects his record title by legal action at Time 4.

CONTINGENT FEE: W, an attorney, enters into a contingent fee contract at Time 1, renders service at Time 2, gets a verdict and judgment in her favor at Time 3 which is upheld on appeal at Time 4 and paid (begrudgingly) at Time 5.

PENSION: W is employed by Employer at Time 1 through Time 10. Payments are made each year into a pension fund. W's rights to payments from the fund vest in percentages and are subject to conditions which are not completely removed until her retirement in Time 10.

At what time in the various examples is the inception of title? When does H or W have a "property interest"? Is the possible claim against an insurance company on a policy which insures the life of a living person a "property" interest? The inception of title theory usually characterizes property at the point in time when it expands from a "mere expectancy" to a property interest. The right to the proceeds of a policy insuring the life of a living person, the forfeitable pension rights of an employee and the not-yet-perfected claim of an adverse possessor have all, at times, been classified as not being a property interest. If they are not a property interest, then there can be no vested right in them.

Although the foregoing issues are presented here in connection with a period which started before and ended after the wedding, it is possible that similar problems will arise over a period which commences during the marriage and ends after the marriage is terminated. Similarly, the period may start while the couple is domiciled in one community (or separate) property state and end while they are domiciled in another community (or separate) property state.

Occasionally, a court will utilize an all-or-nothing approach by declaring that an asset which is the product of both community and separate contributions is entirely community property (or entirely separate property) rather than a portion of each. This all-or-nothing approach is an unwillingness to apply proportionate ownership at the inception of right. The likelihood of this approach varies according to the jurisdiction, the type of asset acquired (realty, life insurance, pensions, business) and the form of the contributions. As a rule of thumb, the all-or-nothing approach varies from strong to weak as the contribution moves from time, through labor to non-cash property items to cash.

B. DETAIL

1. Tracing Commingled Bank Accounts

The most typical and difficult tracing involves bank accounts into which both separate and community property have been deposited. Various techniques are possible to trace the funds:

• Payment of community expenses could be charged to the community property deposited, or, conversely, payment of separate expenses could be charged to the separate property deposited. These methods are sometimes successful in eliminating the character of property which has the smallest amount deposited.

• FIFO ("First In, First Out") is a mechanical accounting method by which the chronology of deposits and withdrawals determines the character of the property acquired by funds from the commingled account.

• Equitable application of selected theories is the most commonly used method. The manager of the community property is treated as a wrongdoer when he (or she) commingles community property with his (or her) separate property. The victim of the wrong is permitted to choose between tracing the funds *into* the commingled account (thus having a claim against the account) or *through* the account to other assets acquired with account money (thus having a claim against those assets). When the victim asserts a claim against the account itself, the victim is entitled to the legal fiction that the wrongdoer first withdrew his or her own separate funds. On the other hand, when the victim wishes to trace a specific withdrawal of cash to a specific asset, the victim is allowed to do so.

One limitation upon either method (tracing "to" or tracing "through") is imposed by the lowest intermediate balance of the bank account. When there are a succession of deposits and withdrawals of separate and community property, the claimant is not entitled to more from the account than the lowest intermediate balance in the account between the time of the commingling and the time as of which the rights in the fund are to be determined. For example, if the order of deposits and withdrawals was that (1) an originally separate account (2) had community property added to it and (3) the funds were dissipated without proceeds, then (4) the subsequent addition of separate funds (unless intended as restitution to the community) to the formerly commingled account should not be deemed to repay the community for its contribution.

• Equitable lien only: In dealing with the commingled bank account, the Restatement of Restitution provides in § 211 for an equitable lien upon the money remaining in the account and upon the proceeds of the part of the account which was withdrawn. Section 212, however, allows a lien only for the lowest intermediate balance when all subsequent deposits were of the depositor's own (i.e., separate) property.

• Restitution: Restatement of Restitution §§ 202 through 215, inclusive, deal with "Following Property Into Its Product" which is a form of tracing. The practical effect of those sections is that tracing gives the innocent party a choice between a constructive trust (i.e., to own a fractional share in the account or its proceeds) or an equitable lien (i.e., to have security for the dollar amount which is owed by the wrongdoer).

Normally, the difference between a constructive trust and an equitable lien is monetary and arises when there is an increase in value of the asset. If there is such an increase, the owner of an interest in the item (by constructive trust) will benefit from the increase in value while the owner of a debt secured by an equitable lien upon the item will have no share in the increase. The question may also arise for non-economic reasons: The psychological difference may be strong between owning one half of a thing and merely owning one half of its value.

The Restatement of Restitution suggests allowing a choice of either an equitable lien ("owes me") or a constructive trust ("I own") as a remedy for wrongdoing. The manager of the community property who commingles it is often placed into the category of "wrongdoer" because of the breach of fiduciary duties. In the community property situation, however, the commingling is often more the product of ignorance than malice. The concept of "fault" in managing the community may be as questionable as the concept of fault in terminating the marriage. Community property is usually divided at death or divorce; "fault" is inappropriate at death and unfashionable at divorce. Should current trends to disregard marital fault extend to managerial fault? Is it a valid assumption that the manager of the community is at fault because he or she is "converting" property by the act of commingling?

Restatement of Restitution § 210 first gives an equitable claim against the property for reimbursement to the owner of money which is wrongfully mingled by another and used to acquire property. The section then allows the alternative remedy of a constructive trust if "the wrongdoer knew that he was acting wrongfully". It is difficult to apply this concept of a "conscious wrongdoer" to the managerial spouse, but courts appear to do so in some cases.

If the parties are equally innocent, i.e., if the concept of fault is eliminated, restitution principles indicate that the fairest ownership between the parties is in proportion to their contributions.

2. Improvements Which Commingle

a. Overview: If property of one character (e.g., community) is used to improve property of another character (e.g., the husband's separate property) generally the improved property does not lose its character, but the owner of the property consumed in the improvement (i.e., the community property) becomes a "creditor".

EXAMPLE: Husband, as manager of the community, used community property funds to build an addition upon his own separate property apartment house. Except in Wisconsin, the community property is given an equitable lien upon or reimbursement from his separate property.

The reimbursement theme is strongest when the following elements exist:

1. Realty, rather than personalty, is improved. Although the rule also applies to personalty, the doctrine of accessions (which destroys the identity of personalty which merges into realty) reinforces the realty situation.

2. The improvements are made with community property upon the separate property of the manager of the community. Variations include all combinations of community, husband's separate and wife's separate property as improving and improved property.

3. Physical improvements of the property are made. Although some states also apply this principle to payments upon indebtedness, there is a blending of the concept of credit acquisitions when the payments reduce the purchase-money obligation.

4. The improving property is cash, as opposed to labor. Labor is often disregarded, sometimes treated as an improvement and occasionally treated as giving an interest in the thing worked upon, e.g., when community property labor contributes materially to a separate property business.

Note that the four distinctions made above merely indicate the areas where the rule is most likely to be applied. The basic theme is that reimbursement (i.e., "creditor" status, as opposed to "contributor" or "co-owner" status,) is permitted when property of one character is used to improve property of a different character.

The variations from this simple theme are multiple:

• "Reimbursement" is stressed by Louisiana and Texas courts (making the contributing party an unsecured creditor); the other courts stress that an "equitable lien" is imposed upon the improved property. The states which impose an equitable lien are not uniform in determining whether that lien arises upon the improvement of the property (giving, in effect, an interest in the property which is improved) or arises only when the court deems it to be appropriate (i.e., it is a remedy within the discretion of the court).

• The lien terminology implies that it secures a debt based upon the right to reimbursement. It is possible (but less likely) that a constructive trust will be imposed for the increase in value due to the addition of the community funds. The subrogation approach is seldom used in this area.

b. Minority Rules:

(i) **Wisconsin (and UMPA)** provide for co-ownership by statute: "Mixed" property (an asset containing a marital property component and a nonmarital property component) retains its various characters so long as the nonmarital component can be traced. If the nonmarital component cannot be traced, the mixed property becomes entirely marital property.

(ii) **Gift to Wife:** California, Idaho and Nevada presume that the husband intended to make a gift to the wife when he used funds or efforts belonging to the community to improve the wife's separate property. The other states do not presume a gift.

Most of the California, Idaho and Nevada cases have been based upon the older pattern of the husband being the manager of the property. Commentators agree that the same principles should apply to the wife when she is manager of the community. Idaho indicated that it would not treat as a gift the wife's separate property used by the husband to improve the community, but linked the reasoning to the husband's duty to support the wife. California, in a more recent case, has extended the presumption of gift to wives who contribute their separate property to improve community property.

The presumption of a gift can be rebutted, for example by an agreement between the parties. Some cases stress that the "consent of the wife to the expenditures" will rebut the presumption of a gift. This leaves the door open for implied and inferred consents and could lead to the resolution of each case on its individual facts.

c. **Amount of Reimbursement:** Except in California, the cases seem to indicate that the amount to be reimbursed is the *lesser* of (a) the improvement money used or (b) the increase in the value of the improved property. California awards the *greater* of those amounts.

Difficult problems of proof are created:

•Enhancement in value can be the result of many factors including intrinsic value of the property, inflation or the increase due to the improvement.

•Only a few cases give interest upon the amount of the lien; fewer still allow the improving property to share in any general enhancement in value of the property.

•The increase in value is measured as of the time of the termination of the community regime.

d. **Improvements v. Repairs:** The cases focus upon the amount by which the value of the separate real property is increased, not the extent to which it is prevented from decreasing. Accordingly, maintenance expenses and normal repairs are not considered to be improvements.

Repairs are distinguished from improvements in a manner reminiscent of the income tax and accounting distinctions. Repairs are short-lived, typically are relatively small in value and maintain (rather than increase) value; they are generally disregarded. Improvements are more permanent, generally cost more and tend to increase the value of the improved property; they are reimbursed (or pro rated over the period for which they are effective).

e. **Family Living Expenses:** Living expenses are closely related to the "improvement" theme. Some of the same concepts are involved in computing the payment of community expenses; the difference in those cases is that there is no product of the sum expended.

Acquisition of an asset rather than payment of an expense is the basis of the distinction between improvements and mortgage principal reduction on the one hand and repairs and mortgage interest on the other hand. Many of the principles concerning reimbursement for improvements parallel principles for reimbursement to the separate property for amounts paid for community property expenses. Expenses of the community are more fully dealt with in Chapter 8.

When community property improvements are made to separate property realty which is used as the family residence, the community is deemed to have received the benefit of the use of the residence during the marriage. Reimbursement for improvements is diminished in at least two ways:

First, operating expenses are deemed to be community expenses. Reimbursement is not allowed for normal maintenance and repairs, whether by labor or cash expenditures. The interest portion of mortgage debt payments is generally regarded as a maintenance expense rather than enhancement of the value of the property. Real property taxes are on the borderline: California cases treat real property taxes as maintenance expenses and Texas cases treat them as the removal of an encumbrance upon the property for which reimbursement is allowed.

Second, the measurement of the improvement value is made at the termination of the marriage. Thus, the improvement is reduced by a factor similar to depreciation for the period between the improvement and the end of the marriage.

f. Situations in Which the Question Arises: The question of whether reimbursement or a lien (or rarely, a proportionate share) will be given to the party whose property was used to improve (or reduce the indebtedness upon) property belonging to his or her spouse typically arises at the termination of the community regime by death or dissolution of the marriage (or dissolution of the community without divorce). The issue between the spouses could arise in the context of a probate proceeding, guardianship, partition, quiet title action, declaratory judgment action, separation or divorce. The rights of third parties, typically creditors, may be involved in mortgage foreclosures, post-judgment collection procedures such as garnishment, bankruptcy, actions for commissions of realtors or tax matters.

3. Credit Acquisitions

a. General Approach and Exercise: Unless a married couple otherwise agrees, property acquired by them during their marriage is presumed to be community property. The character is determined as of the time of acquisition which is generally the inception of title. A logical—but not always satisfactory—corollary of the inception of title rule is that the subsequent use of funds of another character to pay the acquisition debt does not change the character of the property.

EXERCISE

Apply the principles stated in the previous paragraph to determine the character of realty purchased by W for $100,000:

EXAMPLE 1: W pays $100,000 cash from her separate property and receives title prior to marriage.

EXAMPLES 2 through 4: W receives title prior to marriage in exchange for $10,000 of her separate property and a promissory note for $90,000 which is secured by the following:

EXAMPLE 2: A mortgage upon other separate property of W.

EXAMPLE 3: A mortgage upon the property which is purchased, i.e., a "purchase-money" obligation.

EXAMPLE 4: Nothing. The loan is unsecured.

EXAMPLES 5 through 8: The same factual patterns as in Examples 1 through 4, respectively, except that W was married at the time that title was acquired.

EXAMPLE 9: W, prior to marriage, contracts to purchase realty for $100,000. Possession, but not title, is given to W upon her payment of $10,000 from her separate property. The contract for deed provides that W will receive title upon payment of the remaining $90,000. W then marries.

EXAMPLES 10 and 11: In any (and all) of the situations described in Example 2 through 8, the unpaid balance of the promissory note is paid by the use of funds which are community property (EXAMPLE 10) or separate property (EXAMPLE 11).

EXAMPLES 12 through 14: The title to the property is taken in the name(s) of the husband (EXAMPLE 12), the wife (EXAMPLE 13) or both husband and wife (EXAMPLE 14).

EXAMPLES 15 through 17: Husband and wife agree (in a form which satisfies local law requirements) that regardless of the source of the payment and form of the title, the ownership of the property shall be husband's separate property (EX-

AMPLE 15), wife's separate property (EXAMPLE 16) or their community property (EXAMPLE 17).

ANALYSIS

The character of the realty would be determined in the following order:

The valid agreement of the parties will prevail, as in Examples 15 through 17, regardless of other factors, including the form of title. If the parties intend that the property shall be community property, even though title was acquired prior to the marriage, the property will be community property upon the marriage. This is a form of transmutation. The rules stated in this chapter apply in the absence of such transmutation.

The form of the title is not controlling, although it may be indicative of intent to have that character or indicative of a gift (usually from the manager of the property to the non-manager). In California and New Mexico, statutory presumptions exist concerning title to property taken in the name of a wife prior to statutory cut-off dates in the mid-1970's. Thus, the information in Examples 12 through 14 is generally insufficient to rebut the general presumption that property acquired during marriage is community property.

That general presumption will also be the governing factor as to the $90,000 credit in Examples 7 and 8 (W is married at the time of acquisition and purchase is made upon the security of the property purchased or upon no security). The general credit of a spouse is considered to be a community asset. On the other hand, the $10,000 paid from separate funds remains separate property. Thus, the property is 10% separate and 90% community.

Similarly, the tracing of the acquisition to separate funds rebuts the general presumption and proves the separate property character of the entire property in Examples 1 and 5 (W's separate property used for entire purchase price, whether before or after marriage).

The inception of right rule gives a separate property character to the entire property in Examples 1 through 4, since the property was acquired prior to marriage. The same rule, when applied to Examples 5 through 8, invokes the general presumption as to the $90,000 acquired by credit. The general presumption is rebutted by tracing to separate property security only in Example 6.

In Examples 10 and 11 the inception of right rule requires that the character of the property be fixed at the time it is acquired. The character ordinarily does not subsequently change because of satisfaction of the debt by funds of a different character. Therefore the character of the property remains 10% separate and 90% community in Examples 7 and 8 and 100% separate in Examples 1 through 6. In Example 9 the $10,000 down payment is clearly separate property because of tracing principles. The balance of the purchase price is usually characterized as separate using the concept of equitable conversion to consider the right or title to the property as acquired prior to marriage. On rare occasions, courts look to the actual passage of title (which will occur after the marriage). On those occasions, the general presumption and tracing will be applied at the time that title is delivered, i.e., when the full amount has been paid.

ANSWER

In summary, the character of the property and the governing principle in each example are as follows:

Example 1: 100% separate both because acquired before marriage and because acquired in exchange for separate property.

Examples 2 through 4: 100% separate because acquired before marriage.

Example 5: Although acquired after marriage, the general presumption is deemed to be rebutted by the tracing of the funds to separate property; therefore, the property is 100% separate.

Example 6: 100% separate property because the same reasoning is applied in Example 6 as in Example 5. The difference is that in Example 5, the separate property was used to purchase in a direct exchange while in Example 6, the separate property merely served as security. The use of the property as security is considered to be an "exchange" of the property rather than a "rent, issue or profit". Therefore, the rule applies even in those states which consider the rents, issues and profits of separate property received during marriage to be community property.

Examples 7 and 8 generally result in 10% separate property and 90% community property. The community property character arises from the general presumption which is rebutted only to the extent of the 10% down payment which was traced to separate funds. Some courts have had difficulty in seeing the circularity when the very property acquired is the source of the funds used to acquire it. Variations include treating the entire property as separate based upon the 10% down payment or arriving at the same 10% separate and 90% community division based upon the actual source of funds used to pay the debt. (This is particularly easy in those states in which the income from the property received during marriage would be community property regardless of the separate or community property of the asset which produced it.) Another approach would examine the motivation of the lender to see what character asset was primarily (or entirely) relied upon.

Example 9: Generally, the property will be considered 100% separate when an equitable conversion approach is used to declare the inception of title to arise at the time the contract for deed was created. On rare occasions, courts apply the inception of title test at the time of the actual passage of title; at that time W in Example 9 was married;

therefore the property is community to the extent that the general presumption is not rebutted. The 10% down payment was clearly separate property; in the absence of proof to the contrary, the remainder will be presumed to be community property under the general presumption.

Examples 10 and 11: Except in Wisconsin (UMPA), the actual source of payment is irrelevant.

Examples 12 through 14: This factor is not determinative of the character of the property unless there is a presumption of gift or a statutory presumption concerning title taken by a married woman (as exists in California and New Mexico for certain past acquisitions). In California, if the title is taken by husband and wife as joint tenants, the Calif.Civ.Code § 5110 presumption (for the purpose of dissolution of the marriage, the property is community property) is stronger than the general presumption in that it is not rebutted by tracing the source of the funds to separate property. Wisconsin has detailed statutory provisions.

Examples 15 through 17: The valid agreement of the parties is binding, regardless of the source of funds, at least between the spouses. Whether the rights of creditors can be reduced by such an agreement is not as certain.

b. Theories Applied in Credit Acquisitions: There are many different theories to determine the character of property acquired on credit. In some cases, the theories produce results similar to the improvement situation: A lien or right to reimbursement is given to one character of property. In a few cases, the theories produce results similar to most pension situations: The ownership is given in proportion to the contributions. Jurisdictions are seldom entirely consistent in choice and application of theories.

The general presumption is that property acquired during marriage is community property. One method of rebutting the general presumption is to trace the acquisition to separate property. The next link in the approach to credit acquisitions during marriage is to trace the asset acquired during marriage to the separate "credit" of one of the spouses. This commonly used link is weak because credit is not an asset, but the means of obtaining an asset.

Credit is not "property" in the traditional sense. Although a purchase on credit could be treated as an arrested sale, most of the cases in this area use the inception of right theory and disregard the character of funds which were actually used to pay for the asset. Most cases deal with credit as an asset which can be exchanged, but some (usually older) cases state that a credit acquisition does not rebut the general presumption. In addition, a few cases disregarded the credit portion of the purchase entirely (thereby making the character of the down payment the character of the property).

Most cases treat "credit" as if it were an asset; this gives rise to further issues: How is the character of credit determined? Whose intention is controlling? Should the focus be upon collateral or upon the capacity to pay the debt?

As a rule, it is possible to trace credit to separate property on an exchange basis; thus, the presence of some separate property is necessary in order to say that the credit is separate. The general credit of the wage earners, being based upon earning capacity, is treated as community property; no jurisdiction has applied hindsight to say that the now-separated couple had future separate property earned income because of the possibility of separation.

California has led the way in asserting that the intention of the lender should be the determinative force. Most courts emphasize the existence of separate property collateral of the spouse asserting a separate property interest.

The conceptual support for characterizing credit acquisitions by the character of the property used as collateral is questionable; lenders resort to collateral only when there is a default; the collateral is security for the payment, but not necessarily the source of it. Collateral is a spare tire, a reserve for the lender; the repayment mileage is normally taken out of the income (capacity to pay); it makes little sense to measure the mileage on the spare tire.

Although the emphasis is often placed upon the intention of the lender, the intention is not expressly based upon the signatures which are demanded. The identity of the parties who actually sign the promissory note is not determinative of the character of the property; courts often disregard the signature of a spouse when the signature was made as an accommodation even though creditors can enforce the debt against either party.

A theoretical approach which is appealing, but not adopted by many courts, is to examine the actual liability imposed by the promissory notes. In older cases, the signature of the wife was not sufficient to bind the community. In some states, the wife could not even bind her own property. Therefore, the signature of the wife on the promissory note did not use community credit. Newer provisions for management and control of the community and revised considerations of the liability of the wife's separate property for debts make this older theoretical approach less logical.

An approach which has almost never received direct support is to attribute loans from family members to the separate property of the spouse related by blood, rather than marriage, to the lender. The thin line between a gift and an intrafamily loan is not broken. Thus, property purchased with the proceeds of a loan to the husband from his mother is considered to be community property rather than the separate property of the husband.

Note that the use of separate property as collateral is treated as an exchange rather than a "rent, issue or profit" of the separate property. If the use of the property as credit was treated similarly to the use of the property for habitation, the credit based upon separate property during marriage, as a rent, issue or profit, would be separate property in five states and community property in Idaho, Louisiana, Texas and Wisconsin (UMPA). No cases are known in which credit has been treated as a "rent, issue or profit".

Courts have been surprisingly reluctant to admit evidence of the character of property actually used to pay the debt in order to determine the character of the property purchased on credit. This reluctance is consistent with the inception of right theory by which the character of the property is determined at the time of its original acquisition and that character is not changed by subsequent payments or additions. Under the proportionate system, the actual source of payments would be considered; the character of the property could be held in different percentages with each payment. California has generally been in the forefront of the proportionate method of determining the character of property. Yet, even California has been reluctant to consider the actual source of the payments in determining the character of property acquired in credit. The most recent California cases (and a few cases in other jurisdictions) have considered the actual sources of payment.

While California determines the character of property acquired on credit during marriage to be separate property if the lender *intended* to rely upon the separate property of one spouse as security, Washington determines the character of such property to be separate if the creditor *actually* could reach the separate property of one of the spouses.

There is an inherent circularity in determining the character of property when it has been purchased with its own proceeds. Some courts have not noted the circularity which is involved when they determine the character of the property by the character of the property which was used to pay for it and that property was derived from the thing itself.

Another circularity is involved when there is no personal liability because property is acquired subject to existing indebtedness. In California, there could be no personal liability on certain purchase-money obligations even though a promissory note and a trust deed have been signed by the purchaser. If there is no personal liability, the intent of the lender is irrelevant and the lender is not able to reach other separate or community assets of the couple. It would seem that any portion of property acquired during marriage subject to indebtedness for which neither spouse is personally liable should be community property under the general presumption, but what of property inherited during marriage or purchased prior to marriage subject to an existing debt?

Some of the difficulties experienced with credit acquisitions are traceable to the limited view of the community regime taken by most of the community property states. In classic civil law theory, the community was a regime of assets and liabilities. Louisiana has maintained the civil law theory and Washington appears to be approaching it.

4. Life Insurance

a. Background:

(i) **Terminology:** Life insurance progresses from the premiums to the policy to the proceeds. The death of the insured is the usual cause of what is euphemistically phrased as the maturity of the policy, but some policies pay their face amount upon the expiration of a set number of years or upon the insured attaining a very advanced age.

The two major functions of a life insurance policy are (1) indemnity by means of the current insurance risk and (2) investment by means of the accrued cash value element. The current insurance risk is the protection element; it has no permanent value except to the extent there would be a refund of the unearned portion of the last premium in the event the policy was cancelled. "Term" insurance, which includes most group life insurance policies, is purely risk coverage. Ordinary or whole life and endowment insurance policies, on the other hand, have an accrued cash value element, a value which is built up over a period of time and which can be obtained by borrowing against the security of the policy or by surrendering the policy.

(ii) Who owns the insurance? The revocably-designated beneficiary of an unmatured life insurance policy sometimes is said to have a "mere expectancy" and not a property interest. The analogy is often made to the beneficiary of a will of a living person. On the other hand, an irrevocably-designated beneficiary is modernly said to have a vested property interest in the policy.

For federal estate tax purposes, consideration is given to the possession by the insured of *any* incident of ownership including, but not limited to the right to change beneficiaries, the right to surrender the policy for cash and the right to borrow money against the policy.

EXAMPLE: I is the insured under a policy of life insurance of which B is the beneficiary.

• If the designation is revocable, B has no interest during the life of I and the owner of the policy is as designated by the policy, usually I.

• If, however, beneficiary B was trustee of an otherwise unfunded life insurance trust, the beneficiary designation would be enough of a property interest under case law or statute in many states to be a trust res, that property interest which is an essential element to create a trust.

• If the beneficiary designation is irrevocable, B is said to have a property interest rather than a mere expectancy.

• When the beneficiary is irrevocably designated, do other rights such as the right to surrender the life insurance policy for its cash value give I an interest in the insurance policy? For federal estate tax purposes, I does have such a right.

• If I and B are married to third and fourth parties is the property community property?

(iii) **Early theoretical problems:** Although there was no difficulty in seeing that there was a property interest in the premiums and in the proceeds, some courts did not recognize that the contract right, the chose in action which was the policy, is a property interest.

Initially, courts had difficulty in classifying life insurance policies within the community property system. Conceptual problems, now largely ignored, include the following:

• The proceeds of the policy do not exist until the death of the insured; therefore, there can be no property until the death of the insured. This illogic (which denies the ability of a contract right to be "property") can be combined with the concept that community property only arises during the marriage and the fact that after the death of one party, the marriage no longer exists. Therefore, there could never be community property life insurance.

• Term insurance has no value until death; therefore there is no community interest during the marriage. Term insurance is entirely risk indemnity; it has no investment value. Thus, it is similar to casualty insurance which is an expense. As an expense, it is considered to be consumed during the accounting period in which paid; it is not an asset which carries value forward. Some courts still echo this approach. Others have answered it in the past by pointing out that the renewability feature and level premium feature also have value.

• There cannot be property because there is no vested right in the beneficiary who is revocably designated.

• The designation of the spouse (usually the wife) as the beneficiary of the life insurance policy is often treated as a transmutation by gift, so that she receives separate property when the policy matures. If the revocable designation of a beneficiary does not create a property interest in the beneficiary, how can there be a gift without property being given?

b. Theories for Tracing Insurance Premiums: All three of the following theories trace the cash used for the payment of premiums of a life insurance policy in order to determine the character of the policy and its proceeds. The difference is in which premium(s) are determinative. Inception of title looks at the first premium; annual policy looks at the last premium; and apportionment looks to all premiums paid.

(i) Inception of title: The inception of title characterization of an asset looks at the time of acquisition and traces the property used in its acquisition to its source. Thus, where the first premium of a life insurance policy is paid from separate funds, subsequent payments with community property funds do not divest the interest of the insured's separate estate, although the community estate may have a right to reimbursement.

The inception of title theory is justified by analogy to installment purchases or improvements of land and a stressing of uniformity and simplicity. The insurance policy is treated as a single life-long contract rather than a series of annual contracts. The latter would be analogous to *casualty* insurance such as automobile liability insurance.

On the other hand, the inception of title rule permits some inequities. There is a slow drain upon the estate which pays subsequent premiums, yet that estate does not share in the growth in value when the policy matures; indeed, it does not even earn interest.

Louisiana, New Mexico and Texas have adopted the inception of title rule for some or all life insurance cases.

(ii) Apportionment: The apportionment theory is the application of the tracing or source doctrine to all payments which are involved in the acquisition of an asset. The apportionment theory, also known as the pro rata theory, could be better characterized by being called the *subsequent* apportionment rule since the inception of title rule also permits apportionment *at the time of original acquisition*. The difference is that the inception of title rule then freezes the proportion of ownership while the proportionate test permits continual shifting.

Life insurance policies often have a windfall-type growth in value when the policy matures early. The apportionment theory allows the community and separate estates to divide the appreciation in value in proportion to their contribution to the policy premiums. The computations are less complicated if the policy has matured at the time of apportionment of the proceeds.

When the insurance policy is being divided upon divorce, additional problems of computation, maintenance and liquidity are encountered.

California and Washington follow the apportionment rule; Arizona and Idaho have tended to follow that rule in the past, but may be inclining toward the annual policy theory.

Nevada has not had sufficient cases in which its theoretical approach could be determined. It is possible that it will follow the California lead in the apportionment theory.

Wisconsin (and UMPA) apportion the marital property components by statutory provisions which go beyond the usual apportionment rules and which favor the marital property classification.

(iii) **Annual policy theory:** Disregarding the investment feature of the cash surrender value (which generally does not exist with term insurance), the insurance policy has a risk element which is purchased on an annual (or semi-annual, monthly or other periodic) basis. The insurance may be viewed as a series of voluntary unilateral contracts, rather than a single contract. Thus, only the last premium purchases the risk portion of the life insurance policy and that premium is the one to which the character of the policy should be traced. The voluntary, repetitive and periodic payments can be contrasted against the mandatory installments of a previously agreed total purchase price of, for example, a parcel of realty. In the latter case, the right originates once. At the time that the total price is agreed upon, it is a single purchase. The life insurance indemnity feature is more like a rental agreement in which each payment is discrete and voluntary and in which there is little more than a psychological expectation of continuation of the policy or rental for another period.

The annual policy theory has been rejected by some courts which emphasized that renewability and level premium features of policies have values that are ignored by the annual policy theory. Proponents of the annual policy theory counter by stating that a fraction of the value, rather than all of it, can be attributed to the renewability or level premium feature in the same way that a fraction of the value can be attributed to the accrued cash surrender value of an ordinary or whole life policy. The balance, after such attribution, could then be assigned to the estate which paid the final premium which purchased the current annual (or semi-annual or other period) policy.

Arizona and Idaho have had cases which seem to adopt the annual policy theory, at least for term insurance in which no subdivision of the policy is required. The Arizona authority is not fully developed.

Wissner v. Wissner, 338 U.S. 655, 70 S.Ct. 398, 94 L.Ed. 424 (1950) held that state community property law could not be applied to National Service Life Insurance proceeds because of the congressional directives that "No person shall have a vested right" to the proceeds and that the insured "shall have the right to" designate and change beneficiaries within classes specified by Congress. See Chapter 12.

5. Deferred Compensation

a. **Types of Deferred Compensation:** Tax advantages have sponsored and nurtured many types of deferred compensation—stock options, educational assistance, medical and dental plans, life insurance, retirement plans, disability plans and thrift plans. Usually, these deferred benefits are part of the compensation for services rendered by an employee, although the employee may be working for his own corporation, e.g., a doctor, lawyer or dentist who uses a professional corporation. There are also retirement plans which are not associated with an employment, such as the Individual Retirement Account (IRA).

Some of the employment benefits, such as the medical and dental plans do not create assets, but are in the nature of expense-reducers. Other benefits, like bonuses, thrift plans and employer-guaranteed loans are so routine that they do not raise special community property problems. The remaining benefits have caused problems of characterization. The form of deferred compensation which will be dealt with in the most detail in this nutshell is the pension form of retirement benefit.

b. Death, Disability and Retirement Benefits: Employers often provide, as a form of deferred compensation, one or more benefits designed to alleviate financial problems caused by the death, disability or retirement of an employee. Each raises problems and issues in community property states:

• Life insurance problems include unresolved contingencies, dramatic value change and differing state approaches. Employers often have other death benefits which are similar to unfunded life insurance programs. The "right" to receive benefits may be more tenuous; sometimes a right is created by estoppel doctrines applied to past payments by the employer.

• Disability plans have an evitable contingency, as opposed to the inevitable contingency of life insurance. Until the contingency has occurred, there is no right to payment. When the contingency has occurred, the right ripens and is spoken of as being vested. What was an expectancy becomes a vested right. At that point, the inception of title theory looks to the marital status of the recipient to determine the character of the payments. However, disability payments are often designed to replace salary and are further contingent upon the survival of the intended recipient. Should each payment be considered separately to determine its character? If not, a spouse may divorce the disabled employee and take one-half of all benefits. The difficulty of characterizing recoveries for personal injuries was analyzed in Chapter 3; many of the same principles apply to disability payments. Courts have also struggled with the problem of an employee who is entitled to either disability pay or retirement pay, but not both. Generally they have held that the employee option cannot defeat the spouse's right to one half of the community retirement benefits; therefore the disability receipts are characterized as community to the extent that retirement pay would have been so characterized.

• Retirement pay is often in the form of a pension or an annuity, i.e., a set dollar amount payable for the life of the retired employee. There are usually a number of contingencies such as the continued employment and life of the employee for a number of years and the attainment of a certain age. The contingencies may relate to "vesting" in the sense of having a property interest in the retirement benefit, or the contingencies may relate to "maturation", the immediate right to receive payments from the retirement fund. The amount of the payment is often uncertain because it is dependent upon the highest salary received by the employee, is attributed to profit-sharing or is coordinated with social security benefits to give a determined total amount. Both disability and retirement payments are usually contingent upon the survival of the annuitant.

c. Inception of Title and Apportionment: Retirement income annuities are typically earned by a prolonged period of service. That period may overlap married and unmarried periods and periods of domicile in both community and non-community property states during the employee's life, thus calling for an allocation to or apportionment between the separate and community components.

Upon initial employment, there is no "right" to a pension. As the employee accumulates time on the job, the hope for a pension grows from an expectancy into a contingent right. "Vesting" is used here to indicate when a property right arises; it is at this point that inception of title would apply. "Maturation" is used to indicate the time when the benefits under the program commence. The plan benefits are said to "vest" as the employer becomes legally obligated to supply the pension. (In some cases, estoppel may impose the obligation at an earlier time.) It is possible that a plan will be vested, but not yet matured. For example, a pension plan could provide for payments to commence when the employee is 62 years old provided the employee both has been employed for 20 years and retires at age 62. A 50-year-old employee who was employed for 20 years has a vested, but not a matured, right to a pension.

Modernly, courts tend to agree that there is a property right before the pension is matured and probably even before it is vested. This property right is capable of being characterized as community. Difficulties arise in valuing and dividing the pension asset upon divorce.

Is a retirement pension one asset or a series of payments? Vesting of the plan is often incremental. The work process by which the pension is earned consumes a period of time which can be broken down into smaller periods. The benefits are also capable of being paid in a series of installments with no predetermined total amount. A retirement annuity is an asset which produces a stream of income payments, but the asset is consumed in the process. Because of the discounted present value of future payments, the total of the "income" payments usually exceeds the "value" of the asset. Should the court determine the character of the retirement fund on the theory that it is one asset or should it be examined in the same manner as a savings account into which regular monthly payments have been made?

Most of the community property states apportion the proceeds of retirement funds even though they do not necessarily apportion other community property assets. While California and Washington apportion both life insurance and retirement funds by the contribution of the separate and community estates, Idaho, Louisiana and Texas apportion retirement plan benefits between the two (or more) contributing estates, but apply inception of title or other tests for characterizing life insurance proceeds.

When the proceeds are apportioned, what basis should be used? Apportionment by respective time periods appears to be the most commonly used method. The time method bases the percentage upon the respective community and non-community periods during which the retirement benefits were earned. The earliest contributions to the plan were smaller than those paid in subsequent years because the amount contributed is often a percentage of a generally-increasing salary. On the other hand, the accumulated income from the earlier contributions (which would be separate property if earned upon separate property in all states except Idaho, Louisiana, Texas and Wisconsin) is greater because the amounts have been held for a longer time. An alternative method of apportionment is by actual money contributions, sometimes augmented by an interest factor for the period that the funds have been held by the retirement fund.

California usually apportions upon the time basis, but recognizes that either spouse may offer evidence that the time basis distorts the contribution and that actual money contributions should be used as the basis for apportionment. Louisiana has held that the court should apportion on the basis of the money contributed by each estate. Wisconsin (and UMPA) describe the marital property element by statute.

d. Division Upon Divorce of Retirement and Disability Benefits: Since both retirement and disability provisions are dependent upon the outcome of so many contingencies, divorce courts have had particular difficulty in dividing the community property while providing for pre-vesting and post-vesting contingencies (further employment, election to retire, not dying etc.) including options within the control of the employee. The divorce court also has problems of division and assignment. California has set the theme that normally the wage-earner is given the retirement plan if there are balancing assets which can be given to the non-wage-earner.

See Chapter 9 for further problems which arise in connection with termination of the community upon divorce.

e. Public and Private Retirement Plans: A dividing line between governmental and private retirement plans has long existed. The statutory schemes by which public employees are granted retirement benefits have adopted an imperious attitude: The recipient had no right to the retirement or other benefits; they are given as a matter of governmental largess. None of the states follows the old Spanish distinction by which bonus payments to married soldiers who received other compensation were treated as gifts and therefore separate property. The statutory language and approach of governmental employee retirement plans did, however, emphasize the "non-vested" nature of the retirement allowance; this emphasis led the courts in California and Texas to adopt a short-lived doctrine that retirement funds subject to certain contingencies were not "vested" and therefore could not be community property. Both jurisdictions have reversed the holding, but the dichotomy between governmental and private pension plans has been retained.

McCarty v. McCarty, 453 U.S. 210, 101 S.Ct. 2728, 69 L.Ed.2d 589 (1981) held that federal military retirement benefits could not be characterized as community property because the valid federal retirement plan objectives would be injured. The application of the federal supremacy clause (U.S.Const. art. 6, cl. 2) to community property is more fully treated in Chapter 12. The result of the McCarty case was reversed by the enactment of the Uniformed Services Former Spouse's Protection Act, 10 U.S.C.A. § 1408, which permitted the states to apply "the law of the jurisdiction of such court" to treat certain "disposable retired or retainer pay" as "property of the member and his spouse".

Federal statutes by which retirement benefits are awarded often state that the benefits are for the benefit of the employee only and that such rights cannot be reached by process or attachment.

These two separate characteristics—the non-transferable personal interest and the spendthrift provision—are found in many federal statutes including the various military retirement plans as in *McCarty*, the railroad employees plan involved in *Hisquierdo* and the social security old age benefits.

The federal social security program has the most widespread retirement coverage of any retirement plan. Although there is no definitive statement that such benefits are the separate property of the recipient, it is probable that the Supreme Court of the United States will characterize all benefits received under the social security program as separate property of the recipient.

f. ERISA and Private Retirement Plans: Federal law has two attitudes toward retirement plans: As to pensions *from* the *government*, the employee has no vested right until the prescribed term of service has been rendered; the emphasis is upon the absence of enforceable rights of the employee. On the other hand, The Employee Retirement Income Security Act of 1974 (ERISA), 29 U.S.C. §§ 1001 to 1381 demands that *private* retirement plans do not act like the government; the emphasis is upon the vesting of rights in the employee.

ERISA regulates, at the federal level, retirement funds and other employee benefits. Under the supremacy clause of the federal constitution, federal law preempts the field if the federal statute is constitutionally authorized and the statute is intended to preempt the field.

The intention of the federal government to preempt the field by ERISA is shown in 29 U.S.C. § 1144, which declares that ERISA's provisions "shall supersede any and all State laws insofar as they may now or hereafter relate to any employee benefit plan. . . ."

Areas where community property laws of the individual states appear to conflict with ERISA include the definitions of "employee", "participant" and "beneficiary", the application of the spendthrift and non-attachment provisions and the provisions for joint and survivor annuities.

The United States Supreme Court has not yet decided how far the ERISA federal preemption extends—does it negate any community property interest of the non-employee spouse or does it suspend some of the attributes of community property which conflict with ERISA? Lower court decisions have tended to find no preemption.

Federal law is also inconsistent in recognizing community property rights in federal governmental benefits and private annuity plans: Social security old age (retirement) benefits are separate property of the recipient employee despite state community property laws. The REACT amendment to ERISA, on the other hand, created a "super community property" interest for the surviving spouse in death benefits. The REACT right of a surviving spouse applies not only in communi-

ty property states to community property interests
but also applies in non-community property states
and to non-community property interests in community property states.

6. Community Labor in a Separate Business

EXAMPLE: A man who owns a large percentage, or all, of the stock of a corporation (or an
unincorporated business or a partnership) marries.
During coverture, he is active in the management
of the business.   The value of the business increases.   Upon the dissolution of the community, is
the community estate entitled to a portion of the
otherwise-separate property business as compensation for the community property labors of the
owner-spouse?

Frequently the community property labors of
one or both spouses are devoted to a business
venture.   If the business itself is community property, no characterization problems occur.   However, problems similar to commingling arise when
the business is separate property (usually because
it was acquired before marriage).

In this chapter, the term "business" is used in a
broad sense to include not only entrepreneurs such
as the butcher, baker and candlestick maker, but
also farmers and investment managers.   The common thread is that a commingling of separate
property capital and community property labor in
an enterprise intended to produce revenue.   It is
possible, but rarer, to have community property

capital and separate property labor; this could occur, for example, during separation in some states.

Areas to consider include the elements of the commingled business, methods of apportionment, variances in the extent of the gain and the type of business organization involved.

a. Elements of the Commingled Business: In the typical business situation, four of the elements shown in the illustration on page 81 are involved:

(i) The original value of the business itself: Marriage does not change separate property into community property in the United States. Thus, in the absence of a transmutation, the premarital business remains separate property.

(ii) Natural increase in the value of the business due to its intrinsic value or due to inflation: A mere change in value does not change the character of the property. If the business owns realty valued at $100,000 at the time the businessperson marries and the parcel of land increases in value to $150,000 solely because of market conditions, the increase in value is separate property. Ordinarily, the values represented by items (i) and (ii) remain in the business and are not distributed except in liquidation.

(iii) The income from the capital described in items (i) and (ii): Rents, issues and profits of separate property received during marriage are generally community property in Idaho, Louisiana, Texas and Wisconsin (UMPA), but are separate property in the remaining American jurisdictions. In the four civil law states, the task of separation of the community and the separate property elements would divide items (i) and (ii) from items (iii) and (iv); the other states would be concerned with separation of items (i), (ii) and (iii) on the one hand from item (iv) on the other hand. The value represented by item (iii) may be partly or completely left in the business or partly or completely withdrawn from the business in the form of cash or stock dividends.

(iv) Community property labor of one or both spouses during marriage: This contribution may have been partly or completely withdrawn (or overdrawn) in the form of salary.

Ideally, the business will contain enough value to equal the total of the contributions and the return on capital and salary. Ideally, the four items (original contribution, enhancement, return on capital and salary for labor) will equal all value which is in the business. Ideally, information is available and offered concerning the relative contributions of labor and capital to the business profit. It is only because the ideal situation is seldom, if ever, found in reality that adjustments of the type described in this chapter are necessary.

Usually a dispute arises after there has been a large increase in the value of the business. The dispute normally is about the extent to which the separate estate is entitled to the increase because of the contribution of capital and the extent to which the community estate is entitled to the increase because of the contribution of labor.

b. Methods of Apportionment: When community property efforts have been devoted to a separate property business, the increase in value can be allocated entirely to property of one character or apportioned between them.

(i) Allocating to one character: The major reasons (in addition to transmutation) for allocating the increase entirely to one character or the other include the *de minimis* amount of the contribution of the other character, the adequacy of compensation of the other character (by salary, dividends or other withdrawals from the business) or the application of the commingling presumption to deem the property all community property unless the claimant can prove the separate property contribution. The "all-or-nothing" approach of attributing the growth to the principal item—labor or capital—which produced it has been discredited and generally abandoned.

•The *de minimis* application is often found in occupations in which the labor of the owner is not a significant factor, either because of the nature of the business or the use of hired managers. An owner of separate property is allowed to exert a reasonable amount of effort during the marriage without creating a community element to the property. How much is a reasonable amount is a difficult question generally left to the discretion of the court. A minimal amount of labor (such as receiving and depositing a dividend check) is disregarded, but it is also possible that a spouse may expend much effort in the maintenance of investments such as stock holdings or rental apartments. The now-discredited all-or-nothing allocation of the entire growth to the *principal* contributing factor, capital or labor, was an expansion of the *de minimis* technique of disregarding a minor contribution.

• The compensation received as salary by a spouse or as return on the separate property capital may be presumed to be the "correct" amount, i.e., a reasonable salary or reasonable rate of return.   Therefore, the portion of the increase remaining in the business is of the opposite character, usually the original separate property. Problems with this approach are caused by the fact that the amount, timing and nomenclature of the distribution from the business is often within the control of one of the spouses. Additionally, considerations such as liquidity and taxation (rather than fair return or reasonable salary) often influence decisions about payments from the business to the owner-employee.

• Commingling and its presumption: The commingling principle (that separate property which is so commingled with community that it cannot be traced loses its separate identity) is more widely used with bank accounts than with businesses. The commercial valuation of capital, labor and businesses makes tracing and reimbursement easier.

(ii) Apportioning between separate and community: Methods of apportioning tend to do one or more of the following:

• Emphasize a particular attribute of the business (apportioning by labor, capital, interest or rental). This technique was the basic theme of the all-or-nothing rule which allocated all of the business income to one or the other character. Remnants of this theme remain in the determination of the correct formula to use by a consideration of the factor most responsible for any increase in the value of the business.

• Attribute most of the growth to one type of property by allocating reasonable compensation to the other estate. This technique is exemplified by the leading *Pereira* and *Van Camp* decisions.

In Pereira v. Pereira, 156 Cal. 1, 103 P. 488 (1909), the court seemed to presume that *labor* was the main reason for an increase in value of the assets. The other element (the separate property capital) was given the 7% legal rate of interest upon its investment; the community element was therefore entitled to the balance of the increase in value of the business.

In Van Camp v. Van Camp, 53 Cal.App. 17, 199 P. 885 (1921), the court seemed to presume that *capital* had the major responsibility for the increase in the value of the business. The community property was allowed a reasonable salary for services rendered (with any amounts actually paid as salary deducted); the balance of the increase was separate property.

• Seek a mathematical certainty by an apportionment ratio. The respective proportions of reasonable salary and a fair return on the capital are used to divide the actual increase. Few decisions have followed this favorite approach of the theoreticians. Strictly speaking, only this method "apportions" business profits; the other methods merely reimburse one character or the other for its contribution.

• Leave the method of apportionment to the discretion of the trier of fact by using the vague test of "substantial justice" for each case. The trial court is thus free to select the formula which is most appropriate to the individual case in accordance with the information available to the court.

There is greater variation within each jurisdiction than between jurisdictions in the methods of apportioning the increase in value of a business between separate and community property. Among the factors which are relevant in determining which method of apportionment is used in a particular case are the amounts actually withdrawn from the business, the extent of the gain, whether the business is incorporated, the nature of the business, and the relative importance of capital or labor for the particular business.

c. **Extent of the Gain:** The decided cases have almost always dealt with a successful business. Generally unmentioned in the cases which divide up the profit of a business is the appropriate method of apportioning losses. While emphasis is placed upon rewarding the community for its labor contribution to a separate property business which grows, rarely is the community paid for its services in a separate property business which loses money. The apportionment formulae are capable of making such an allocation, but are seldom so used. It appears that if there is a loss in the value of the separate property business, the community will not receive any allowance on account of community labor. Of course, a controversy could arise as to whether there was a loss. Some accounting variables, such as the rate of creation of a depreciation reserve, may turn an otherwise profitable business into an unprofitable one.

The application of the various formulae can be very result-oriented. Not only is an examination made to see if there is a profit in the business, there are also examinations of the actual withdrawals from the business and how they are characterized and the expenses of the community. For example, in some cases the courts have refused to make any apportionment of amounts remaining in the business because there were withdrawals from the business which were consumed for living expenses of the married couple.

d. Type of Business Organization: Although the rules of this section apply to unincorporated sole proprietorships and partnerships as well as corporations, the existence of a close (i.e., entirely or predominately owned by a married person) corporation seems to increase the problems and lead to more apportionment questions:

• The separate entity for tax purposes causes greater formality in the arrangement and business records. A salary is more likely to be paid because it has more income tax advantages than a dividend. Accountants may compute the fair market value of the business by including an asset known as "good will" to account for the profitability of the business. If that item is included in a computation at the time of the divorce of the owner, it may create a paper profit which belongs in part to the spouse of the owner. The owner usually then purchases the share of the spouse as part of the property settlement, thus being required to pay for one half of the good will which often presumes the future labor of the owner.

• The divorce court occasionally disregards the corporate entity in its discretion, especially if it seems to have been used in an effort to conceal assets or obtain undue advantage in the divorce proceedings for the shareholder spouse.

Often it makes more sense to distinguish between the close corporation on the one hand and a publicly traded corporation on the other hand (even though both are "corporations") than it does to distinguish between corporations and unincorporated businesses.

e. Contrasts to Community Property Doctrines: There are a number of areas where different rules seem to apply to the separate property business into which community property labor is combined:

• The nonapplication of commingling rules has been mentioned.

• The concept that the spouses contribute equally to the community is the foundation of the rationalization for the community property system. This is an irrebuttable presumption; it is irrelevant whether the spouses actually were helpful. In the case of the community property labor which is added to the separate property business, however, the *actual* labor performed is examined to determine the extent of the community contribution.

• In retirement plans, the employed spouse has a number of options such as when to retire and whether to take disability retirement in lieu of normal retirement pay. A self-employed businessperson similarly can make a number of decisions (such as the amount of salary paid) which affect the community. Cases are currently developing the extent to which a court can compensate for community retirement benefits by the property division or alimony and the extent to which the court can direct the management and control of those benefits by the employed spouse. Similar control has not been exerted over businesses.

• In California and New Mexico, community property law is altered because of express modification of the Uniform Partnership Act to state that a partnership interest is not community property. In California the courts have recognized that the community may have some rights in the partner's partnership interest as distinguished from his right to participate in the management of the firm or rights in specific partnership property.

• Credit acquisitions by a business, especially a corporation, may be subject to the business rules as opposed to the rules concerning credit acquisition of community property assets generally.

C. INDIVIDUAL STATES

ARIZONA

Cockrill v. Cockrill, 124 Ariz. 50, 601 P.2d 1334 (1979) abandoned the "all-or-nothing" rule in favor of apportioning the increase in value of separate property between the inherent value of separate property and the product of the community work effort during marriage. That case also reconciled the conflict between the presumption that property acquired during marriage is community property and the presumption that increases in value of separate property are also separate property by placing the burden of proof upon the spouse who contends that the increase is also separate property.

Arizona has been generous in measuring the amount of the lien for **improvements** made to property of another; the measure is the value of the improvements at the time of the trial and is not limited to the amount of the improving property which was consumed. This generosity is in marked contrast to the Arizona practice of allowing only reimbursement for the amount of premiums paid by the community property upon (rather than a share of the proceeds of) matured separate **life insurance** policies payable to someone other than the spouse.

Different rules for **credit** acquisitions have been applied by the Arizona Supreme Court. When a married person acquires property with a down payment from separate property and the balance of the purchase price is originally represented by a promissory note which is subsequently paid with community property, Arizona starts with the usual approach: The inception of title rule fixes the character at the time that it is acquired. The down payment is traced to an exchange of separate property and therefore rebuts the general presumption. However, the cases have made a number of divergent paths from that beginning:

• The intent of the lender test, used in California, is not used. In fact, the intention of the lender is used to weaken a factor considered important by other courts: If both spouses sign the promissory note and mortgage for the credit acqui-

sition at the request of the lender, the importance
of such signing is diminished.

• The usual inception of title rule (as opposed to
the apportionment approach) is that the character
of the property is fixed at the time that it is
acquired and the character of the funds subsequently used to pay the debt is irrelevant.   The
character of the property which is used to pay the
debt is entitled, at most, to reimbursement or a
lien for reimbursement.

• Some Arizona cases have appeared to ignore
the credit portion of the acquisition and thus determine the character of the property by tracing it
entirely to the down payment.

• The Arizona Supreme Court on at least two
occasions has stated the rule to be that property
purchased during marriage with a separate property down payment is entirely separate property
unless the promissory note was subsequently paid
with community funds.

• In Kingsbery v. Kingsbery, 93 Ariz. 217, 379
P.2d 893 (1963), the balance of the purchase price
after a separate property down payment was subsequently paid with community property funds, but
the community property was, in turn, repaid by
the separate property.   The court held that the
entire property was separate property (disregarding its own rule about payment with community
property) and did not give a lien to the community
(because it had already been repaid).

Arizona has touched all three of the theories for life insurance—inception of title, apportionment and annual policy—without clearly indicating which is preferred:

• Inception of title was given support in a dictum in Rothman v. Rumbeck, 54 Ariz. 443, 96 P.2d 755 (1939) which indicated that that rule would be applied to life insurance with the non-owning character of property being entitled only to reimbursement of one half of premiums paid. In that case community property was allegedly paid for premiums upon a premarital life insurance policy upon the husband's life and payable to someone other than the wife.

• The proportionate approach was the choice of the legislature in dealing with life insurance upon the life of a child in Ariz.Rev.Stat. § 20–1128(B).

• The "annual policy" theory is reflected in more recent decisions, Gaethje v. Gaethje, 7 Ariz.App. 544, 441 P.2d 579 and 8 Ariz.App. 47, 442 P.2d 870 (1968) and Lock v. Lock, 8 Ariz.App. 138, 444 P.2d 163 (1968).

Luna v. Luna, 125 Ariz. 120, 608 P.2d 57 (Ariz.App.1979) apportioned on a time basis the benefits of a **retirement pension** which the court found to be partly earned during the period when the couple was married and domiciled in Arizona. That case held that disability pay, being designed to replace future income of the now-divorced husband, was separate property.

CALIFORNIA

California has been the most reluctant of the states to allow a married person to recover the value of *separate* property **improvements** *to community* property. See v. See, 64 Cal.2d 778, 51 Cal.Rptr. 888, 415 P.2d 776 (1966) created the presumption that a gift is intended unless there is an agreement for reimbursement when separate property of a spouse is used to pay community expenses. This rule was extended to a wife who contributed her separate property for the improvement of community property in Marriage of Lucas, 27 Cal.3d 808, 166 Cal.Rptr. 853, 614 P.2d 285 (1980). The legislature modified the rule of Lucas, prospectively and retroactively, in Calif.Civ.Code § 4800.1 for divorce purposes. The retroactive application of § 4800.1 was declared unconstitutional in Marriage of Griffis, 187 Cal.App.3d 156, 231 Cal.Rptr. 510 (1986). A similar fate is possible for retroactive application of the following statute:

Calif.Civ.Code § **4800.2** now allows a claim as creditor (but not as co-owner) for divorce purposes when community property is improved by separate property:

. . .[U]nless a party has made a written waiver of the right to reimbursement or signed a writing that has the effect of a waiver, the party shall be reimbursed for his or her contributions to the acquisition of the property to the extent the party traces the contributions to a separate property source. The amount reimbursed shall be without interest or adjustment for change in monetary values and shall not exceed the net value of the property at the time of the division. As used in this section, "contributions to the acquisition of the property" include downpayments, payments for improvements, and payments that reduce the principal of a loan used to finance the purchase or improvement of the property but do not include payments of interest on the loan or payments made for maintenance, insurance or taxation of the property.

Calif.Civ.Code § 4800.3 which allows interest on certain community property contributions to education or training is in contrast to Calif.Civ.Code § 4800.2 denying interest.

On the other hand, California has been among the most liberal in allowing spouses both to recover their contributions and to share the appreciation in value when *community* property is used *to* improve (and occasionally to pay off indebtedness upon) *separate* property. Marriage of Moore, 28 Cal.3d 366, 168 Cal.Rptr. 662, 618 P.2d 208 (1980) allowed a pro tanto interest to the community (which had appreciated greatly in value) as well as reimbursement for community property principal payments upon a separate obligation purchase-money promissory note.

Although California is a leader in the application of the proportionate ownership theory (rather than adhering to the inception of title theory), its courts have been slow to apply proportionate ownership in **credit** acquisition cases. California tends to agree with other jurisdictions that the character of the property at the time of acquisition is determinative and that credit is a community asset unless the lender bases the extension of the credit upon the separate property of one spouse. The prime factor under the California cases has been to examine the intent of the lender. If the primary intent of the lender was to rely upon the purchaser's separate property (and occasional cases seem to treat the credit as a discrete item without specific separate assets) in extending credit, then the credit portion of the acquisition is separate, regardless of the character of the funds actually used to repay the debt. The intent of the lender even prevailed over the fact that signatures of both spouses to the promissory note and mortgage were requested by the lender.

Despite the strength and repetition of the rule to disregard the actual source of payments, the California Supreme Court traced payments in Marriage of Moore, 28 Cal.3d 366, 168 Cal.Rptr. 662, 618 P.2d 208 (1980).

California has consistently and frequently used the apportionment rule for determining ownership of **life insurance** since early in its history, although most of the cases are at the intermediate appellate level. The initial case was Estate of Webb, Myr.Prob. 93 (Cal.1875); the most frequently cited case is Modern Woodmen of America v. Gray, 113 Cal.App. 729, 299 P. 754 (1931). In both cases, the proceeds of matured life insurance policies were apportioned between the community and the separate estates in the ratio that the premiums were paid from each of those estates.

Calif.Civ.Code § 4800.8 was enacted in an attempt to eliminate the unique California "terminable interest" rule for **retirement** benefits. The terminable interest rule eliminated community property rights of a non-employee spouse at the death of either spouse.

California has differed in deciding its basic approach to apportioning profits of a separate property **business:**

The formula of Pereira v. Pereira, 156 Cal. 1, 103 P. 488 (1909) reimburses the separate property an amount deemed to be a fair return on the capital; any excess is given to the community. The owner-spouse (usually the husband) has the burden of proving that the separate property is entitled to a higher rate of return than the legal rate of interest.

The *Pereira* approach was weakened by a number of cases including Van Camp v. Van Camp, 53 Cal.App. 17, 199 P. 885 (1921) which held that the community was entitled to a reasonable salary for the efforts of the owner-spouse, but the balance of the profit belonged to the separate property as growth of the business. Additionally, one pair of tax cases (involving the same couple) utilized a true apportionment by giving to each, separate and community, an amount of the increase based upon the proportions of fair rate of return and reasonable salary. The formula has not been used in dissolution cases in California.

The *Pereira* rule, apparently downgraded, was given new life by Estate of Neilson, 57 Cal.2d 733, 22 Cal.Rptr. 1, 371 P.2d 745 (1962) which indicated that the *Pereira* approach was to be used unless the party urging another approach showed why it should be more appropriate.

Beam v. Bank of America, 6 Cal.3d 12, 98 Cal.Rptr. 137, 490 P.2d 257 (1971) backed away from the *Pereira* approach to state the current California rule: The trial court may select whichever formula "will achieve substantial justice between the parties".

IDAHO

Gapsch v. Gapsch, 76 Idaho 44, 277 P.2d 278 (1954) is the leading Idaho case on commingling of separate and community property. The case elaborately explained why the community is entitled to reimbursement for funds expended in **improvement** of the husband's separate property (unless a gift was intended). Subsequent cases have clarified that the measure of the reimbursement is not the amount expended but rather the amount of increase in value of the improved property. A gift of the husband's share to the community is no longer presumed when he uses community property to improve his wife's separate property, Brazier v. Brazier, 111 Idaho 692, 726 P.2d 1143 (App.1986).

Credit acquisitions have received a number of different treatments in Idaho. An early case, Wilkerson v. Aven, 26 Idaho 559, 144 P. 1105 (1914) seemed to allow the separate property character of the down payment to determine the character of the property and to ignore the credit acquisition by an unsecured promissory note signed by the wife alone. The actual source of payments was used on a condition subsequent basis in Cargill v. Hancock, 92 Idaho 460, 444 P.2d 421 (1968) in which the court quoted with approval from an Arizona case that when "the balance is borrowed on a mortgage on the property and a note signed by both spouses at the instance of the mortgagee, as between the spouses, *unless the mortgage was afterwards paid from community funds,* the property is separate." The more traditional approach of refusing to consider the actual source of payments was utilized in Estate of Freeburn, 97 Idaho 845, 555 P.2d 385 (1976) in which the Supreme Court of Idaho upheld a District Court finding that the general presumption had not been rebutted by evidence that the $30,000 down payment was derived from an unsecured promissory note for $35,000 which was paid a week later with part of $40,000 borrowed from an insurance company upon the security of the husband's separate property. The parties stipulated that "It is believed that [bank which loaned the $35,000 apparently unsecured] had an oral assignment of the insurance company loan proceeds."

The Idaho case dealing with community property **life insurance**, The Travelers Insurance Company v. Johnson, 97 Idaho 336, 544 P.2d 294 (1975) rejected both the inception of title approach to life insurance and the apportionment rule in favor of the annual policy theory. In that case, the insured purchased a term life insurance policy and designated his divorced first wife as beneficiary; nine months later the insured married his second wife. He died over ten years later without changing his designated beneficiary. Assuming that premiums were paid in advance on an annual basis, one payment was made before the second marriage and ten payments during the second marriage. The Idaho Supreme Court did not apportion the proceeds one eleventh to separate property and ten elevenths to community property; it did not consider apportionment. The court did hold that when an insurance policy is issued on the life of a married person without the knowledge or consent of the other spouse and someone other than the spouse is the gratuitously named beneficiary of the policy and (the last, some, most or all?) premiums are paid with community property, a community interest exists as to one half of the proceeds of the policy upon the death of the insured. The court also indulged in semantics which raised the question of whether there was a community property interest prior to the death of the insured; it stated of the policy in question "As a term policy it had no value except in the event of the death of the insured." It is not certain that the court meant to imply that there was no property interest as opposed to a property interest of no present value; the distinction may be important in future cases.

Employee deferred compensation **retirement** benefits do not suffer from the same uncertainty as to the proper characterizing technique. Pensions are apportioned on a time basis between periods when the employee was or was not married and domiciled in Idaho, Ramsey v. Ramsey, 96 Idaho 672, 535 P.2d 53 (1975).

Idaho Code § 32–712 provides that the existence and extent of retirement benefits (including social security, military and railroad retirement benefits) is a factor which bears upon whether a division of community property shall be equal and the manner of division. This provision may run counter to the reasoning of Hisquierdo v. Hisquierdo, 439 U.S. 572, 586, 99 S.Ct. 802, 810–811, 59 L.Ed.2d 1, 14 (1979), which held that to allow an offsetting award to the non-employee spouse would defeat the purpose of barring the anticipation of benefits.

Although the natural enhancement in the value of separate property during coverture does not constitute community property, any income received during coverture in the form of rents or profits from the separate property does constitute community property. In Speer v. Quinlan, 96 Idaho 119, 525 P.2d 314 (1974), the court held that because the retained earnings of a closely held corporation were never disbursed by the corporation, the retained earnings could not be considered to be "income" or "rents and profits" within the meaning of the Idaho statute. Therefore, the retention of the earnings in the corporation did not present a case of community funds being invested in a separate property business. While the court was thus unwilling to give a share of the separate property **business** as the "income" of the separate property business during coverture, it did point out that one mechanism by which an inequity might be remedied was the discretionary division of community property upon divorce. This remedy is not available when third parties are involved, such as in intestacy.

Not only does Idaho not seem to reimburse the community for retained earnings from separate property, it uses a relatively strict test to determine the amount of the business to attribute to the community estate as compensation for labor. *Speer v. Quinlan* stated that the trial court should adequately compensate the community for the labor of the owner-employee. In so deciding, compensation was denied for the wife who made "considerable effort in entertaining business clients and contacts" and the trial court was told to consider "salaries of other business executives with similar responsibilities and skills located within the Pacific Northwest."

LOUISIANA

Louisiana historically required greater clarity in order to preserve the separate character of property acquired by exchange during marriage. Formerly, immovables acquired by exchange during the marriage would be considered community unless the husband made the **double declaration** that the purchase was made with the proceeds of a sale of separate property and that the purchase was made for his separate account. Similarly, the wife who obtained property during marriage in exchange for her separate property had the burden of proving that she purchased the property as her separate property, by the investment of her paraphernal funds, which she administered separately and apart from her husband. Modernly, the double declaration requirement is faintly echoed by La.Stat.Ann.—Civ.Code art. 2342.

Louisiana has been hesitant to recognize the proportionate sharing of ownership between separate or community; it tends to find that an asset belongs to one or the other, but not both.

While construing the title of property more toward community property *or* separate property, the Louisiana courts were the most liberal of the community property states in giving a right of reimbursement to the separate property for the funds which were used for the **improvement** or purchase of community property.

The inception of title rule had a variation in Louisiana which has been gradually reduced in its breadth of application. This variation looked not at the *inception* of *title* but at the *time* of *vesting*. Thus, in a bond for deed (called a "contract for deed" in other jurisdictions) for the purchase of immovables, the *inception* of *title* arises when the contract for the sale of realty is made, but the *time* of *vesting* in the purchaser does not occur until the deed is delivered, often years later. Currently, this rule applies only to the acquisition of immovables by purchase, homestead or prescription; recent decisions have refused to apply this doctrine to life insurance, pensions and other personal property acquisitions.

La.Stat.Ann.—Civ.Code art. 2341 acknowledges by statute what other community property states declare by decision: If the value of community property which is commingled with and inseparable from separate property is inconsequential in comparison with the value of the separate things used, the character of the property remains separate.

Louisiana has detailed statutory provisions dealing with the use of property of one character to satisfy an obligation of, or improve, property of the other character: **La.Stat.Ann.—Civ.Code articles 2364 and 2365** deal with the use of separate and community property, respectively, to satisfy obligations of property of the opposite character; **articles 2366 and 2367,** respectively, deal with the use of community or separate property to improve property for the benefit of the other character:

Article 2364. If community property has been used to satisfy a separate obligation of a spouse, the other spouse is entitled to reim-

bursement upon termination of the community property regime for one-half of the amount or value that the property had at the time it was used.

Article 2365. If separate property of a spouse has been used to satisfy a community obligation, the spouse, upon termination of the community property regime, is entitled to reimbursement for one-half of the amount or value that the property had at the time it was used.

Reimbursement may only be made to the extent of community assets, unless the community obligation was incurred for the ordinary and customary expenses of the marriage, or for the support, maintenance, and education of children of either spouse in keeping with the economic condition of the community. In the last case, the spouse is entitled to reimbursement from the other spouse even if there are no community assets.

Article 2366. If community property has been used for the acquisition, use, improvement, or benefit of the separate property of a spouse, the other spouse is entitled upon termination of the community to one-half of the amount or value that the community property had at the time it was used.

Article 2367. If separate property of a spouse has been used for the acquisition, use, improvement, or benefit of community property, that spouse, upon termination of the community, is entitled to one-half of the amount used or one-half of the value that the property had at the time it was used, if there are community assets from which reimbursement may be made.

In credit acquisitions which a wife claims to have been made with her credit, Louisiana required in Fortier v. Barry, 111 La. 776, 35 So. 900 (1904) that the wife establish "(1) the possession of some paraphernal funds under her administration, and available for investment, (2) that the cash portion of the price bears such a relation to the whole as to make the property purchased sufficient security for the credit portion, and (3) that her paraphernal property and revenues are such as to enable her to make the purchase with reasonable expectation of meeting the deferred payments."

The three requirements have been condensed in Betz v. Riviere, 211 La. 43, 29 So.2d 465 (1947) to "that she not only made the down payment out of her separate and paraphernal funds, but that she had sufficient separate revenues and funds to make the purchase with reasonable certainty of being able to meet the deferred payments."

The strict requirement to rebut the presumption of community property status was matched with an "all-or-nothing" approach in a number of cases: Even though the wife proved that she paid *some* of the purchase price from her separate assets and that she possessed *some* separate resources, she was required to prove that she was able to pay *all* of the deferred payments. If she could not prove the ability to pay for the entire asset from separate resources, the property was community because the presumption was not entirely rebutted. The separate property was, however, entitled to reimbursement. Modernly, some cases such as Curtis v. Curtis, 388 So.2d 816 (La.App.1980), recognize that reimbursement is not adequate in inflationary times; that case granted proportionate ownership to the wife's separate property (from which the down payment was made) and to the community property (from which the payments were intended to be made).

Louisiana has consistently applied the inception of title rule to **life insurance** policies and proceeds, Succession of Verneuille, 120 La. 605, 45 So. 520 (1908). The potential unfairness of this rule in situations in which the community is terminated by court order rather than by death is increased by the limitation upon reimbursement to one character property for funds expended for premiums on insurance of a different character: The reimbursement is not in the amount of the premiums paid, but is the amount by which the cash surrender value of the policy increased as a result of the premiums paid. Thus, there is no right to reimbursement when the policy is term insurance without a cash surrender value, Connell v. Connell, 331 So.2d 4 (La.1976).

In Sims v. Sims, 358 So.2d 919 (La.1978) the Supreme Court of Louisiana apportioned **retirement** benefits between the separate and community estates of the married couple on the basis of the money contributions. This use of the apportionment technique is in sharp contrast with the usual Louisiana application of the inception of title theory. In the public retirement fund area, Louisiana tracks the federal approach of deciding that some retirement funds do not belong to the community of acquets and gains. This is done by construing statutory language which (1) limits plan participants to "employees" or (2) purports to exempt the proceeds of the funds from legal process, or both. Cases such as Kennedy v. Kennedy, 391 So.2d 1193 (La.App.1980) concerning the Firefighter's Pension and Relief Fund and Scott v. Scott, 179 So.2d 656 (La.App.1965) concerning the State Teachers' Retirement System can be explained as statutory changes of the community property system. Some relief from the harshness of this rule is given in the form of the right of reimbursement of the community of acquets and gains for the contributions made to the separate property retirement system.

Formerly, a now-repealed statute required the all-or-nothing approach (tempered by a right of reimbursement) to community labor expended in increasing the value of a separate property **business**. The increase or amelioration of a separate property business was treated as part of the community regime "if it be proved that the increase or ameliorations be the result of the common labor, expenses or industry". On the other hand, the increase or amelioration was allocated entirely to the separate property of the business person "if it be proved that the increase is due only to the ordinary course of things, to the rise in the value of property, or to the chances of trade." The all-or-nothing approach has been abandoned in favor of a statutory scheme for retention of separate property character with reimbursement to the community for the value of any labor resulting in an increase in value. La.Stat.Ann.—Civ.Code art. 2368 provides:

Article 2368. If the separate property of a spouse has increased in value as a result of the uncompensated common labor or industry of the spouses, the other spouse is entitled to be reimbursed from the spouse whose property has increased in value one-half of the increase attributed to the common labor.

NEVADA

There are very few Nevada cases dealing with the problems of this chapter. **Credit** acquisition of stock was involved in Zahringer v. Zahringer, 76 Nev. 21, 348 P.2d 161 (1960) which upheld the trial court's finding of separate property character of stock. The stock was traced to premarital separate property of the husband despite the husband's testimony that he borrowed the purchase price from his parents. The Supreme Court of Nevada stated in dictum that "The proceeds of the loans received by the husband from his parents must be presumed to be community property." It added: "The fact that the stock was issued only in the name of the husband did not affect the presumption that it was community property."

The Supreme Court of Nevada seems to have confused the character (community or separate) of the **life insurance** policy and its proceeds on the one hand with the beneficiary designation on the other hand. In Peters v. Peters, 557 P.2d 713 (Nev.1976), the premiums for a life insurance policy upon the life of the husband were paid from community property and the wife was designated as the beneficiary. The Supreme Court of Nevada held that all proceeds vested at the moment of the insured's death in the surviving spouse as her separate property. It was not stated whether this was because (a) death terminated the community, (b) the husband had made a gift to the wife or (c) she received the policy proceeds after the termination of the marriage or gratuitously.

Nevada's reliance upon California community property precedents is evidenced by declarations such as in Cord v. Neuhoff, 94 Nev. 21, 26, 573 P.2d 1170, 1173 (1978) that the preferred method of apportioning profits when community labor has been added to a separate property **business** is the *Pereira* method. That method of allowing a fair return upon the capital and then allocating the balance of the profits to the community estate is to be used "unless the owner of the separate estate can establish that a different method of allocation is more likely to accomplish justice." Apportionment by the *Van Camp* method has been held to achieve substantial justice when the community was fully compensated by salary for the community labor. It is not clear how far Nevada is following Beam v. Bank of America, 6 Cal.3d 12, 98 Cal.Rptr. 137, 490 P.2d 257 (1971) in emphasizing substantial justice rather than the basic *Pereira* approach.

Nevada has also applied the general commingling rule in cases where the business was not incorporated, records were not made available and the court suggested that the manager of the business might be concealing assets and income, as in Ormachea v. Ormachea, 67 Nev. 273, 217 P.2d 355 (1950).

NEW MEXICO

Credit of a spouse has been treated as separate property in some New Mexico cases. One case disregarded the credit portion of an acquisition in which the $18,000 purchase price was represented by a $10,000 down payment and the assumption of promissory notes secured by mortgages on the purchased property. Otherwise, New Mexico appears to follow the inception of title theory and allow a right of reimbursement when funds of another character are used to pay the debt upon the purchased property.

New Mexico applies the inception of title rule for determining the character of **life insurance**, White's Estate, 43 N.M. 202, 89 P.2d 36 (1939), but apportions **pension** funds which are earned both during and outside the marriage, LeClert v. LeClert, 80 N.M. 235, 453 P.2d 755 (1969).

TEXAS

Texas cases recognize the presumption which arises when separate and community property are commingled so that they cannot be separately traced.   In addition, Vernon's Ann.Tex.Stat. Family Code § 5.22(b) provides a presumption concerning management, control and disposition of commingled property; see Chapter 7.

Texas allows reimbursement to either the community estate or the separate property of either spouse for **improvements** made upon property of the other character.   The amount of the reimbursement is the lesser of the amount expended or the enhancement of the value of the improved property.   Trial courts may, in their discretion, grant an equitable lien upon property which is improved in order to secure collection of a reimbursement claim.

Property acquired during marriage is presumed to be community property, including property acquired on **credit**.   Thus, in both Gleich v. Bongio, 128 Tex. 606, 99 S.W.2d 881 (1937) and Broussard

v. Tian, 156 Tex. 371, 295 S.W.2d 405 (1956), property was held to be community property to the extent of the credit acquisition despite separate property down payments and no payments being made from community property.

Credit acquisitions in Texas are determined by this general rule subject to other community property rules:

•One who is a party to the transaction cannot offer parol evidence to contradict a recital in the deed. Parol evidence to contradict the recital is admissible if offered by one not a party to the transaction, Messer v. Johnson, 422 S.W.2d 908 (Tex.1968).

•The intention of the lender is given great emphasis in Texas in determining the character of property acquired on credit. Property acquired on credit by a married person is community property unless the creditor agreed to look only to the separate property of the contracting party for satisfaction of the credit extended, Goodloe v. Williams, 302 S.W.2d 235 (Texarkana Civ.App.1957, writ refused). One weakness of this rule is that rents, issues and profits received from separate property during marriage are community property; thus the creditor would need to look to an exchange of a separate property item itself.

•The actual source of payment is irrelevant under the inception of title rule; once the title has passed, payment from property of another character gives a right of reimbursement, at most. If payments are made *before* title has passed, a tenancy in common is created.

Texas has experienced intellectual convulsions in dealing with community property **life insurance.** Initial problems, both of which have been remedied by legislation, were the inability to decide that a life insurance policy is community property and the problem of a divorced spouse not having the required continuing insurable interest. Continuing problems revolve around the different treatment given to the life insurance policy before maturity, as opposed to the proceeds of the policy upon maturity.

Texas courts insist that a distinction should be made between ownership of the insurance contract during the life of the insured (which in itself is a valuable property right) and ownership of the proceeds payable on death. In McCurdy v. McCurdy, 372 S.W.2d 381 (Tex.Civ.App.1963, error refused), the inception of title rule was selected to determine ownership of the contract, but earlier Texas Supreme Court cases have hinted that either the apportionment or the annual policy theory might be used, at least for term insurance. Case law has consistently held the proceeds of a community property life insurance policy payable to a widow or widower to be the separate property of that survivor as a gift.

Texas courts are reluctant to trace the proceeds of an insurance policy back to the policy itself. Different rules of ownership have been created for the caterpillar and the butterfly, without extensive consideration of the fact that they are successive forms of the same thing. While the divorce cases have been able to give one half of cash value of the community property life insurance policies to each spouse, cases involving matured policies have not been able to surmount the beneficiary designation. Although entitled to one half of the policy's cash surrender value, the holder of community property rights in a life insurance policy has not been allowed to take one half of the proceeds.

The characterization of the policy as separate, community or partly each is not always determinative of the question of the rightful taker of either the policy upon divorce or the proceeds upon death. Among the variations involved in the cases are whether the insured's spouse survives the insured, whether the insurance beneficiary designation is irrevocable and the identity and relationship of the beneficiary—the spouse, the estate of the insured or third parties.

The right of a married person having insurance "issued in his or her name" to manage, control and dispose of such contracts of life insurance without the joinder or consent of the other spouse is set out in Vernon's Ann.Tex.Stat. Insurance Code § 3.49–3.

Retirement funds are apportioned between the separate and community estates upon a time basis to the extent that the employee was married and domiciled in Texas during the period when the retirement benefits were earned, Taggart v. Taggart, 552 S.W.2d 422 (Tex.1977).

In allocating and apportioning profits from a separate property **business** to which community property efforts have been added, Texas has retained many aspects of the all-or-nothing rule and has created a seemingly contradictory pattern. The form of the business organization—sole proprietorship, partnership or corporation—affects the approach and outcome. In dealing with sole proprietorships, Norris v. Vaughn, 152 Tex. 491, 260 S.W.2d 676 (1953) presents many of the rules and distinctions of the Texas approach:

• A reasonable amount of community time and talent can be expended upon separate property by the owner of that separate estate without converting the asset or its profit to community property.

• Certain types of depleting asserts remain separate property even if community property labor is added. Seeming inconsistencies arise between oil and gas interests (which remain separate real property until severance) on the one hand and bricks and lumber (which require more labor to process) on the other hand.

Other Texas rules dealing with the determination of character of a separate property business to

which community property labor has been added
include the following:

• Crops grown on separate property land are
community property with community property labor being attributed even when it did not exist.
Other cases have held that separate property cattle
fattened with community labor and materials remained separate property.

• Stock dividends and undistributed accumulated
profits of an incorporated business are of the same
character as the stock to which they relate, but a
few Texas cases have used the alter ego theory to
attribute to the community estate undistributed
profits of a separate property close corporation.

WASHINGTON

Washington has granted an equitable lien for the
amount of **improvements** not only when separate
and community property are commingled by the
improvement by one character property to the
other, but also when the separate property of one
spouse is used to improve the separate property of
the other spouse, as in Estate of Trierweiler, 5
Wash.App. 17, 486 P.2d 314 (1971). Washington
also indicates that the measure of the lien is the
amount expended rather than the amount by
which the value of the improved property is en-
hanced.

In determining the character of property acquired on **credit**, Washington has followed the
general presumption but has matched benefits and

burdens and has developed a number of local peculiarities and inconsistencies:

• Washington's original approach to credit acquisitions was to classify the portion of property acquired on credit during marriage as community property; some exceptions appeared almost immediately.

• Washington determines the character of such property to be separate if the creditor *actually* could reach the separate property of one of the spouses. This change in emphasis is consistent with the Washington system of classifying debts as separate and community and preserving property of one character from claims of the other character. The large number of Washington cases in this area is partially caused by the efforts of creditors to reach, and spouses to protect, assets.

• The Washington "ability of the lender to reach" test does not solve the circularity involved when the purchased property is the sole security relied upon or reachable. It is possible that there is no personal liability because property is acquired subject to existing indebtedness. Without personal liability, the lender is not able to reach other separate or community assets of the couple; the intent of the lender is therefore irrelevant. In Merkel v. Merkel, 39 Wash.2d 102, 234 P.2d 857 (1951), the husband acquired two parcels of land, each of which was subject to existing indebtedness for which neither spouse was liable. The asset portion of each parcel was the husband's separate property: The first was inherited from the husband's father; the second was purchased prior to marriage. Although community property was used to discharge portions of the indebtedness, the community was held to be entitled to only reimbursement for amounts expended and not entitled to any part of the ownership of the asset.

• When separate property of the wife was used as security for the purchase price, the Washington Supreme Court has delivered varied results by emphasizing different aspects of the transactions, such as whether both parties signed the note, in whose name or names title was taken, whether there was an interspousal agreement etc.

Life insurance is apportioned in the ratio which the separate and community estates have contributed to the payment of premiums, Coffey's Estate, 195 Wash. 379, 81 P.2d 283 (1938). The same method of apportionment on a time basis of **pension** benefits was applied in Marriage of Jacobs, 20 Wash.App. 272, 579 P.2d 1023 (1978).

In allocating the profits of a separate property **business** to which community labor has been added, the courts in Washington have looked at the respective importance of labor or capital in the particular business and have considered the sufficiency of amounts withdrawn from the business as salary. The corporate form has not prevented the courts from apportioning a part or allocating the accumulated undistributed profits or the entire corporate value to the community in appropriate cases.

WISCONSIN (and UMPA)

Wisconsin (and UMPA) classify by statute property which combines two or more components—marital, individual or predetermination date. Wisconsin differs from UMPA by using the term "property which is not marital property" and thereby includes predetermination date property for application of its "mixing" rule and "active" appreciation rule.

Wis.Stats. 1985–86 §§ 766.63 states the general rules for commingled property in part (1) and for improvements and businesses in part (2):

(1)   [M]ixing marital property with property having any other classification reclassifies the other property to marital property unless the component of the mixed property which is not marital property can be traced.

(2)   Application by one spouse of substantial labor, effort, inventiveness, physical or intellectual skill, creativity or managerial activity to either spouse's property other than marital property creates marital property attributable to that application if both of the following apply:

(a)   Reasonable compensation is not received for the application.

(b) Substantial appreciation of the property results from the application.

The following provisions (as summarized in Wisconsin Legislative Council Staff, "Wisconsin's New Marital Property Law" 13) govern the determination of the marital property component of **life insurance** benefits:

1. If the policy designates the insured as owner and the policy is issued after [the latest of] the date of marriage, January 1, 1986, or establishment of a Wisconsin domicile, the ownership interest and proceeds are marital property, regardless of the classification of property used to pay premiums.

2. The ownership interest and proceeds of a policy which designates the spouse of the insured as the owner are individual property [of the spouse designated as owner] regardless of the classification of property used to pay premiums on the policy.

3. For other situations, in which at least one premium is paid with marital property, the marital property component is that portion of the ownership interest and proceeds generally representing a ratio of the period during marriage after which a premium is paid with marital property to the entire period the policy is in effect.

4. The interest of the owner or beneficiary of a policy acquired under a judgment or property settlement incident to a prior marriage is not marital

property, regardless of what property is used to pay the policy's premiums.

The marital property law also allows a spouse to consent in writing to designation of a third person as the beneficiary of a policy or to the use of property to pay premiums on an insurance policy. The consent, according to its terms, relinquishes or reclassifies the consenting spouse's interest in premiums, the policy or its proceeds.

Wis.Stats. 1985–86 § 766.62 apportions **deferred employee benefit plans** by allocating to the marital property component the ratio of the employment years during marriage to the total employment years. Wisconsin goes beyond UMPA by terminating the marital property interest of the non-employee spouse in the deferred compensation plan if the non-employee predeceases the employee spouse.

PART III

DURING THE MARRIAGE

CHAPTER 7

MANAGEMENT AND CONTROL

A. OVERVIEW

1. History of Management and Control

Management and control is the collective name for a number of important property rights including the rights to use, transfer, abandon, lease, expend, assign, create a security interest in, mortgage, dispose of, institute or defend a legal action regarding, buy, consume, exchange, encumber, sell or donate the property as well as the right to dictate the manner by which the property will be used or not used. Management and control therefore constitutes an important element of ownership, although not the entire bundle of ownership rights.

Until 1970, management and control of community property was vested in the husband in all states with a few items of property (such as the wife's earnings or her personal injury recoveries) being excluded. Since the right of management and control is so extensive and important, this meant that the "equal" right of the wife in commu-

nity property was "less equal" than that of the
husband. Equality existed in general theory and
perhaps existed through actual practice, but it did
not exist at the level of the law's view of management and control.

In the 1970's the then eight community property
states made major changes in the management and
control provisions of their statutes. All states except Texas elected to have a one-spouse system of
management for most assets. The phrasing of the
one-spouse system ranged from saying that the
spouses have "equal management" (Arizona) or
that "either spouse" has the right to manage (California, Idaho, Nevada, New Mexico) to saying that
"each spouse" has the sole management (Louisiana, Washington and Texas as to certain community assets). Texas uses as its basic premise the
concept of joint management which is a two-spouse
system of management.

Within the one-spouse management system, most
of the management is by *either* spouse. The provisions for *each* spouse to serve as manager of designated property are remnants of the former system
by which one designated spouse (usually the husband) had the sole management and control. In
Louisiana, for example, significant amounts of the
management and control are given to that spouse
who has any of movables issued or registered in his
or her name, a partnership interest or a community enterprise as to its movables which are not

issued in the name of the other spouse (with an exception for certain other provisions of the law).

Texas, on the other hand, uses the designated one-spouse system to allow each spouse the full management and control of the community property which he or she would have owned if single until the managed property is mingled with community property subject to the sole control of the other spouse.

California, Louisiana, Nevada, Washington and Wisconsin (UMPA) recognize the right of a spouse who is operating or managing a business to have the sole management and control of the assets of that business without the consent of the other spouse. California uses the term "primary control".

2. Statutory Patterns

Each of the statutory schemes contains exceptions. In the one-spouse manager states (i.e., other than Texas), there are certain items which require the action of both spouses, for which the appropriate statute should be consulted. The major statutes are set out for each state in Part C of this chapter, below. Generally the items requiring joint action include encumbrance or alienation of realty and one or more of the following items:

●Acquisition of community realty (Arizona, Nevada, Washington).

●Guaranty, indemnity or suretyship transactions (Arizona).

• Sale of community furnishings of the home and clothing of the other spouse (Louisiana, Nevada, Washington).

• Sale of either substantially all assets of a community enterprise (Louisiana), or any such assets if both spouses participate in the management of the business (Nevada and Washington).

Specific statutory provisions allow the spouses to agree to a different scheme of management and control in Idaho, Texas and Wisconsin (UMPA). In Louisiana a spouse may expressly renounce the right to concur in actions which would otherwise require joint action of the spouses. The consent of a spouse may be obtained in advance by a power of attorney in accordance with statutory provisions in Idaho, Nevada and Texas.

Certain exceptions to the management and control by either spouse are found in California, Louisiana, Nevada and Washington which restrict gifts made by either spouse alone.

Arizona, Texas and Wisconsin (UMPA) considered it provident to point out that each spouse has the exclusive right to manage and control his or her separate property. Modernly, the same rule holds true in the other community property states without the benefit of a statute.

In Texas, joint management and control is the rule unless the parties otherwise agree or a party is dealing with "community property that he or she would have owned if single." That category includes, but is not limited to personal earnings, revenue from separate property, personal injury recoveries and the increase, mutations and revenue from property subject to the sole management of the spouse.

Protection of the other spouse is seldom provided by statute. California and Wisconsin (UMPA) have codified a good faith rule for the management and control of the community property.

Protection of third parties is furnished by a number of provisions without much uniformity among the states. California, Idaho and Wisconsin (UMPA) included express provisions which validate certain prexisting documents. Washington protects mechanics' liens. New Mexico has express provisions for management based upon the form of documentary title to personal property. Nevada and Wisconsin (UMPA) have a specific provision concerning payments from employee benefit plans.

3. Application of Management and Control Theories

Statutes concerning management by the husband or by either spouse probably do not change the way that a happily-married couple manages its finances. Individuals decide these issues as a practical matter without the aid of the law. When, however, marital discord arises, the law is consulted to see what should be or should have been done.

When husbands generally had management and control of community property, legal consequences flowed from that power. In any case where a wife had some or all of the actual management and control despite the legal rules, her husband was, nonetheless, responsible because of his nominal management and control. The one-spouse management system which gives control and management to either spouse acting alone gives at least nominal management and control to both spouses; the system probably will not change intrafamily allocations of responsibilities. It is not certain how the legal consequences which flow from nominal management and control will be changed: Will they be applied to neither spouse, to both spouses or to the spouse who has actual (rather than nominal) management and control?

The following rules or applications of community property law were originally based upon the concept of the husband being the manager of the community property and need to be reevaluated in light of the new provisions:

• Community property which was registered or titled in the name of the wife was often treated as a gift by the husband to the wife. On the other hand, community property which was registered in the name of the husband remained community property either because his name alone was recognition of his management and control or because an attempt to transmute the community to the husband's separate property without the consent of

the wife was a fraud upon his fiduciary duty as
manager.

• Management and control of community property while the two spouses are living separate and
apart is easiest under the system by which one or
either spouse can manage and control and is hard-
est when joint action is required. Texas varies the
management and control rather than the character
of the property when the members of a married
couple are living separate and apart.

• One spouse or the other may be a necessary or
proper party to bring an action for personal injury
or property damage depending upon the character
of the injured property or of the recovery.

• Disappearance of a spouse (including persons
who are missing in action) may require court assistance where formerly none was required. Formerly, when the husband had management and control, the disappearance of the wife did not require
utilization of statutory and court procedures for
the management of community property. The procedures were required for the wife's separate property or if the manager-husband disappeared. Now,
the disappearance of either spouse requires those
procedures in all those situations in which joint
action is required, but does not cause a problem in
dealing with property which either spouse or the
remaining spouse could manage or control.

• Commingling of community property with the
separate property of the manager put the burden
upon that manager to trace and prove his separate

property; failure to do so resulted in the commingled (and confused) mass being treated as entirely community property. Formerly this operated almost entirely against the husband. It is uncertain whether and how the commingling rule will be changed because of the changes in management and control.

•Statutes designed to protect third parties who deal with one spouse were often based upon the model of male management and control. Changes in the management and control probably should not diminish the protection given third parties since the lack of protection might cause greater hardship to married persons in the future.

•Liability for debts is often linked to management and control. See Chapter 8.

4. The Fiduciary Standard

Under the husband-management model, a fiduciary standard of varying stringency was generally imposed upon the husband. It is uncertain what standard of care is now to be applied to the manager of the community property. Two extremes can be identified:

a. Some statutes emphasized that the husband was (and the present manager of the community is) free to deal with the property as if it were his (or her) own property. Some hints of this language remain in the California and Nevada provisions which describe the power (but not the right) of the manager to deal with the community "with the same power of disposition as the . . . spouse has over his separate property. . . ." The apparent freedom of this standard should not be taken literally.

b. On the other extreme, some cases have gone so far as to suggest that the husband as manager of the community was a trustee for his wife's share. This, also, is too absolute a standard. Some of the duties of a trustee are never applied to the manager of community property. Two examples (and typical remedies for breach) are the duty to make the trust property productive (or suffer surcharge against one's own property) and the duty to account periodically (or suffer removal from the trustee position). The type of accounting made by the manager of the community typically occurs at the end of the marital regime and usually lacks the detail and certainty of the trustee's accounting.

Between these extremes are a number of other possible positions, most of which have had adherents from some community property states at some point in time:

• The duty not to commit fraud is clearly a part of the manager's obligation in every jurisdiction. Contrast, however, gross negligence or incompetence of the manager which are risks of the marriage. Success of an employed spouse in his or her career is not required by the law. A manager is permitted to be inept, inefficient or clumsy, so long as he or she is honestly so.

•Good faith is the standard imposed by California and Wisconsin (UMPA). The manager must not use the managerial position to take unfair advantage of the non-managing spouse.

•Partnership fiduciary standards are relatively close to the standard which is applied in most situations. While acknowledging the individual desires to further his or her own interests, this standard recognizes that an obligation is owed to the other party.

The manager of the community is usually called to account for his or her stewardship at the termination of the marital regime, which most frequently occurs at death or divorce. The termination could also occur by court action or by agreement, dependent upon the law of the applicable jurisdiction.

B. DETAIL

1. Gifts

a. **Historical Development:** Why, you may ask, should a spouse who owns only one half of the community property, but is given management and control of both halves, be able to give away both halves of the community property to a third person? That's a good question.

The power to make gifts has historically been included in the enumeration of the attributes of management and control. This inclusion was neither necessary nor logical. Although the manager of the property needs the ability to convert an asset from one form to another, there was seldom a pressing need to eliminate an asset.

Spanish law gave the husband the right to make gifts of community property to third persons as part of management and control so long as he did not thereby defraud his wife. Most community property states followed the Spanish lead, but statutes in California, Louisiana, Nevada and Washington now require the non-manager spouse to consent to gifts. California requires the "written consent" while Nevada and Washington require only the "express or implied consent" of the non-manager spouse. In Louisiana "concurrence of the spouses" is required except that "a spouse acting alone may make a usual or customary gift of a value commensurate with the economic position of the spouses at the time of the donation."

Wisconsin (UMPA) requires that both spouses "act together" to create gifts which exceed both $1,000 (UMPA suggested $500.) per donee in a calendar year and "a larger amount if, when made, the gift is reasonable in amount considering the economic position of the spouses."

If the non-manager spouse consents to the gift or authorizes it in advance by giving a power of attorney and the consent or authorization was not obtained by fraud, undue influence, mistake or misrepresentation, the gift is valid.

Fraud by the manager (usually the husband) upon the spouse is the minimum standard in all states by which any gift of community property could be set aside.

b. Gifts of Community Property to a Spouse: Gifts of community property from the manager to the non-manager pose few problems; it is really a matter of transmutation from community to separate property. See Chapter 2. On the other hand, gifts from the non-manager wife to the manager husband were not as quickly found. The husband, as manager, could not convert the community into his separate property without being accused of breach of his fiduciary duty as manager if not outright fraud of the wife.

The law presumes the existence of a confidential relationship between husband and wife. This confidential relationship precludes either spouse from procuring an unfair advantage over the other by fraud or undue influence. Although the mere existence of the husband-wife relationship does not create a presumption of fraud or undue influence, it often shifts the burden to the person who obtained the advantage to show that it was free from fraud or undue influence.

For the purposes of this chapter, gifts will be presumed to have been made to a third person, i.e., other than to a spouse, with neither the consent of, nor fraud upon, the non-manager spouse, unless otherwise expressly stated.

c. Gifts to Third Parties: The manager of the community property (formerly the husband in most cases) has power to make gifts of community property, but that power is limited:

• Gifts made with the fraudulent purpose of injuring the spouse can be set aside.

• The law does not bother with trifles. Therefore, small customary gratuities are fully within the management power. Louisiana has codified and extended this rule by stating in La.Civ.Code— art. 2349 that "a spouse acting alone may make a usual or customary gift of a value commensurate with the economic position of the spouses at the time of the donation."

• Between the trifle and the fraud is a broad area. Gifts in this broad ground have generally been upheld by the states which do not have statutes restricting the power of the manager of the community to make gifts, although there is some uncertainty as to the standard applied in Idaho.

Among the factors which are considered in determining whether a gift is in fraud of the spouse's right in Arizona, Idaho, New Mexico and Texas are the relationship of the donee to the donor, the respective amounts of the gift and the community estate and the motivation for the particular gift.

d. Portion of the Gift Which Is Set Aside: If the manager of the community property makes a gift to a third person without the consent (in four states) or in excess of the permissible standard (in Wisconsin and UMPA), or in fraud (in the other four states) of the non-manager spouse, what reme-

dies are available? Is the purported gift void or
voidable? How much should be set aside—one half,
all in excess of the standard, all or a fraction based
on the value at the time of the gift?

Ordinarily, the gift is voidable, rather than void.
The gift can be avoided at the request of the
injured spouse and the gift cannot (short of collusion) be avoided at the request of the manager
spouse.

The amount of the gift which can be declared
void and brought back into the community estate
is dependent upon whether the community regime
is still in existence at the time that the issue
arises:

• The injured spouse brings back the entire gift
into the community if the community is still in
existence. This prevents the manager spouse from
giving progressive halves of the community by
successive gifts. In Wisconsin (and UMPA) the
non-donor spouse may recover the property or a
compensatory judgment equal to the amount by
which the gift exceeded the permissible standard.
The recovered property is characterized as community property.

• If the community has been terminated (whether by agreement, court action or death), the injured
spouse has the right to recapture only one-half of
the donated property. The other half is allowed to
remain with the donee on a variety of theories
including that the transfer is tantamount to a
testamentary transfer and should be permitted as

a devise, that the gift and setting aside comprise a transmutation or that the manager-spouse should not be allowed to undo his or her portion of the gift.

Another remedy which is possible at the termination of the community is to award to the injured spouse so much of the community property remaining on hand as will equal in value the half of the community which was improperly donated. With this technique, if enough community wealth remains on hand, the injured spouse need not pursue the donees.

e. Gifts by Life Insurance Policy: One of the most frequently litigated issues concerning gifts of community property is the designation by the insured spouse of a third party as the beneficiary of community property life insurance. Typically, there are also threshold questions as to the character of the life insurance premiums, policy and proceeds.

When is the gift of life insurance made—at the time that each premium is paid or when the proceeds are paid? Among the issues which turn upon the answer to that question are the relative amount of the gift, the time for examination of the size of the remaining community property and the applicable law:

• If the gift is made with each premium payment, then the amount of the gift is the small annual premium and it is measured against the community property remaining each year to determine if there has been a fraud upon the spouse. Possibly statutes of limitation or laches may prevent subsequent invalidation of the multiple gifts.

• If the gift occurs when the beneficiary receives the proceeds, a larger gift has been made. The gift is measured against the net community estate remaining after the payment of debts. Statutes of limitation have not run and the present law of management and control applies.

Generally, courts use the revocability or irrevocability of the beneficiary designation as the touchstone for determining whether the gift is made when the premium is paid or when the proceeds are collected. Normally the beneficiary designation is revocable, and the gift is therefore not made until the maturation of the policy. An irrevocable beneficiary designation, however, effects an immediate gift; and all subsequent premium payments are additional gifts. Some uncertainty exists concerning the retention of other rights which can indirectly change the beneficiary, such as the right to surrender the insurance policy, the right to borrow against the policy or the right to allow coverage to expire by the nonpayment of premiums. Generally such rights are disregarded or considered to be in the nature of conditions subsequent upon an otherwise-completed gift of the life insurance premiums.

Insurance company practices and protective statutes reduce the probability the insurer will be called upon to pay the proceeds twice. Many companies have special procedures for married insured persons who are domiciled in community property states; the companies request the signature of the spouse of the insured when the beneficiary designation is not to the spouse. Additionally, most states have enacted statutes which permit insurance companies to pay in accordance with the beneficiary designation unless the surviving spouse asserts his or her claim in a timely manner. This practice permits insurance companies to make fast payouts in cases where no other question arises as to coverage and beneficiary designation. If the spouse does assert a claim contrary to the beneficiary designation, the company usually pays the money into court and interpleads the claimants. These statutes protect the insurance company from paying twice, but do not determine the right to the proceeds between the spouse and the designated beneficiary. Thus the spouse asserts his or her claim first against the insurance company, but if it has already paid the proceeds, the spouse asserts the claim against the designated beneficiary.

Do these life insurance rules apply when there is consideration for the transfer? The source of the rules is the limitation upon gifts which is an aspect of management and control. It is possible that a reciprocal arrangement between partners, for example, may be treated as a contract, at least to the extent that it is not a gift to the partner which the spouse of the insured partner can set aside.

C. INDIVIDUAL STATES

ARIZONA

Arizona aggregates life insurance and other formerly community property assets upon the death of the insured-manager. If there are sufficient other provisions for the widow or widower, whether by joint tenancy, trust, life insurance or probate estate, so that the survivor receives at least one half of the community, there has been no fraud upon his or her rights and the gifts (including life insurance beneficiary designations) stand effective. To the extent that the widow or widower does not receive his or her half of the community from the manager's estate and probate substitutes, there is a constructive fraud upon the survivor's rights; the gifts and beneficiary designations are ineffective to the extent of such constructive fraud.

The management and control statute is as follows:

Ariz.Rev.Stat. § 25–214:

A. Each spouse has the sole management, control and disposition rights of his or her separate property.

B. The spouses have equal management, control and disposition rights over their community property, and have equal power to bind the community.

C. Either spouse separately may acquire, manage, control or dispose of community prop-

erty, or bind the community, except that joinder of both spouses is required in any of the following cases:

1. Any transaction for the acquisition, disposition or encumbrance of an interest in real property other than an unpatented mining claim or a lease of less than one year.

2. Any transaction of guaranty, indemnity or suretyship.

CALIFORNIA

The current management and control provisions are as follows:

Calif.Civ.Code § 5125:

(a) Except as provided in subdivisions (b), (c), and (d) and Sections 5113.5 and 5128, either spouse has the management and control of the community personal property, whether acquired prior to or on or after January 1, 1975, with like absolute power of disposition, other than testamentary, as the spouse has of the separate estate of the spouse.

(b) A spouse may not make a gift of community personal property, or dispose of community personal property without a valuable consideration, without the written consent of the other spouse.

(c) A spouse may not sell, convey, or encumber the furniture, furnishings, or fittings of the home, or the clothing or wearing apparel of the other spouse or minor children which is community personal property, without the written consent of the other spouse.

(d) Except as provided in subdivisions (b) and (c) and in Section 5127, a spouse who is operating or managing a business or an interest in a business that is all or substantially all community personal property has the primary management and control of the business or interest. Primary management and control means that the managing spouse may act alone in all transactions but shall give prior written notice to the other spouse of any sale, lease, exchange, encumbrance or other disposition of all or substantially all of the personal property used in the operation of the business (including personal property used for agricultural purposes) whether or not title to that property is held in the name of only one spouse. Written notice is not, however, required when prohibited by the law otherwise applicable to the transaction.

Any change in the form of a business is not subject to the requirement of written notice.

Remedies for the failure of a managing spouse to give prior written notice as required by this subdivision are only as specified in Section 5125.1. A failure to give prior written notice shall not adversely affect the validity of the transaction nor of any interest transferred.

(e) Each spouse shall act in good faith with respect to the other spouse in the management and control of the community property in accordance with the general rules which control the actions of persons having relationships of personal confidence as specified in Section 5103, until such time as the property has been divided by the parties or by a court. This duty includes the obligation to make full disclosure to the other spouse of the existence of assets in which the community has an interest and debts for which the community may be liable, upon request. . . . In no event shall this standard be interpreted to be less than that of good faith in confidential relationships. . . .

Calif.Civ.Code § 5125.1 provides remedies in the form of an action for an accounting, to add the name of the other spouse to the title of assets (with some business exceptions) or for damages.

§ 5127: Except as provided in Sections 5113.5 and 5128, either spouse has the management and control of the community real property, whether acquired prior to or on or after January 1, 1975, but both spouses either personally or by duly authorized agent, must join in executing any instrument by which such community real property or any interest therein is leased for a longer period than one year, or is sold, conveyed, or encumbered; provided, however, that nothing herein contained shall be construed to apply to a lease, mortgage, conveyance, or transfer of real property or of any interest in real property between husband and wife; provided, also, however, that the sole lease, contract, mortgage or deed of the husband, holding the record title to community real property, to a lessee, purchaser, or encumbrancer, in good faith without knowledge of the marriage relation, shall be presumed to be valid if executed prior to January 1, 1975, and that the sole lease, contract, mortgage, or deed of either spouse, holding the record title to community real property to a lessee, purchaser, or encumbrancer, in good faith without knowledge of the marriage relation, shall be presumed to be valid if executed on or after January 1, 1975. No action to avoid any instrument mentioned in this section, affecting any property standing of record in the name of either spouse alone, executed by the spouse alone, shall be commenced after the expiration of one year from the filing for record of such instrument in the recorder's office in the county in which the land is situate, and no action to avoid any instrument mentioned in this section, affecting any property standing of record in the name of the husband alone, which was executed by the husband alone and filed for record prior to the time this act takes effect, in the recorder's office in the county in which the land is situate, shall be commenced after the expiration of one year from the date on which this act takes effect.

IDAHO

The management and control statutes in Idaho are as follows:

Idaho Code § 32–912:

Either the husband or the wife shall have the right to manage and control the community property, and either may bind the community property by contract, except that neither the husband nor wife may sell, convey or encumber the community real estate unless the other joins in executing and acknowledging the deed or other instrument of conveyance, by which the real estate is sold, conveyed or encumbered, and any community obligation incurred by either the husband or the wife without the consent in writing of the other shall not obligate the separate property of the spouse who did not so consent; provided, however, that the husband or wife may by express power of attorney give to the other the complete power to sell, convey or encumber community property, either real or personal. All deeds, conveyances, bills of sale, or evidences of debt heretofore made in conformity herewith are hereby validated.

§ 32–916: The property rights of husband and wife are governed by this chapter, unless there is a marriage settlement agreement entered into prior to or during marriage containing stipulations contrary thereto.

LOUISIANA

The thoroughness of the Louisiana statutory provisions reflects both the civil law tradition and the fact that Louisiana was the last of the eight original community property states to enact "equal" management:

La.Stat.Ann.—Civ.Code art. 2346:

Each spouse acting alone may manage, control, or dispose of community property unless otherwise provided by law.

Art. 2347: The concurrence of both spouses is required for the alienation, encumbrance, or lease of community immovables, furniture or furnishings while located in the family home, all or substantially all of the assets of a community enterprise and movables issued or registered as provided by law in the names of the spouses jointly.

Art. 2348: A spouse may expressly renounce the right to concur in the alienation, encumbrance, or lease of a community immovable or all or substantially all of a community enterprise. He also may renounce the right to participate in the management of a community enterprise. The renunciation may be irrevocable for a stated term.

Art. 2349: The donation of community property to a third person requires the concurrence of the spouses, but a spouse acting alone may

make a usual or customary gift of a value commensurate with the economic position of the spouses at the time of the donation.

Art. 2350: The spouse who is the sole manager of a community enterprise has the exclusive right to alienate, encumber, or lease its movables unless the movables are issued in the name of the other spouse or the concurrence of the other spouse is required by law.

Art. 2351: A spouse has the exclusive right to manage, alienate, encumber, or lease movables issued or registered in his name as provided by law.

Art. 2352: A spouse who is a partner has the exclusive right to manage, alienate, encumber, or lease the partnership interest.

Art. 2353: When the concurrence of the spouses is required by law, the alienation, encumbrance, or lease of community property by a spouse is relatively null unless the other spouse has renounced the right to concur. Also, the alienation, encumbrance, or lease of the assets of a community enterprise by the nonmanager spouse is a relative nullity.

NEVADA

The basic management and control provisions in Nevada are as follows. A special provision in Nev.Rev.Stat. 123.240 protects the payors of amounts from retirement, death or other employee benefit plans or savings plans.

Nev.Rev.Stat. 123.230:

A spouse may, by written power of attorney, give to the other the complete power to sell, convey or encumber any property held as community property or either spouse, acting alone, may manage and control community property, whether acquired before or after July 1, 1975, with the same power of disposition as the acting spouse has over his separate property, except that:

1. Neither spouse may devise or bequeath more than one-half of the community property.

2. Neither spouse may make a gift of community property without the express or implied consent of the other.

3. Neither spouse may sell, convey or encumber the community real property unless both join in the execution of the deed or other instrument by which the real property is sold, conveyed or encumbered, and the deed or other instrument must be acknowledged by both.

4. Neither spouse may purchase or contract to purchase community real property unless both join in the transaction of purchase or in the execution of the contract to purchase.

5. Neither spouse may create a security interest, other than a purchase money security interest as defined in NRS 104.9107, in, or sell,

community household goods, furnishings or appliances unless both join in executing the security agreement or contract of sale, if any.

6. Neither spouse may acquire, purchase, sell, convey or encumber the assets, including real property and goodwill, of a business where both spouses participate in its management without the consent of the other. If only one spouse participates in management, he may, in the ordinary course of business, acquire, purchase, sell, convey or encumber the assets, including real property and goodwill, of the business without the consent of the non-participating spouse.

NEW MEXICO

The management and control sections are as follows:

N.Mex.Stat.1978 § 40–3–14:

A. Except as provided in Subsections B and C of this section, either spouse alone has full power to manage, control, dispose of and encumber the entire community personal property.

B. Where only one spouse is:

(1) named in a document evidencing ownership of community personal property; or

(2) named or designated in a written agreement between that spouse and a third party as having sole authority to manage, control,

dispose of or encumber the community personal property which is described in or which is the subject of the agreement, whether the agreement was executed prior to or after July 1, 1973; only the spouse so named may manage, control, dispose of or encumber the community personal property described in such a document evidencing ownership or in such a written agreement.

C.   Where both spouses are:

(1) named in a document evidencing ownership of community personal property; or

(2) named or designated in a written agreement with a third party as having joint authority to dispose of or encumber the community personal property which is described in or the subject of the agreement, whether the agreement was executed prior to or after July 1, 1973; both spouses must join to dispose of or encumber such community personal property where the names of the spouses are joined by the word "and." Where the names of the spouses are joined by the word "or," or by the words "and/or," either spouse alone may dispose of or encumber such community personal property.

40–3–15: A married person under the age of majority may join with his or her spouse in all transactions for which joinder is required by Section 40–3–13 NMSA 1978 and such joinder shall have the same force and effect as if the

minor spouse had attained his or her majority at the time of the execution of the instrument.

TEXAS

Texas has retained the civil law "fraud" test for setting aside a gift by the manager of the community, but has expanded the coverage of the test by utilizing the concept of constructive fraud. Additionally, the person who attempts to uphold the gift has the burden of proof to show that the gift was reasonable under the circumstances in which it was made.

Texas upholds many community property life insurance beneficiary designations when the beneficiary is a relative or former relative to whom a duty, even a moral duty, to support exists. The existence of the duty negates fraud upon the spouse so long as the community funds expended for the insurance are not unreasonably out of proportion to the community assets remaining.

The new provisions for joint control of many community property assets apparently will permit setting aside of gifts by a showing that joint control was required, but not obtained.

The statutory provisions for management, control and disposition of separate and community property and the protection of third parties are as follows:

Vernon's Ann.Tex.Stat. Family Code § 5.21:

Each spouse has the sole management, control, and disposition of his or her separate property.

§ 5.22: (a) During marriage, each spouse has the sole management, control, and disposition of the community property that he or she would have owned if single, including but not limited to:

(1) personal earnings;

(2) revenue from separate property;

(3) recoveries for personal injuries; and

(4) the increase and mutations of, and the revenue from, all property subject to his or her sole management, control, and disposition.

(b) If community property subject to the sole management, control, and disposition of one spouse is mixed or combined with community property subject to the sole management, control, and disposition of the other spouse, then the mixed or combined community property is subject to the joint management, control, and disposition of the spouses, unless the spouses provide otherwise by power of attorney in writing or other agreement.

(c) Except as provided in Subsection (a) of this section, the community property is subject to the joint management, control, and disposition of the husband and wife, unless the spouses provide otherwise by power of attorney in writing or other   agreement.

§ 5.24: (a) During marriage, property is presumed to be subject to the sole management, control, and disposition of a spouse if it is held in his or her name, as shown by muniment, contract, deposit of funds, or other evidence of ownership, or if it is in his or her possession and is not subject to such evidence of ownership.

(b) A third person dealing with a spouse is entitled to rely (as against the other spouse or anyone claiming from that spouse) on that spouse's authority to deal with the property if:

(1) The property is presumed to be subject to the sole management, control, and disposition of the spouse; and

(2) the person dealing with the spouse:

(A) is not a party to the fraud upon the other spouse or another person; and

(B) does not have actual or constructive notice of the spouse's lack of authority.

WASHINGTON

Washington's tradition of voiding community property gifts preceded the present statutory provisions. The amount of the gift which is set aside after the death of the manager-spouse has changed, however. In reversing a prior case, Francis v. Francis, 89 Wash.2d 511, 573 P.2d 369 (1978) held that only one half of the life insurance proceeds could be set aside by the widow; previously, the entire beneficiary designation was set aside.

The statutory provisions for management and control in Washington are as follows:

Rev.Code Wash.Ann. 26.16.030:

Property not acquired or owned, as prescribed in RCW 26.16.010 and 26.16.020, acquired after marriage by either husband or wife or both, is community property. Either spouse, acting alone, may manage and control community property, with a like power of disposition as the acting spouse has over his or her separate property, except:

(1) Neither spouse shall devise or bequeath by will more than one-half of the community property.

(2) Neither spouse shall give community property without the express or implied consent of the other.

(3) Neither spouse shall sell, convey, or encumber the community real property without the other spouse joining in the execution of the deed or other instrument by which the real estate is sold, conveyed, or encumbered, and such deed or other instrument must be acknowledged by both spouses.

(4) Neither spouse shall purchase or contract to purchase community real property without the other spouse joining in the transaction of

purchase or in the execution of the contract to purchase.

(5) Neither spouse shall create a security interest other than a purchase money security interest as defined in RCW 62A.9–107 in, or sell, community household goods, furnishings, or appliances, or a community mobile home unless the other spouse joins in executing the security agreement or bill of sale, if any.

(6) Neither spouse shall acquire, purchase, sell, convey, or encumber the assets, including real estate, or the good will of a business where both spouses participate in its management without the consent of the other: *Provided*, That where only one spouse participates in such management the participating spouse may, in the ordinary course of such business, acquire, purchase, sell, convey or encumber the assets, including real estate, or the good will of the business without the consent of the nonparticipating spouse.

26.16.040: Community real estate shall be subject to the liens of mechanics and others for labor and materials furnished in erecting structures and improvements thereon as provided by law in other cases, to liens of judgments recovered for community debts, and to sale on execution issued thereon.

WISCONSIN (and UMPA)

Wis.Stat. 1985–86 § 766.15(1) prescribes and makes non-waivable the duty of good faith between spouses as follows:

Each spouse shall act in good faith with respect to the other spouse in matters involving marital property or other property of the other spouse. This obligation may not be varied by a marital property agreement.

The management and control statute, **Wis.Stat. 1985–86 § 766.51**, reads as follows:

(1) A spouse acting alone may manage and control:

(a) That spouse's property that is not marital property.

(am) Except as provided in subs. (2) and (3), marital property held in that spouse's name or not held in the name of either spouse.

(b) Marital property held in the names of both spouses in the alternative, including marital property held in a form designating the holder by the words "(name of one spouse) or (name of other spouse)".

(d) A policy of insurance if that spouse is designated as the owner on the records of the policy issuer.

(e) Any right of an employe under a deferred employment benefit plan that accrues as a result of that spouse's employment.

(1m)(a) **Notwithstanding any provision in this section except par. (b), for the purpose of obtaining an extension of credit for an obligation** [incurred by a spouse in the interest of the marriage or the family], **a spouse acting alone may manage and control all of the marital property.**

(b) **Unless the spouse acting alone may otherwise under this section manage and control the property, the right to manage and control marital property under this subsection does not include the right to manage and control marital property** [consisting of an interest in a partnership or joint venture held as a general partner or as a participant in a professional corporation, professional association or similar entity, an unincorporated business as operator or manager of a non-publicly traded corporation] **or the right to assign, create a security interest in, mortgage or otherwise encumber marital property.**

(2) **Spouses may manage and control marital property held in the names of both spouses other than in the alternative only if they act together.**

(3) **The right to manage and control marital property transferred to a trust is determined by the terms of the trust.**

(4) **The right to manage and control marital property permits gifts of that property, subject to remedies under this chapter.**

(5) The right to manage and control marital property does not determine the classification of property of the spouses and does not rebut the presumption [that all property of spouses is presumed marital property].

(6) The enactment of this chapter does not affect the right to manage and control any property of either or both spouses acquired before the determination date.

(7) A court may appoint a conservator or guardian . . . to exercise a disabled spouse's right to manage and control marital property.

(8) This section does not affect [the requirement that both spouses sign a conveyance of their homestead].

(9) If an executory contract for the sale of property is entered into by a person having the right of management and control of the property, the rights of all persons then having or thereafter acquiring an interest in the property under this chapter are subject to the terms of the executory contract. This subsection applies to contracts entered into before or after the determination date.

The standards for gifts of marital property to third persons are set out in **Wis.Stat. 1985–86 § 766.53:**

A spouse acting alone may give to a 3rd person marital property that the spouse has the right to manage and control only if the value of the marital property given to the 3rd person does not aggregate more than either $1,000 in a calendar year, or a larger amount if, when made, the gift is reasonable in amount considering the economic position of the spouses. Any other gift of marital property to a 3rd person is subject to [§ 766.70(6)'s recovery remedy during the marriage] unless both spouses act together in making the gift. Under this section and for the purposes of [§ 766.70(6)'s recovery remedy during the marriage], in the case of a gift of marital property by a spouse to a 3rd person in which the donor spouse has retained an interest, the gift shall be valued at the full value of the entire transfer of marital property, regardless of any retained interest or interest donated to the other spouse. For purposes of this section only, a gift of a life insurance policy by a spouse to a 3rd person shall be valued at the amount payable under the policy if the insured died at the time the gift was made.

The remedies available to a nondonor spouse regarding gifts by the other spouse of marital property to a third person are set out in **Wis.Stat. 1985–86 § 766.70(6) to (8).**

CHAPTER 8

LIABILITIES

A. OVERVIEW

1. Gross and Net Liabilities

a. Civil Law Contrasted with Common Law Approach: The nine community property states diverge the most from each other in their treatment of liabilities that concern the community. The civil law model has been widely abandoned. The statutes do not resemble one another. The case law differs in approach, language and results.

The traditional civil law approach to the community asserts that there is a regime of assets *and liabilities*. Of the American community property states, only Louisiana follows this pattern, although some aspects of the Washington system are close to the civil law model. The common law states, on the other hand, consider community property to be a method of holding assets, without regard to accompanying liabilities. The difference can be characterized by the following equation:

IN DETERMINING WHAT IS "COMMUNITY PROPERTY"

COMMON LAW STATES LOOK TO THE   **GROSS ASSETS**

CIVIL LAW JURISDICTIONS DEDUCT   **(LIABILITIES)**

AND LOOK TO THE NET COMMUNITY: **NET ASSETS**

b. Liabilities, Debts and Expenses: The term "liabilities" is used generically without regard to the method of obligation or the time of payment. In Louisiana, the term "obligations" is used in lieu of "liabilities". "Liabilities" does not distinguish between the two major categories of liabilities, contract and tort, while the term "debts" implies contractual rather than tort liability. A time of payment distinction is connoted between "debts" (amounts unpaid) and "expenses" (amounts paid). If the manager of the community is willing and able to pay the amount of the liability, then the "debt" can be transformed into an "expense".

Theoretically, the same rules should apply to both present and past liabilities. In practice, trial courts tend to disregard liabilities which have been paid, probably because of an unwillingness to re-open completed transactions except in case of fraud. Unpaid liabilities, on the other hand, force a court to determine their character.

c. Types of Liabilities: This portion of community property law seems to have been designed to make the heads of students reel. (Really!)

Both assets and liabilities can be divided into three major categories: His separate, her separate and their community. Chapters 3 through 6 indicated the methods used to characterize assets. There were many similarities among the states. His, her and their assets are the target areas for his, her and their creditors; one target area or the other may be more desirable or accessible to certain creditors. Which assets can be reached by whom? The community property rules for dealing with liabilities do not enjoy the same degree of consensus as the rules for assets.

Among the areas of divergence in treatment given by various states are the following, in order of importance:

• The three targets areas—his, hers and theirs;

• The method by which the liability is incurred—contractual, tort and statutory (especially including taxes);

• Time that the debt is incurred—premarital, marital and postmarital;

• Person incurring—him, her or the manager of the community;

• Purpose for which contracted—The purpose ranges from a center point of support of the family, through "the benefit of the community" to an outer ring of protection of separate property.

2. Do "Community Debts" Exist?

Is there, in law, such an entity as "their debt" or are obligations purely "his" or "hers" with some debts being "both his and hers"? There are different views of whether there is such a thing as a "community debt" and, if so, what constitutes a community debt:

• Spanish civil law authorities proclaimed that any liability incurred during the marriage for the benefit of the community was a community liabili-

ty. The incurring of the expense was presumed to
be for the benefit of the community, but debts
incurred by the manager (then the husband) for his
or her separate benefit or account were not community liabilities. The wife, not being the manager, did not have a full right to bind the community
by her contracts. The civil law approach "marshaled the assets" (i.e., indicated the *order* in which
they should be liable) but subjected both community and separate property to liability for community
contractual debts. The right of reimbursement
diminished the distinction between debts and expenses; payment of a liability from the inappropriate character property gave rise to a right of reimbursement.

• Louisiana remains the most faithful to the
community regime approach. It has the most detailed statutes describing community and separate
obligations.

• Washington used an "entity" approach by
which the community was regarded as a separate
juristic entity. The liability itself was classified as
separate or community. This led to a rigid distinction (subsequently watered down by statutes and
cases) that the separate property was liable for
separate debts and the community was liable only
for community debts (which excluded both premarital debts and many torts).

• Most of the community property states follow
neither the "regime" approach of Louisiana nor
the "community debt" of Washington, but instead

have developed a common law approach of considering community property a form of holding gross assets without regard to the liabilities. These states determine liability by a complex and inconsistent pattern based upon the nature (tort or contract), time (during the marriage or not) and purpose (necessaries, community or separate) of the debt and the identity (husband, wife or manager of the community) of the person incurring the debt and the ownership or management (his, hers or theirs) of the property sought to be attached.

• California originally denied that there were "community debts" but recognized the existence of debts collectible from the community. The divorce statute now directs the court to characterize debts as community or separate.

3. Marshaling the Assets

"Marshaling" is the process of arranging items such as troops or railroad cars. In collecting debts, "marshaling" is the process by which the creditor is directed to proceed first against one source; and, if that source proves inadequate, to proceed against a second (and perhaps a third, fourth etc.) source. Under the civil law system, a community liability was collected first from the community; if the community assets were insufficient, then the creditor looked to the separate property of the husband because he had management and control. If the husband's separate property also did not satisfy the obligation, the creditor could proceed against the wife's separate property. Marshaling is the middle ground between allowing a creditor to reach all assets or only certain assets; marshaling indicates the order of application which the creditor is required to follow.

B. DETAIL

1. Liability of Community Property

a. For Contractual Obligations During Marriage: The safest ground in this area of quicksand is the sure liability of the community property for contractual debts incurred during marriage for a community purpose (and, in Texas, the liability is limited to the community property under the sole management and control of that spouse or under joint management and control). These debts (which enjoy the favored status by type of claim, time, purpose and manager) always qualify creditors to reach community assets, if such exist. If the creditor proceeds against separate property, the jurisdictions are not as certain whether those assets can be reached second, or at all.

Contractual debts have enjoyed a favored status. The reliance of a creditor upon the existence or status of property was considered to be justified. The tort creditor did not have comparable reliance; however, the issue might be phrased in terms of reasonableness of insuring against most unintentional torts.

What is a "community purpose"?

•The surest center of it is the duty of the spouses (or the husband) to support each other (or the wife) and their children by the present marriage. This duty to provide "necessaries" is often given an overriding importance so that a debt for necessaries can be collected from separate property if the community property is inadequate.

•A bit more difficult are alimony obligations to the prior spouse and the duty to support children of a prior marriage. The support duties are generally so strong that they are not only community purposes, but also are imposed against the separate property (even in Washington which otherwise rigidly separates the two types of liabilities).

•The tendency has been to come in from the other end of the scale: Obligations incurred during the marriage are presumed to be community obligations unless it is clearly shown that they were not for the benefit of the community.

•If the obligation incurred during the marriage was clearly not for the benefit of the community, then it is a separate obligation in most of the states. The benefit to the community is not part of the statutory scheme in California, Idaho, New Mexico, Texas and Wisconsin.

b. **For Premarital Obligations:** Classic civil law concepts exempted community property (or at least one half of it) from liability for premarital obligations because the debts had not been contracted on behalf of the community.

This proved extremely inconvenient for creditors since all income (including most of the income from separate property) was community property. If the only assets of a married couple were community earnings, the creditor could pursue no assets upon the marriage of the debtor. Therefore, for the price of a marriage license, a person could frustrate premarital creditors. This was known as the "Two Dollar (the pre-inflation price of a marriage license) Bankruptcy".

There has been an increasing tendency to subject community property to premarital liabilities.

Sometimes a distinction was based upon whether the debtor was the manager of the community. At other times, the decision turned on whether the debtor was the producer of the community income. Both tended to subject the community to liability when the husband was the debtor. Subjecting the entire community to liability for a premarital obligation was not favored in the civil law.

Statutes may exempt a portion of the community from a portion of the premarital debts of the spouse:

• Arizona subjects community property to debts incurred after September 1, 1973, and "only to the extent of the value of that spouse's contribution to the community property which would have been such spouse's separate property if single." In other words, Arizona ignores the marriage for the purpose of collecting those premarital debts.

• California exempts "earnings of the spouse" from liabilities of the other spouse contracted before the marriage.

• Idaho has permitted a premarital creditor of the manager-husband, but not a premarital creditor of the non-manager wife, to reach community assets. It is not certain how the existing case law rules will be changed by the statutory changes in management and control.

• Louisiana now permits a premarital creditor to reach the community property, but provides for reimbursement between the spouses upon termination of the marital regime.

• Nevada provides that one spouse's "share of the community property" is not liable for the debts of the other spouse contracted before marriage.

• New Mexico, reversing its prior rule of exemption, now allows separate debts (including premarital obligations of either spouse) to be collected from that spouse's half of the community, but only after the separate property of that spouse proves insufficient.

• Texas allows the satisfaction of all premarital debts from community property under joint control, but subjects property under the sole management and control of one of the spouses only to the premarital debts of that spouse and not to the premarital debts of the non-manager spouse.

• Washington, in effect, creates a non-community status of the earnings and accumulations of a spouse for the purposes of satisfaction of liabilities incurred by that spouse prior to marriage.

• Wisconsin (UMPA) provides that an obligation incurred by a spouse before or during marriage that is attributable to an obligation arising before marriage or to an act or omission occurring before marriage may be satisfied only from property of that spouse that is not marital property (including the unique Wisconsin "unclassified" or "other" property) and from that part of marital property which would have been the property of that spouse but for the marriage.

The foregoing range of rules for the nine states illustrates the extent to which the community property states have diverged from their civil law origin and each other.

c. Alimony and Support Obligations: Some jurisdictions assume that alimony for a previous spouse and support payments to the children of a prior marriage are premarital debts, but Louisiana has arrived at the opposite conclusion. The obligation arises not because of the termination of the first marriage, but because of the passage of time during the second marriage; therefore it is a community obligation of the second marriage. The logic of this approach, although sound, is difficult to explain to the second spouse.

d. Tort Liability: There was an exception in the civil law system by which the separate property of one spouse was not liable for the "delict" (roughly, the tort or crime) of the other. Similarly, only the community property managed and controlled by the tortfeasor was subject to liability and then only if the tort was committed while the manager was engaged in an activity for the benefit of the community.

Today, the rules appear to be as follows for tort liability of community property:

• The community is liable in Arizona and Louisiana for a tort committed by the person who is manager of the property (i.e., it is no longer limited to the husband in that role) if the activity which gave rise to the tort was being performed for the benefit of the community.

• In California, the community property is liable, but marshaled if there was a community benefit.

• Idaho and Nevada rules are uncertain.

• New Mexico subjects the community to liability unless the tort was a "separate tort" which could be interpreted along the same lines as the "community benefit" test.

• Texas subjects the community to liability by statute.

• Washington has recently changed from a very liberal interpretation of the benefit to the community to a marshaling approach.

• Wisconsin (but not UMPA) provides that an obligation incurred by a spouse for a tort during marriage may be satisfied from property of that spouse which is not community property (i.e., separate or "unclassified" property) and from that spouse's interest in community property.

e. Liability of One Half of the Community: If a separate debt cannot be collected from *both* halves of the community, may the creditor collect against one half of the community?

A theoretical problem arises. On the one hand, if the community is owned equally by the two spouses, then one half of the community is as much the property of a spouse as his or her separate property. On the other hand, this question arises only in those states and in those situations in which the entire community is not liable for that particular debt. If the civil law "net community" approach is used, the exact amount of the community share cannot be accurately ascertained until the payment of all community debts and the division of the property at the termination of the marital regime. To allow collection of a separate debt against one half of the community would be to allow a preference to this separate obligation over later community obligations (including support needs of the family) and would create difficult bookkeeping problems. Would the earnings of the remaining one half of the community belong entirely to the other spouse, or does the debtor spouse receive one half of the income?

There have been some breaks in the traditional reluctance of the community property jurisdictions to allow collection of a separate debt from one half (but not the whole) of the community property:

• Louisiana has taken the theoretically most accurate approach by allowing reimbursement upon the termination of the regime, but not before.

• Nevada implies that one half of the community is liable for the premarital debts in Nev.Rev.Stat. 123.050 which states that the community share of a married person is not liable for the premarital debts of that person's spouse.

• New Mexico and Wisconsin (UMPA) marshal one half of the community after the separate (and Wisconsin "unclassified") property of a spouse in the order of payment of that spouse's separate debts.

• Texas courts are permitted to adopt this approach; the statute leaves the order of marshaling to the discretion of the court.

• Washington has adopted by case law a marshaling approach to the payment of tort liabilities.

2. Liability of Separate Property

a. **For One's Own Separate Debts:** There is no controversy about the rule that separate (and Wisconsin "unclassified") property of each spouse is liable for his or her own separate debts.

Often, there is an initial question as to whether the debt is a separate debt of the individual spouse. The liability may arise as a matter of civil, con-

tract or tort law and may be individual or joint
with the other spouse:

•Civil liability may occur by reason of the duty
of support although most other provisions imposing
liability by virtue of the marital relationship (other
than the support and community property rules)
have been abolished. The separate debt of one
spouse may become the separate debt of the other
because of a duty to provide items necessary for
support.

•Contract liability may arise as a result of one's
own promise (alone, jointly or as guarantor of the
other spouse's promise), by consent or other agreement (including transmutations) or by giving authority to the other spouse, such as by a power of
attorney or other agency arrangement.

•Tort liability in addition to being for one's own
torts may be vicarious or derivative. The other
spouse may commit a tort which is attributed to
the first spouse by virtue of the agency doctrine of
respondeat superior or because of ownership such
as vehicle registration liability. There can also be
owner liability derived from community property
ownership.

b. Liability as Manager of the Community:
There is still some authority for subjecting the
separate property of the manager of the community to liability for acts done as manager of the
community.

One part of the old law which is definitely eliminated is the liability of the separate property of the husband only (and no liability of the separate property of the wife) for community debts because the husband had management and control of the community. Now, either the separate property of both spouses is bound or the separate property of neither is bound.

Two variations reflect the fact that males have a preference as a matter of economics: First is the ability of a spouse to bind the property over which he or she would have had control if not married, typically his or her earnings. The second is the provision in Louisiana under a "separation of property regime" making the spouse liable for family expenses; that liability is charged, not on an equal basis, but in proportion to his or her means, La. Stat.Ann.—Civ.Code art. 2373. Assuming that men more frequently receive higher monetary compensation for their labor than women, then husbands have a greater economic exposure to liability than their wives. This liability by economic reality is not as absolute and unchangeable as the older liability imposed on the husband-manager of the community.

c. **Liability for Separate Debts of Spouse:** Generally, there is no liability of a married person's separate property for the debt of the other spouse. California and Washington make exceptions for "the necessaries of life" and "the expenses of the family and the education of the children", respectively.

d. Liability for Community Debts: If both spouses signed or agreed to the contract imposing a debt, the separate property of both can be used to satisfy the debt. If only one spouse did the contracting, the separate property of that spouse is liable for that community debt. Arizona and New Mexico specify by statute that the separate property of the manager shall be marshaled after the community property.

C. INDIVIDUAL STATES

ARIZONA

Community property is liable in Arizona for the payment of postmarital community liabilities (contract and tort) and some premarital liabilities.

The separate property of each spouse is liable for his or her own debts, but not liable for the separate debts of the other spouse unless there is an agreement to the contrary. Separate property of the contracting spouse is liable for community debts, but is marshaled after community property.

Arizona reversed prior case law specifically by statute in order to subject community property to liability for premarital debts, but only for debts incurred after September 1, 1973, and "only to the extent of the value of that spouse's contribution to the community property which would have been such spouse's separate property if single."

The selection of that particular portion of the community property to be liable for the premarital contract and tort liabilities of a spouse is an abandonment of the basic community property principle of sharing. In effect, a creditor can disregard community property principles which would otherwise apply.

In Schilling v. Embree, 118 Ariz. 236, 575 P.2d 1262 (1977), the Court of Appeals of Arizona interpreted the "other liabilities" in Ariz.Rev.Stat. § 25–215(B) to mean "other *premarital separate* liabilities", thus limiting the statute's application so that the community is not liable for payment of postmarital separate liabilities.

The controlling statute reads as follows:

Ariz.Rev.Stat. § 25–215:

A. The separate property of a spouse shall not be liable for the separate debts or obligations of the other spouse, absent agreement of the property owner to the contrary.

B. The community property is liable for the premarital separate debts or other liabilities of a spouse, incurred after September 1, 1973 but only to the extent of the value of that spouse's contribution to the community property which would have been such spouse's separate property if single.

* * *

D. Except [when joinder of both spouses is required] in § 25–214, either spouse may con-

tract debts and otherwise act for the benefit of the community. In an action on such a debt or obligation the spouses shall be sued jointly and the debt or obligation shall be satisfied: first, from the community property, and second, from the separate property of the spouse contracting the debt or obligation.

CALIFORNIA

California is gradually resolving its semantic difficulties with the concept of a community debt. The original approach is reflected in the language of Calif.Civ.Code §§ 5120.010 through 5122 which refer to the debt as being the "liability of the community property" or the "liability of a married person". In contrast, Calif.Civ.Code § 4800 defines the term "community estate" as "both the community and quasi-community assets and liabilities of the parties." That section requires that for the "purposes of division and in confirming or assigning the liabilities of the parties for which the community estate is liable, the court shall characterize liabilities as separate or community and confirm or assign them to the parties. . . ."

In the following sections, "community property" is defined to include quasi-community property (Calif.Civ.Code §§ 5120.020 and 5120.120) and "debt" is broadly defined in Calif.Civ.Code § 5120.030 to mean "an obligation incurred by a married person before or during marriage, whether based on contract, tort, or otherwise."

Calif.Civ.Code § 5120.110 is the basic statute:

(a) Except as otherwise expressly provided by statute, the community property is liable for a debt incurred by either spouse before or after marriage, regardless which spouse has the management and control of the property and regardless whether one or both spouses are parties to the debt or to a judgment for the debt.

(b) The earnings of a married person during marriage are not liable for a debt incurred by the person's spouse before marriage . . . . they remain not liable so long as they are held in a deposit account in which the person's spouse has no right of withdrawal and are uncommingled with other community property, except property insignificant in amount. . . .

The corollary statute, Calif.Civ.Code § 5120.130, provides that separate property is liable for the debts of its owner, but not of the owner's spouse except for necessaries of life.

A statutory right of reimbursement, described in Calif.Civ.Code § 5120.210, is available in situations involving the provision of "necessaries", post-divorce settlements and for "a child or spousal support obligation of a married person that does not arise out of the marriage."

Tort liability of the community property and the separate property of the tortfeasor involves a marshaling order which begins with one or the other, dependent upon whether the tort was committed "while the married person was performing an activity for the benefit of the community".

Calif.Civ.Code § 5122 provides in part:

(a) A married person is not liable for any injury or damage caused by the other spouse except in cases where he or she would be liable therefor if the marriage did not exist.

(b) The liability of a married person for death or injury to person or property shall be satisfied as follows:

(1) If the liability of the married person is based upon an act or omission which occurred while the married person was performing an activity for the benefit of the community, the liability shall first be satisfied from the community property and second from the separate property of the married person.

(2) If the liability of the married person is not based upon an act or omission which occurred while the married person was performing an activity for the benefit of the community, the liability shall first be satisfied from the separate property of the married person and second from the community property.

IDAHO

Idaho's statutory and case law on debts are less extensive than most of the other community property states. The major statutory provision is Idaho Code § 32–912, set forth in Chapter 7, which provides that either husband or wife may bind the community property by contract with an exception for the sale, conveyance or encumbrance of realty. Joint action is then required.

The separate property of a married person who signed a promissory note may be executed upon by a marital debt creditor, regardless of the purpose of the contract, i.e., whether it was for separate or for community purposes, Williams v. Paxton, 98 Idaho 155, 559 P.2d 1123 (1977).

Idaho exempts some separate property from liability for certain community obligations. Idaho Code § 32–912 provides, in part: "any community obligation incurred by either the husband or the wife without the consent in writing of the other shall not obligate the separate property of the spouse who did not consent."

The statutory scheme requires consent of a person to any community *contract* which binds his or her separate property. This suggests that the separate property of a spouse should be exempt from liability for the *tort* of the other spouse.

A prediction that community property would be subject to judicial execution for tort liabilities of either husband or wife if the tort was committed in the furtherance of community business or for the benefit of the community was made by Merlin S. Young in "Joint Management and Control of Community Property in Idaho: A Prognosis", 11 Idaho Law Rev. 1, 7 (1974). The uncertainty about the liability of Idaho community property for the torts of either spouse is described in Terry L. Crapo,

"Equal Management of Community Property: Creditors' Rights", 13 Idaho Law Rev. 177, 185–190 (1976).

LOUISIANA

Louisiana is the purest adherent to the community regime concept. Obligations are classified as separate or community by La.Stat.Ann.—Civ.Code art. 2359. "Community obligation" is defined in **La.Stat.Ann.—Civ.Code art. 2360** as follows:

An obligation incurred by a spouse during the existence of a community property regime for the common interest of the spouses or for the interest of the other spouse is a community obligation.

La.Stat.Ann.—Civ.Code art. 2361 provides that all obligations incurred by a spouse during the existence of a community property regime are presumed to be community obligations, except for the separate obligation enumerated in **La.Stat.Ann.— Civ.Code art. 2363** as follows:

A separate obligation of a spouse is one incurred by that spouse prior to the establishment or after termination of a community property regime, or one incurred during the existence of a community property regime though not for the common interest of the spouses or for the interest of the other spouse. An obligation resulting from an intentional wrong not perpetrated for the benefit of the community, or an obligation incurred for the

separate property benefit of a spouse to the extent that it does not benefit the community, the family, or the other spouse, is likewise a separate obligation.

Upon termination of a community property regime, a spouse may have a claim against the other spouse for reimbursement when property of one character (community or separate) has been used to satisfy an obligation of the other character. The amount of the reimbursement is one half of the amount or value that the property had at the time is was used.

The right of reimbursement to separate from community is limited, however, by the following language in **La.Stat.Ann.—Civ.Code art. 2365:**

Reimbursement may only be made to the extent of community assets, unless the community obligation was incurred for the ordinary and customary expenses of the marriage, or for the support, maintenance, and education of children of either spouse in keeping with the economic condition of the community. In the last case, the spouse is entitled to reimbursement from the other spouse even if there are no community assets.

La.Stat.Ann.—Civ.Code art. 2367 does not similarly restrict the right to reimbursement if separate property was used for the "acquisition, use, improvement, or benefit of community property". In that case, the right of reimbursement is limited only by the existence of community assets from which reimbursement may be made.

The provisions quoted above are concerned with the allocation of the burden between the husband and wife; they do not deal with the rights of creditors, although creditors may intervene and object in the proceeding by which the spouses resolve their rights.

NEVADA

Among the few provisions which give guidance in this area is **Nev.Rev.Stat. 123.050:**

Neither the separate property of a spouse nor his share of the community property is liable for the debts of the other spouse contracted before the marriage.

NEW MEXICO

New Mexico has relatively complete statutory provisions dividing debts into separate and community debts and directing an order of marshaling for satisfaction of liabilities. The order of marshaling is unique in two ways: The residence of the spouses (in excess of the homestead exemption) is separately ranked in the marshaling process and provision is made for two common methods of holding property, joint tenancy and tenancy in common.

The statutory provisions for the definition of separate and community debts and the priorities for satisfaction of them are as follows:

N.Mex.Stat.1978 § 40–3–9:

A. "Separate debt" means:

(1) a debt contracted or incurred by a spouse before marriage or after entry of a decree of dissolution of marriage; [or legal separation]. . . .

(3) a debt designated as a separate debt of a spouse by a judgment or decree of any court having jurisdiction;

(4) a debt contracted by a spouse during marriage which is identified by a spouse to the creditor in writing at the time of its creation as the separate debt of the contracting spouse; or

(5) a debt which arises from a tort committed by a spouse before marriage or after entry of a decree of dissolution of marriage or a separate tort committed during marriage.

B. "Community debt" means a debt contracted or incurred by either or both spouses during marriage which is not a separate debt.

40–3–10: A. The separate debt of a spouse shall be satisfied first from the debtor spouse's separate property, excluding that spouse's interest in property in which each of the spouses owns an undivided equal interest as a joint tenant or tenant in common. Should such property be insufficient, then the debt shall be satisfied from the debtor spouse's one-half interest in the community property or in property in which each spouse owns an undivided equal interest as a joint tenant or tenant in common, excluding the residence of the spouses. Should such property be insufficient, then the debt shall be satisfied from the debtor spouse's interest in the residence of the spouses. . . . Neither spouse's interest in community property or separate property shall be liable for the separate debt of the other spouse.

B. The priorities or exemptions established in this section for the satisfaction of a separate debt must be claimed by either spouse under the procedure set forth in Section 42-10-13 NMSA 1978, or the right to claim such priorities or exemptions is waived as between a spouse and the creditor.

C. This section shall apply only while both spouses are living, and shall not apply to the satisfaction of debts after the death of one or both spouses.

§ 40-3-11: A. Community debts shall be satisfied first from all community property and all property in which each spouse owns an undivided equal interest as a joint tenant or tenant in common, excluding the residence of the spouses. Should such property be insufficient, community debts shall then be satisfied from the residence of the spouses, except as provided in Section 42–10–9 NMSA 1978. Should such property be insufficient, only the separate property of the spouse who contracted or incurred the debt shall be liable for its satisfaction. If both spouses contracted or incurred the debt, the separate property of both spouses is jointly and severally liable for its satisfaction.

B. The priorities or exemptions established in this section for the satisfaction of community debts must be claimed by either spouse under the procedure set forth in Section 42–10–13 NMSA 1978 or the right to claim such priorities or exemptions is waived as between a spouse and the creditor.

C. This section shall apply only while both spouses are living, and shall not apply to the satisfaction of debts after the death of one or both spouses.

TEXAS

Vernon's Ann.Tex.Stat. Family Code § 5.61 provides the basic theme of liability of community property:

• Property subject to the sole management and control of one spouse is liable for that spouse's marital debts but is not liable for either premarital liabilities or any non-tort debts of the other spouse.

• All the community property is subject to liability for torts committed during the marriage.

The text of **Vernon's Ann.Tex.Stat. Family Code § 5.61** is as follows:

(a) A spouse's separate property is not subject to liabilities of the other spouse unless both spouses are liable by other rules of law.

(b) Unless both spouses are liable by other rules of law, the community property subject to a spouse's sole management, control, and disposition is not subject to:

(1) any liabilities that the other spouse incurred before marriage; or

(2) any nontortious liabilities that the other spouse incurs during marriage.

(c) The community property subject to a spouse's sole or joint management, control, and disposition is subject to the liabilities incurred by him or her before or during marriage.

(d) All the community property is subject to tortious liability of either spouse incurred during marriage.

The Texas approach to marshaling is also unique; it is left to the discretion of the judge by **Vernon's Ann.Tex.Stat. Family Code § 5.62**:

(a) A judge may determine, as he deems just and equitable, the order in which particular separate or community property will be subject to execution and sale to satisfy a judgment, if the property subject to liability for a judgment includes any combination of:

(1) a spouse's separate property;

(2) community property subject to a spouse's sole management, control, and disposition;

(3) community property subject to the other spouse's sole management, control, and disposition; and

(4) community property subject to the spouses' joint management, control, and disposition.

(b) In determining the order in which particular property will be subject to execution and sale, the judge shall consider the facts surrounding the transaction or occurrence upon which the suit is based.

WASHINGTON

Washington has been unusual in making community property responsible for the payment of only community liabilities and certain premarital debts. Because most separate debts could not be collected from community property and most community debts could not be collected from separate property, the distinction between community and separate liabilities was more important (and more frequently litigated) than in other community property states. The relative immunity of community property is derived from judicial interpretation of a statute providing that community real property is subject to mechanics' liens and judgment liens obtained for community debts.

Community liabilities are liabilities incurred during marriage which were contracted on behalf of the conjugal partnership. The emphasis is upon the purpose (for the benefit of the community) and is not simply a matter of timing (contracted during marriage).

There is a rebuttable presumption that a liability incurred by either spouse is a community liability. Liabilities incurred in the acquisition or management of community property are clearly community liabilities. On the other hand, clear and convincing evidence that the liability was incurred in the making of a gift to third parties would rebut the presumption of community purpose for the liability. The courts have been liberal in finding community purpose and therefore community liability. Expectation of employment, benefit to a corporation of which the spouse is an officer or director, recreational activities and even a debt for funds borrowed on the security of separate property have been classified as community debts because there was some benefit, direct or indirect, to the community. The clearest ways to rebut the presumption of community business purpose are to show that the transfer was a gift to a third party or was directly related to the separate property of the person applying the community property funds.

If a debt is created by one of the spouses with the intention to benefit the community, enforcement against the community is probable. On the other hand, the court in Northern Bank & Trust Co. v. Graves, 79 Wash. 411, 140 P. 328 (1914) stated that a separate obligation was not transformed into a community obligation merely because both spouses signed the promissory note; the signature of the wife in addition to the husband created her (additional) separate liability, but did not create a community liability.

The community property of a spouse is available for legal process of creditors of him or her for premarital (and therefore separate) debts, in only three situations:

(1) if the liability is reduced to judgment within three years of the marriage of the parties it can be satisfied from the earnings and accumulations of the debtor spouse, Rev.Code Wash.Ann. 26.16.200;

(2) support obligations to children or former spouses; and

(3) taxes.

Until recently Washington did not permit collection of a separate debt from the debtor's one half of the community property, although federal taxes were so collected as a matter of federal supremacy. Recent cases have indicated an abandonment of this position, at least for tort recoveries.

The separate property of a spouse is not liable for the separate debt of the other spouse, except as provided in Rev.Code Wash.Ann. 26.16.205 which states that "The expenses of the family and the education of the children, including stepchildren, are chargeable upon the property of both husband and wife, or either of them.   .   .   ."

In the tort field, the distinction between activities which are a benefit to the community and those which are not has been abandoned as a test of liability of the community; it remains as a determinant of the order of resort. The case of deElche v. Jacobsen, 95 Wash.2d 236, 622 P.2d 835 (1980) ended a long series of distinctions by which the community was gradually held more liable for torts on the theory that the tortfeasor was engaged in an activity for the community benefit. That case reduced the impact of the "benefit of the community" test from making it determinative of the issue of liability to making it determinative of the *order* of liability, i.e., marshaling. Thus, if a tort is not in the management of community business or for its benefit, the separate property of the tortfeasor is primarily (formerly solely) liable and, if there is insufficient separate property, the tortfeasor's one half of the community becomes liable.

WISCONSIN (and UMPA)

Wisconsin adds to the detailed UMPA provisions in specifying which classifications of property are liable for enumerated types of spousal obligations incurred both prior to and during marriage. **Wis. Stat. 1985–86 § 766.55** provides in part:

(1) An obligation incurred by a spouse during marriage, including one attributable to an act or omission during marriage, is presumed to be incurred in the interest of the marriage or the family. A statement separately signed by the obligated or incurring spouse at or before the time the obligation is incurred stating that the obligation is or will be incurred in the interest of the marriage or the family is conclusive evidence that the obligation to which the statement refers is an obligation in the interest of the marriage or family, except that the existence of that statement does not affect any interspousal right or remedy.

(2) After the determination date all of the following apply:

(a) A spouse's obligation to satisfy a duty of support owed to the other spouse or to a child of the marriage may be satisfied only from all marital property and all other property of the obligated spouse.

(b) An obligation incurred by a spouse in the interest of the marriage or the family may be satisfied only from all marital property and all other property of the incurring spouse.

(c) 1. An obligation incurred by a spouse before or during marriage that is attributable to an obligation arising before marriage or to an act or omission occurring before marriage may be satisfied only from property of that spouse that is not marital property and from

that part of marital property which would
have been the property of that spouse but for
the marriage.

2. An obligation incurred by a spouse before, on or after January 1, 1986, that is attributable to an obligation arising before January
1, 1986, or to an act or omission occurring
before January 1, 1986, may be satisfied only
from property of that spouse that is not marital property and from that part of marital
property which would have been the property
of that spouse but for the enactment of this
chapter.

(cm) An obligation incurred by a spouse during marriage, resulting from a tort committed
by the spouse during marriage, may be satisfied from the property of that spouse that is
not marital property and from that spouse's
interest in marital property.

(d) Any other obligation incurred by a
spouse during marriage, including one attributable to an act or omission during marriage,
may be satisfied only from property of that
spouse that is not marital property and from
that spouse's interest in marital property, in
that order.

(2m) Unless the dissolution decree or any
amendment to the decree so provides, no income of a nonincurring spouse is available for
satisfaction of an obligation under sub. (2)(b)
after entry of the decree. Marital property

assigned to each spouse under that decree is available for satisfaction of such an obligation to the extent of the value of the marital property at the date of the decree. If a dissolution decree provides that the nonincurring spouse is responsible for satisfaction of the obligation, the obligation may be satisfied as if both spouses had incurred the obligation.

Wisconsin has two additional statutes: **Wis.Stat. 1985–86 § 766.555** provides for liability of spouses' property under certain open-ended credit plans such as the use of credit cards. **Wis.Stat. 1985–86 § 766.56** prescribes requirements for creditors having transactions with married persons.

PART IV

TERMINATION OF THE COMMUNITY

CHAPTER 9

DIVORCE

A. OVERVIEW

1. Termination of the Community Regime

A community regime continues until one of the following events occurs:

1. An agreement, in a form permitted by the jurisdiction, by the parties to terminate the regime;

2. (In Louisiana only) Separation of property regime by court procedure;

3. Legal separation of the spouses;

4. Divorce; or

5. Death of either spouse.

The methods of terminating the application of the community property laws (other than changing domicile to a separate property state, which operates only prospectively) are given above in their increasing order of complicating factors.

• Termination of the community by agreement is governed by the principles of transmutation de-

scribed in Chapter 2. Louisiana, Washington and
Wisconsin (UMPA) statutes provide for a termination of the community by agreement without court
action.

• Louisiana also permits a nonconsensual "regime of separation of property", i.e., an abandonment of the statutory form of community regime
by means of a judgment decreeing separation of
property.

• Legal separation (which is also known as "divorce from bed and board", "limited divorce" or
divorce *a mensa et thoro*") generally involves all of
the elements of a divorce (right to separate maintenance, custody of children, support of spouse and
children) except termination of the marriage and
change of name. It is the result of a formal,
statutory procedure.

• This chapter concentrates on the procedure by
which the marriage is also ended, i.e., the divorce.
Although local terminology is used in discussion of
particular state law, the general term "divorce" is
intended to include "dissolution of the marriage".
Note the terminology difference between termination of the *community regime* (the subject with
which we are concerned) and dissolution of the
marriage (a term used as a substitute for "divorce"
and which includes, but is broader than, dissolution of the community).

• Termination of the community by death of one
of the spouses is treated in the next chapter of this
work.

2. Types of Marital Termination

There are three general categories of proceedings by which a marriage (as opposed to a community regime) is terminated:

a. **Annulment:** Because of major defects such as bigamy or too close a degree of kinship (incest), certain marriages never came into existence and are considered void from the beginning. Additionally, some marriages are voidable because of defects existing at the time of the marriage such as impotency or defect in formalities of the marriage. Nevertheless, community property (or an analog to it) comes into existence during this "putative" marriage and until a decree of nullity is issued. See Chapter 11. In this situation, there never was a valid marriage.

b. **Divorce from Bed and Board or "Legal Separation":** In this legal procedure, the conjugal relationship is suspended, but the marriage is not ended. The marriage continues to exist; the spouses cannot remarry. In Louisiana, a two-step procedure is the usual route for a full divorce: First, a divorce from bed and board is obtained; then an absolute divorce to terminate the marriage is subsequently obtained. For community property purposes, there are few differences (other than timing) between a legal separation and a divorce.

c. **Absolute Divorce:** This is the termination of the marriage itself. Historically, absolute divorce has proceeded from a status of non-existence (reflecting the Roman Catholic faith as the predominant faith in countries from which the community property system was introduced into the United States) to separate maintenance and, later, absolute divorce for fault (adultery, cruelty, desertion, imprisonment, insanity etc.) to "no-fault" divorce. Today, all community property states permit absolute divorce and the concept of "fault" is largely eliminated.

3. Divorce Division of Property

a. **The Theoretical Model:** As a purely theoretical matter, the disentanglement of property interests upon divorce would call for an acknowledgment of the husband's ownership of his separate and his one half of the community and the wife's ownership of her separate and her one half of the community property in each asset. The theory is seasoned by reality: Co-ownership of each asset is often impractical; often the family has one major asset (the home) and much of the remaining wealth is in non-liquid form, such as life insurance or retirement plans. Property which would otherwise be community property is often held in joint tenancy, a form of separate title.

b. **Separate Property:** Some states purportedly do not allow the court to give the separate property of one spouse to the other spouse. Arizona specifically requires by statute that the divorce court "shall assign each spouse's sole and separate property to such spouse". However, courts are frequently permitted to create a lien upon the separate property of either spouse to satisfy an interest which the other spouse may have in that property (e.g., because of the use of community property to improve the separate property) or to enforce payment of support obligations to the spouse or to the children. Arizona and New Mexico have specific statutory provisions permitting courts to order alimony paid out of separate property. Arizona, California and Nevada statutes allow the divorce court to terminate joint tenancies and divide the property between the spouses. If the Wisconsin court makes a finding "that refusal to divide [certain separate property described below] will create a hardship on the other party or on the children of the marriage", the court "may divest the party of such property in a fair and equitable manner." The property requiring such a hardship finding is described as "property shown to have been acquired by either party prior to or during the course of the marriage as a gift, bequest, devise or inheritance or to have been paid for by either party with funds so acquired". Although the Wisconsin statute provides that all other property is to be divided equally between the parties, the divorce court has the power to divide and transfer title to all other property (community, separate and unclassified).

c. **Community Property:** The states differ in their approach, but are close in result when the issue is the division of the community property. The majority of the statutes give little guidance to

the divorce court (and little basis for appeal from
its decision); they state that the division of the
community property shall be "equitable".   Note
that this is not necessarily "equal" as the theoretical model would seem to require. Washington and
Wisconsin describe relevant factors in their statutes.

Equal division of the community is a stated goal
of Idaho. A list of factors which might compel a
different distribution is set forth in its statute.
California is the most adamant in insistence upon
an equal division, but a number of exceptions are
provided by statute.

Paradoxes exist: An exact equality of the
spouses' shares is imposed during the marriage and
at death, but not upon divorce (if the court is
aware of the asset and asked to make a division of
it). If neither court order nor valid agreement of
the parties disposes of a community asset, it will be
equally divided between the two spouses even
though the divorce court would have had the authority to make an "equitable" as opposed to an
equal, division.

Constitutional questions have arisen in Arizona
and Texas in connection with a division upon divorce which was not equal and therefore deprived
one party of his or her property.

The more rigid the state was in insisting upon
the theoretical model of an equal division of community and non-assignment of separate property to
the other spouse, the more important became the

distinction between separate and community. Adjustment of seeming injustices in the property division were sometimes made by means of court ordered extension of the support obligation to one's spouse, otherwise known as alimony or maintenance payments.

4. The Support Obligation (Alimony)

Alimony represents a continuation of the support obligation beyond the termination of the marriage. It is attributable to two systems which are not operative in community property states:

First, alimony is a vestige of the separate maintenance action (which left intact the marital status) that was carried over to absolute divorces without re-examination. Separate maintenance actions preceded divorces in historical development. In a separate maintenance action, the marriage (and its accompanying duty upon the husband to support the wife) was not terminated. When absolute divorces were permitted, the concept of alimony was carried to it from separate maintenance although the theoretical basis no longer existed. Alimony became "payments for a dead horse."

Second, alimony is a share of the on-going income, while termination of the community property system involves a division of the accumulated assets, if any. In the terminology of business statements, the divorced spouse in a community property state was given one half of the assets on the balance sheet. Those assets represented the amount by which income during the marriage was not consumed for expenses of the community. Alimony gives a share of the future income, i.e., from a period when the couple is not married. It consisted of income which is ordinarily shown on a profit and loss statement.

Whatever the lack of justification of alimony modernly or in the community property system, it exists and probably will continue to exist. Statutory changes have made the obligation reciprocal, but actual imposition of alimony upon wives for the support of their husbands is rare.

5. Reconciliation

Formerly, the reluctance of the courts and legislatures to grant divorces was reflected in various provisions encouraging reconciliation, including interlocutory decrees, decrees nisi or prohibitions upon remarriage for a time period. (Louisiana had a provision which prohibited the female from remarrying for nine months, regardless of the party at "fault" in the divorce.)

If the parties reconcile before the divorce decree is final, the courts differ in their treatment of the income and gains during the period of estrangement or divorce. If the parties divorce and remarry each other, the community property which became separate property upon their divorce does not become community property again since it was acquired prior to the current marriage. The parties may, of course, agree to the contrary and transmute their formerly community property, now separate property, into community property after a remarriage.

B. DETAIL

1. Divorce Division of Community Property

a. The "Ideal" Model: Ideally, in a divorce action, the parties and the court would be fully informed of and agree as to the disposition of all community assets and liabilities, with the net community easily being divided equally or equitably between the parties. Often, however, the ideal situation does not arise. Among the factors causing variations from the ideal are the following:

- Concealment of assets;

- Failure of the parties to agree;

- Omission of an asset from the agreement or decree which dissolves the community;

- Assets which are difficult to value, divide or assign to one (or both) of the spouses;

- Property outside the court's jurisdiction, especially realty located in a non-community property state.

These problems of divergence from the ideal are examined in the following material.

b. Concealed Assets: The cynic may comment that only the imperfectly-concealed assets are involved in division of spouses' property.

Traditionally, the husband (who was in the economically superior position because of management and control of the community property) was obligated not to conceal any community property, but rather to make full disclosure as to its existence and reveal material factors as to its value at the time that a property settlement was made. If the manager did not adhere to that standard of disclosure, then the property settlement could be invalidated at the request of the other party. With the changes in management and control, it appears that the principle should apply to either spouse who conceals community property.

Jurisdictions which require the divorce court to make an "equal" division of the community property occasionally make an exception for the situation in which concealment of assets is suspected, See Calif.Civ.Code § 4800(b)(2).

    c.   **Agreement of the Parties:** If the parties do not agree as to the disposition of community property, the court will divide it between them. Statutory schemes vary as to whether the court is to make an "equal" division (with some exceptions) or an "equitable" division. The latter term allows the court greater discretion and reduces the ground for appeal that the division was not "equal".

If the parties do agree, the interaction of the court and the agreement varies from state to state and from action to action. It is desirable to allow parties to settle their own differences, but the courts have traditionally been wary of collusive or coerced agreements. Assuming the permissibility and fairness of a marriage settlement agreement, the further question arises as to the effect of the court decree upon the agreement: Is the agreement merged in the decree so that it can be enforced by contempt proceedings? Who can change the terms of the agreement, the court or the parties? Tax and other consequences have flowed from the answers to these questions.

d. **Omitted Community Assets:** If an asset is omitted from the division of the community, whether because of concealment, honest error or difference of opinion as to character, the asset is converted from community to tenancy in common by the divorce of the parties. Life insurance policy proceeds and retirement plan benefits of a deceased divorced person may require apportionment to determine the share of a former spouse of the decedent. A sale to a third person may be defective because a former spouse has an interest derived from the property's former character as community.

e. **Assets Which are Difficult to Divide:** Some assets are difficult to divide because they cannot be liquidated or because they are subject to severe fluctuation in value.

Life insurance is difficult to liquidate during the life of the insured and subject to a great increase in value upon the insured's death. Some courts may award the spouse one half of the value of the premiums or contributions paid; other courts award off-setting property to the spouse; but either method prevents the spouse of the insured from participating in any increase in value due to the death of the insured.

Retirement plans raise the issue of whether they are property for division, pose problems of management and are difficult to value because of contingencies.

If an annuity is viewed as "property", it is an asset for division upon divorce. This is the common approach. On the other hand, the stream of income produced by the annuity can be viewed as income of one spouse. Support for the other spouse (or their children) may be ordered, based upon the income right. Obviously, the non-employee spouse is being given two bites of the apple if the retirement fund is divided in half and the non-employee is given both the non-employee's half and also a share of the income from the employee's half.

If the retirement benefit is community property and both spouses are entitled to participate in the management and control, then it would follow that options given to "the employee" under the retirement plan belong to both spouses.

Federal law requires a state court order to be a "qualified domestic relations order" in order to direct payments from a pension, annuity, profit-sharing or stock bonus plan, 26 U.S.C.A. § 414(p), ERISA § 206(d)(3). A qualified domestic relations order must relate to child support, alimony payments or marital property rights for a spouse, former spouse, child or other dependent of the plan participant pursuant to a state domestic relations law, including community property laws.

The Retirement Equity Act of 1984 (REA) amendments to the Employee Retirement Income Security Act of 1974 (ERISA) require benefit distributions which commence while a participant is alive to be in the form of a qualified joint and survivor annuity unless there is a formal consent by the non-employee spouse.

Among the options which are likely to be found in retirement plans are the following:

• Disability retirement income in lieu of ordinary retirement income. If the employee is entitled, at his or her election, to receive either *community* property *retirement* benefits or *separate* property *disability* benefits, the court may require the employee to apply the higher disability benefits as if they were retirement income to the extent that retirement benefits would have been received.

• Lump sum payment or an annuity. Should the spouses be required to select the same plan or could one (typically the non-employee) "cash out" and leave the other half as an annuity?

• Self or Self-and-survivor (or Joint) annuity.

• Whether to retire or continue in employment. Occasionally, a court will order a spouse who elects not to retire to pay benefits to his or her divorced spouse as if retirement had occurred.

f. Conflict of Laws: The marital or separate property may be outside the jurisdiction of the divorce court. A court may not enter *in rem* orders affecting the title to realty outside the forum, but it may enter an *in personam* order which purports to direct a person over whom the court has personal jurisdiction to convey, transfer or take other action with reference to realty located outside the forum.

At the other end of the scale is property acquired outside, and then brought in to, the community property forum state. Arizona, California and Texas have statutes defining "Quasi-Community" property. Quasi-community property is property which would have been community property except that the spouses were not domiciled in the forum community property state at the time that the property was acquired. For further discussion see Chapter 12.

2. De Facto Separation

The theoretical basis for the equal sharing of the income and property acquired during marriage is the living together and sharing of burdens by a married couple.

Often there is a period of psychological and physical separation of husband and wife prior to the divorce. If the period is short and a divorce is ultimately obtained, the period tends to be disre-

garded; the date of the divorce is used as the
termination point for the community. On the other hand, if the separation in fact continues, but is
not accompanied by court action, readjustment of
the community property regime is necessary.
Some states provide that the income of one or both
spouses is separate property during such an estrangement. Texas provides for the separate management and control in such circumstances. See
Chapter 3. When the couple voluntarily ceases to
live together, except because of health or business
reasons, the theoretical basis for sharing of income
and gains no longer exists.

C. INDIVIDUAL STATES

ARIZONA

Upon dissolution of the marriage or legal separation, Ariz.Rev.Stat. § 25–318 authorizes an "equitable" (and therefore not necessarily equal) division
of not only the community property, but also property owned by the husband and wife as joint tenants or tenants in common with each other.
Fault is not relevant for the division, according to
that statute. Arizona does not permit the divorce
court to award the separate property of one spouse
to the other, but liens may be imposed against that
property for reimbursement or to secure payment
of support obligations. Provision is specifically
made for quasi-community property.

The major portions of **Ariz.Rev.Stat.** § **25–318** are as follows:

A. In a proceeding for dissolution of the marriage, or for legal separation, . . . the court shall assign each spouse's sole and separate property to such spouse. It shall also divide the community, joint tenancy and other property held in common equitably, though not necessarily in kind, without regard to marital misconduct. For purposes of this section only, property acquired by either spouse outside this state shall be deemed to be community property if the property would have been community property if acquired in this state. Nothing in this section shall prevent the court from considering excessive or abnormal expenditures, destruction, concealment or fraudulent disposition of community, joint tenancy and other property held in common.

B. The community, joint tenancy and other property held in common for which no provision is made in the decree shall be from the date of the decree held by the parties as tenants in common, each possessed of an undivided one-half interest.

C. The court may impress a lien upon the separate property of either party or the marital property awarded to either party in order to secure the payment of any interest or equity the other party has in or to such property, or in order to secure the payment of an allowance

for child support or spousal maintenance or both.

CALIFORNIA

California grants dissolutions of marriages upon the ground of incurable insanity or the "no fault" ground of "irreconcilable differences". The basic theme for division of the property upon the dissolution of the marriage or legal separation is an "equal" division, which has a number of statutory exceptions, as set out in **Calif.Civ.Code § 4800:**

(a) . . .[T]he court shall, either in its judgment of dissolution of the marriage, [or] in its judgment decreeing the legal separation of the parties, . . . divide the community estate of the parties . . . equally. . . .

California now uses the concept of "community estate" in its divorce statute. For the purposes of divorce, liabilities are classified as either separate or community. "Community estate" includes both the community and quasi-community assets and liabilities of the parties.

The equal division of the community estate may be varied by written agreement or oral stipulation in open court of the parties.

Among the numerous statutory exceptions to the general concept of equal division of the community estate are the following:

•Division need not be an equal one half of each asset; the court may award an asset entirely to one party "as it deems proper to effect a substantially equal division of the property . . . [w]here economic circumstances warrant."

• Additional award or offset is possible if the court determines that one party has deliberately misappropriated a part of the community estate.

• A net community estate of less than $5,000 may be awarded entirely to one spouse if the other spouse cannot be located.

• Community estate personal injury damages, as defined in Calif.Civ.Code § 4800(b)(4), are assigned at least one half and potentially entirely to the party who suffered the injuries.

Detailed provisions for the allocation of debts are contained in Calif.Civ.Code § 4800(b)(5), (c), (d) and (e).

California does not permit the divorce court to award the separate property of one spouse to the other, but liens may be imposed against that property for reimbursement or to secure payment of support obligations, Fox v. Fox, 18 Cal.2d 645, 117 P.2d 325 (1941).

California created a new category of property which it called "quasi-community" property. Although different definitions are used for dissolution, probate and taxation, the basic theme is that quasi-community property consists of property which the parties would have held as California community property had they been domiciled in California instead of another state. For dissolution of marriage purposes, quasi-community property is treated as if it were California community property. The definition of quasi-community property given in **Calif.Civ.Code § 4803** for the purposes of dissolution of marriage is as follows:

As used in this part, "quasi-community property" means all real or personal property, wherever situated, heretofore or hereafter acquired in any of the following ways:

(a) By either spouse while domiciled elsewhere which would have been community property if the spouse who acquired the property had been domiciled in this state at the time of its acquisition.

(b) In exchange for real or personal property, wherever situated, which would have been community property if the spouse who acquired the property so exchanged had been domiciled in this state at the time of its acquisition.

IDAHO

In Idaho the court terminates the community by a divorce granted for any of seven traditional grounds or for the "no fault" ground of "irreconcilable differences".

Idaho does not permit the divorce court to award the separate property of one spouse to the other, but liens may be imposed against that property for reimbursement or to secure payment of support obligations, Radermacher v. Radermacher, 61 Idaho 261, 100 P.2d 955 (1940).

Idaho provides for a generally equal division of the community property between the spouses upon divorce but allows the court to determine the equality and manner of division of the community by considerations of a number of factors set out in **Idaho Code § 32–712:**

In case of divorce by the decree of a court of competent jurisdiction, the community property and the homestead must be assigned as follows:

1. The community property must be assigned by the court in such proportions as the court, from all the facts of the case and the conditions of the parties, deems just, with due consideration of the following factors:

(a) Unless there are compelling reasons otherwise, there shall be a substantially equal division in value, considering debts, between the spouses.

(b) Factors which may bear upon whether a division shall be equal, or the manner of division, include, but are not limited to:

(1) Duration of the marriage;

(2) Any antenuptial agreement of the parties; provided, however, that the court shall have no authority to amend or rescind any such agreement;

(3) The age, health, occupation, amount and source of income, vocational skills, employability, and liabilities of each spouse;

(4) The needs of each spouse;

(5) **Whether the apportionment is in lieu of or in addition to maintenance;**

(6) **The present and potential earning capability of each party; and**

(7) **Retirement benefits, including, but not limited to, social security, civil service, military and railroad retirement benefits.**

LOUISIANA

Louisiana has unique procedures for a regime of separation of property, by which the parties by agreement (or one member for cause) may agree (or obtain a judgment) that the community regime shall not arise or shall cease to exist, see La.Stat.Ann.—Civ.Code art. 2370 through 2376. The protective nature of the non-voluntary form can be inferred from the causes for which a judgment of separate property regime can be obtained. La.Stat.Ann.—Civ.Code art. 2374 permits a judgment decreeing separation of property when "a community property regime is threatened to be diminished by the fraud, fault, neglect, or incompetence of the other spouse".

In Louisiana, immediate divorces are granted only because of adultery or conviction of a felony and sentence to death or imprisonment at hard labor. Divorce is also granted after a separation from bed and board has been granted. A separation from bed and board, in turn, is granted on any of eight statutory grounds or when the parties have lived apart for a period of time (one year without reconciliation or six months if both spouses swear that there are irreconcilable differences). A separation from bed and board must first be obtained before an absolute divorce can be obtained a year later. The separation from bed and board immediately terminates the community regime and entitles the parties to division of the community property.

Upon divorce Louisiana generally divides community property equally, usually on an asset by asset basis. The authority for such division is derived more from case law than from statutes.

NEVADA

Nevada, which earned a national reputation for a liberal attitude toward divorces, grants divorces upon the grounds of insanity, living apart for one year or "incompatibility". The divorce court is required to divide the property "as appears just and equitable" as opposed to "equally" and has jurisdiction over and power to divide property placed in joint tenancy after July 1, 1979. Additionally, a limited power over separate property is given in **Nev.Rev.Stat. 125.150**:

4. In granting a divorce, the court may also set apart such portion of the husband's property for the wife's support, the wife's property for the husband's support or the property of either spouse for the support of their children as is deemed just and equitable.

NEW MEXICO

New Mexico has two statutory procedures for termination of the community:

(1) a division of property (without a dissolution of the marriage) in N.Mex.Stat.1978 § 40-4-3, and

(2) dissolution of marriage on the grounds of "incompatability", cruel and inhuman treatment, adultery or abandonment. The "no fault" ground of "incompatibility" is declared in N.Mex. Stat.1978 § 40–4–2 to exist when "because of discord or conflict of personalities, the legitimate ends of the marriage relationship are destroyed[,] preventing any reasonable expectation of reconciliation."

The division of property is governed by N.Mex.Stat.1978 § 40–4–7B, which also gives the divorce court power to order alimony in a single sum or in installments out of a spouse's separate property. An additional provision permits the divorce court to "set apart out of the property of the respective parties, such portion thereof, for the maintenance and education of their minor children, as may seem just and proper". The statute does not specifically permit an unequal division of the community property upon divorce, and the courts appear to require equal division of the community property, Michelson v. Michelson, 86 N.M. 107, 520 P.2d 263 (1974).

TEXAS

Vernon's Ann.Tex.Stat.Family Code § 3.01 provides:

On the petition of either party to a marriage, a divorce may be decreed without regard to fault if the marriage has become insupportable because of discord or conflict of personalities that destroys the legitimate ends of the mar-

riage relationship and prevents any reasonable expectation of reconciliation.

Texas is the only community property state which does not permit the divorce court to award permanent alimony. The flexibility lost by that rule is partly recaptured (when there are assets, as opposed to earning power) by allowing the divorce court to divide the quasi-community property and community property "as the court deems just and right" (i.e., unequally) and to award the separate personal property of one spouse to the other spouse.

It would seem that Texas has further reduced the chance of alimony because it does not permit the divorce court to divest either spouse of the title to separate real estate, Vernon's Ann. Tex.Stat.Family Code § 3.63 as construed in Eggemeyer v. Eggemeyer, 554 S.W.2d 137 (Tex.1977). The analysis used by the Texas Supreme Court in that case suggests that it would be unconstitutional to award *any* separate property (realty or personalty) of one spouse to the other spouse upon divorce. However, a little knowledge can be a dangerous thing in this field. Liens may be imposed against separate property for reimbursement or to secure payment of support obligations. The statutory protection of separate property from divorce obligations has been further weakened by cases permitting a divorce court to award one spouse a homestead for life in the separate property of the other spouse and authorizing subjection of the income, rents or revenues of the separate real

estate to the support of the other spouse or to the
education and support of the children, Hedtke v.
Hedtke, 112 Tex. 404, 248 S.W. 21 (1923). The
logic of the *Eggemeyer* case has not been carried
out by subsequent lower court cases.

Community property assigned to one spouse can
be the justification for payments to the other
spouse. Those payments "referable to property"
can be similar to alimony in structure such as
periodic payments during life or until remarriage
for the support of the former spouse. Payments,
otherwise clearly alimony, can be "referred to" any
property received by the spouse ordered to make
the payments, even non-productive community
acreage paid for by separate property and sold at a
loss. Thus, permanent alimony can be simulated,
if not actually obtained, in many Texas cases. A
danger for the unwary is that protections which
are built into awards of alimony—termination upon death or remarriage, modification for change of
circumstances—are not available from the alimony
surrogates.

Perhaps in reaction to the restrictiveness of the
legislative unwillingness to grant permanent alimony, the Texas Supreme Court has narrowly defined "alimony". It refers to "only those payments
imposed by a court order or decree on the husband
as a personal obligation for support and sustenance
of the wife after a final decree of divorce" according to Francis v. Francis, 412 S.W.2d 29, 33
(Tex.1967). The definition needs reworking to include the wife as the payor of alimony and the

definition does not emphasize the periodic payment
for an indefinite period characteristic of alimony.
The definition does, however, distinguish court approval of family settlement agreements which impose the obligation of support by contracts (which
were so enforced by the court) from forbidden
permanent alimony orders imposed by the court
itself.

The parties may also enter into a property settlement agreement which provides for payments
which are similar to permanent alimony.

WASHINGTON

Washington grants a "no fault" dissolution of
marriage or legal separation upon a finding that
the marriage is "irretrievably broken", Rev.Code
Wash.Ann. 26.09.030. Additionally, the parties to
a marriage may contract to live separate and apart
without any court decree; Rev.Code Wash.Ann.
26.09.070 authorizes the recording and publishing
of notice of such a contract. The contract may
dispose of any property owned by both or either of
them.

Rev.Code Wash.Ann. 26.09.080 permits an unequal division of community property between the
spouses:

**In a proceeding for dissolution of the mar-
riage [or] legal separation . . . the court
shall, without regard to marital misconduct,
make such disposition of the property and the
liabilities of the parties, either community or
separate, as shall appear just and equitable**

after considering all relevant factors including, but not limited to:

(1) The nature and extent of the community property;

(2) The nature and extent of the separate property;

(3) The duration of the marriage; and

(4) The economic circumstances of each spouse at the time the division of property is to become effective, including the desirability of awarding the family home or the right to live therein for reasonable periods to a spouse having custody of any children.

WISCONSIN (and UMPA)

In Wisconsin, a court may grant a judgment of divorce or legal separation only upon finding that a marriage is "irretrievably broken", **Wis.Stat. 1985–86 § 767.07(2) and 767.12(2).**

Property division is prescribed by **Wis.Stat. 1985–86 § 767.255** as follows:

Upon every judgment of annulment, divorce or legal separation, or in rendering a judgment in an action [for property division], the court shall divide the property of the parties and divest and transfer the title of any such property accordingly. . . .

Any property shown to have been acquired by either party prior to or during the course of the marriage as a gift, bequest, devise or inheritance or to have been paid for by either party with funds so acquired shall remain the property of such party and may not be subjected to a property division under this section except upon a finding that refusal to divide such property will create a hardship on the other party or on the children of the marriage, and in that event the court may divest the party of such property in a fair and equitable manner. The court shall presume that all other property is to be divided equally between the parties, but may alter this distribution without regard to marital misconduct after considering:

(1) The length of the marriage.

(2) The property brought to the marriage by each party.

(2r) Whether one of the parties has substantial assets not subject to division by the court.

(3) The contribution of each party to the marriage, giving appropriate economic value to each party's contribution in homemaking and child care services.

(4) The age and physical and emotional health of the parties.

(5) The contribution by one party to the education, training or increased earning power of the other.

(6) The earning capacity of each party, including educational background, training, employment skills, work experience, length of absence from the job market, custodial responsibilities for children and the time and

expense necessary to acquire sufficient education or training to enable the party to become self-supporting at a standard of living reasonably comparable to that enjoyed during the marriage.

(7) The desirability of awarding the family home or the right to live therein for a reasonable period to the party having custody of any children.

(8) The amount and duration of an order . . . granting maintenance payments to either party, any order for periodic family support payments . . . and whether the property division is in lieu of such payments.

(9) Other economic circumstances of each party, including pension benefits, vested or unvested, and future interests.

(10) The tax consequences to each party.

(11) Any written agreement made by the parties before or during the marriage concerning any arrangement for property distribution; such agreements shall be binding upon the court except that no such agreement shall be binding where the terms of the agreement are inequitable as to either party. The court shall presume any such agreement to be equitable as to both parties.

(12) Such other factors as the court may in each individual case determine to be relevant.

The discovery of concealed property after entry of a judgment dividing the spouses' property is dealt with by **Wis.Stat. 1985–86** § 767.27(5):

If any party deliberately or negligently fails to disclose information required . . . and in consequence thereof any asset or assets with a fair market value of $500 or more is omitted from the final distribution of property, the party aggrieved by such nondisclosure may at any time petition the court granting the annulment, divorce or legal separation to declare the creation of a constructive trust as to all undisclosed assets, for the benefit of the parties and their minor or dependent children, if any, with the party in whose name the assets are held declared the constructive trustee, said trust to include such terms and conditions as the court may determine. The court shall grant the petition upon a finding of a failure to disclose such assets as required. . . .

The Uniform Marital Property Act (UMPA) is not a divorce statute. UMPA must be coordinated with divorce (and other) statutes of the states adopting it. As the Prefatory Note to UMPA points out, UMPA is a property statute; it takes the parties "to the door of the divorce court" only and leaves to existing dissolution procedures in the several states the selection of the appropriate procedures for dividing property.

CHAPTER 10

DEATH

A. OVERVIEW

1. Death and Ownership, Generally

Upon the death of a married person, both the marriage and the community regime terminate. A probate estate comes into existence. The term "probate estate" is used here to indicate the assets of a decedent subject to the scheme of distribution under probate administration set forth below.

The trend of the Uniform Probate Code to offer an alternative to formal probate is disregarded in this generalization. See, generally, Lawrence H. Averill, *Uniform Probate Code in a Nutshell.* Arizona, Idaho and New Mexico have enacted, with some individual modifications, the Uniform Probate Code.

In a non-community property state, the probate estate includes the separate property possessed by the decedent at death. Obvious exclusions from the probate estate are assets which do not belong to the decedent (including the surviving spouse's separate property) and assets which are disposed of by other means. Alternatives to probate administration include joint tenancy which passes to the surviving joint tenant and trusts and life insurance which pass to the designated beneficiary.

The law provides means by which creditors of the decedent can prove and collect (to the extent of the decedent's estate) debts owing by the decedent. Certain obligations to the family are given priority over even the creditors. The assets of the decedent's estate are consumed or distributed in the following order:

a. Administration expenses, taxes and debts.

b. Homestead, exempt property, elective share of the spouse and family allowance to the surviving spouse or dependent children or both.

c. Beneficiaries designated by a valid will (which includes codicils) or those indicated as substitute beneficiaries in cases involving lapse, renunciation or other circumstances affecting the devolution of testate estates.

d. Heirs (intestate takers) or those indicated as substitutes for them in cases involving renunciation or other circumstances affecting the devolution of intestate estates.

e. Escheat to the state (or its designated agency).

Only those assets remaining after the exhaustion of the preceding categories pass to subsequent categories. Thus, a decedent's spouse or children or both may exhaust a small estate by taking exempt property or family allowance. A person could die with assets insufficient to pay all creditors and nothing would pass to his or her will beneficiaries. A valid will which effectively disposes of the entire estate to will beneficiaries deprives the heirs of any inheritance.

2. Community Property Variations

Since the death of a married person terminates the community character of property, the property dealt with in this chapter is "former community" rather than community property. Nevertheless, for convenience of expression, the former status is spoken of as if it continued to exist.

In community property states, it would seem that only the separate property of the decedent and his or her half of the community should be in the probate estate of a married person. In most states, this is now the case. Formerly, however, the management and control of the husband produced non-parallel probate situations: The entire community was administered if the husband died first, but the wife's estate included only her half of the community and was not always subject to probate administration.

If property in joint tenancy form was determined to be community property, then probate administration (and liability for debts and expenses of administration) necessarily followed upon the death of one of the owners. If the property is truly joint tenancy property, or, in Wisconsin was held as survivorship marital property, it is owned by survivorship and not subject to the decedent's debts nor included in his or her probate estate.

Liability for debts in a probate estate usually follows the same rules as the liability of the community for debts during the marriage, but Washington imposes a greater liability upon the community half of a decedent for separate debts.

The rights of the surviving spouse to family allowance, although based upon historical granting of a period of quarantine to a widow, is similar to the divorce award of alimony in that it is designed as a continuation of the obligation of support owed by one spouse to the other and as alleviation of the economic difficulties caused by the termination of the marriage. The concept of exempt property and homestead was initiated in Texas and has been adopted in one form or another by almost all of the United States. For a more detailed description of these rights, see—or better yet, buy—Robert L. Mennell, *Wills and Trusts in a Nutshell.*

The surviving spouse could also be a creditor of the decedent. The basis for the claim can be a ground also found in non-community property states or a ground unique to community property states such as a claim for reimbursement for community funds used to improve the separate property of the decedent.

The net probate estate, after payment of administration expenses, taxes, debts and family support priority items, is distributed in accordance with the effective provisions of the decedent's last will (including any codicils). Assuming that the character of the property has been determined to be community, there are two areas where litigation tends to occur:

a. To the extent that the provisions made by the will are less generous to the surviving spouse than the intestacy statutes, there is motivation for the surviving spouse to instigate a will contest.

b. The decedent may attempt to dispose of more than he or she is entitled to dispose of by will or may attempt to impose conditions or restrictions upon the share which the surviving spouse is entitled to receive outright and in kind. The surviving spouse may be required to make an election to take under the provisions made by the will rather than keep the property to which he or she is entitled by law.

3. Intestacy Statutes

The laws of intestacy set forth a distribution pattern for the property of a decedent who dies without effectively disposing of his or her entire estate by will. If a decedent dies intestate, all of the separate property of the decedent but only one half of the community property is subject to the laws of intestacy. In all the community property states except Arizona, a different distribution scheme exists for community property as opposed to separate property.

The widow or widower owns one half of the community property. The decedent's half of the community passes as follows:

• In California, Idaho, Nevada, New Mexico and Washington, to the widow or widower regardless of the number of issue of the decedent;

• In Arizona and Wisconsin, to the issue of the decedent who are not the issue of the surviving spouse (i.e., they are the survivor's step-children); if there are no step-children, to the widow or widower;

• Texas, Louisiana and Wisconsin have more detailed provisions for the decedent's half of the community property.

Separate property of the decedent is subjected to a different and usually more complicated distribution scheme, except in Arizona and Wisconsin.

B. DETAIL

1. Probate Administration of Community Property

a. Background: Administration of the estate of a decedent (loosely called "probate" after the proof of a will) is the process by which a personal representative (executor or administrator) is appointed by the local court to gather the assets of the decedent, to pay debts, taxes and administration expenses and to distribute the estate to the will beneficiaries or heirs. The process is also used to prove or clear title to assets. The probate administration provides a forum in which the community or separate character of property can be determined.

The probate administration process is designed to protect both the objects of the decedent's bounty and those creditors who file their claims in the appropriate manner within the relatively short time allowed. Probate administration has not been popular with the ultimate takers of the estate because of the processing time and the estate shrinkage, the latter being caused largely by death taxes and administration expenses, including attorneys' fees.

Is probate administration necessary? Some states, including California, have held that probate administration is necessary even when the beneficiaries are in possession of the decedent's property, no creditors are known and all death taxes have been paid. On the other hand, the tendency has been to simplify or make optional parts or all of the probate administration process. Texas and Washington were leaders in this movement with the concept of the "independent executor" who qualified with, and reported a list of assets to, the probate court, but then operated "informally", i.e., independent of probate court supervision. The Uniform Probate Code allows both formal and informal probate administration.

b. Administration of Community Property:
The functions of the personal representative dupli-

cate some, but not all, of the functions of the manager of community property.

If the non-manager of the community property dies, should the (former) community property be subjected to probate? Many of the community property states did not, and some still do not, require probate administration of the community property when the non-manager dies, especially when the decedent's half of the community property passed by intestacy to the surviving spouse. In some states, and in Texas today, the need for probate administration turns on whether the decedent died with or without a will.

On the other hand, when the manager of the community property (historically, the husband) died first, both halves of the community were often administered in his estate. A justification for subjecting the surviving spouse's half of the community to probate administration was the convenience of paying community debts from the total community property. The weakness of this justification is shown by examining the treatment of tenancy in common or joint tenancy properties which are subject to debts, mortgages, mechanics' liens or real property taxes. In tenancies in common, only the decedent's portion of the property was administered; in the case of joint tenancy, the property was held by the survivor without the necessity of probate administration. Procedures exist to prove the death of the joint tenant and the payment of death taxes without the intervention of a court.

Administration of both halves of the community property when the husband died was justified as a continuation of the management and control exerted by the husband during the marriage. When the management and control was wrested from husbands, a re-examination was made of the need for probate administration.

How much, if any, of the community property should be subject to probate administration? Each combination has advantages: If the community property is entirely included in the probate administration, proof of title and collection of debts are simplified. If only the decedent's half of the community is included in probate administration, the equal ownership of each spouse is recognized. If probate administration is completely avoided, there are savings in time and cost for the surviving spouse, but less protection to the tax collector, creditors and will beneficiaries.

Probate administration of community property produces difficulties: In Texas, which permitted a separate administration of the community property by the surviving spouse, conflicts arose between that survivor and the personal representative who was charged with administering the balance of the probate estate. In California, in which the estate of a deceased husband included both halves of the community but the deceased wife's estate required no administration unless she devised it by will, the statutory probate fees of the personal representative and his or her attorney were almost twice as much when the husband died first. The California probate fee schedule is based upon the size of the probate estate. In practice it is more difficult to administer one half of an asset than to administer the entire asset; the coordination with a co-owner of each payment and receipt complicates administration.

c. Present Rules for the Administration of Community Property: Three of the community property states—Arizona, Idaho and New Mexico—have adopted, with modifications, the Uniform Probate Code which permits less formal probate procedures when simplicity, rather than protection, appears appropriate. Those states and Washington require that the whole of the community property be subject to probate administration upon the death of either spouse.

California, Nevada and Wisconsin provide that only the decedent's half of the community shall be subject to probate administration, and California requires that much administration only when the community estate is devised other than to the spouse outright.

Texas provides that when the surviving spouse is the heir of community property, i.e., when the intestate left no issue, the surviving spouse may take the entire community without administration. Louisiana similarly sends the spouse and other heirs into possession without administration if they are competent, they accept the succession unconditionally and the succession is relatively free of debt.

2. Forced Shares and Elections

Elections can be forced by or against a will:

•Forced shares against the will may be permitted by statute. The provisions in the Uniform Probate Code for a forced share to the spouse of the "augmented estate" (as defined in the Uniform Probate Code) are typical: If the decedent's will does not make adequate provision for the surviving spouse, he or she may assert the right to take a specified fraction of the estate (or additional assets up to that fraction of the estate). The election, when made, is to take *against* the provisions of the will. This type of provision, which exists in Wisconsin, is more commonly found in non-community property states as a minimum protection for the surviving spouse. Theoretically, the community half of a spouse in a community property state achieves the same purpose.

•A trade-off may be proposed by the will. The testator may, in effect, make an offer to a devisee to trade. For example, a testator could bequeath "my automobile to my older son, provided he gives his automobile to my younger son" or "my farm, Blackacre, to my son, provided he pay $100,000 to my daughter." A testator has power to dispose by will only of the property which the testator owns at death (or, in the case of powers of appointment, over which the testator has a valid testamentary power of appointment) and which is not otherwise disposed of by joint tenancy, contract or trust. An attempt by a testator to dispose by will of property which is not owned is a nullity unless it can be given effect as a "forced election". The law recognizes the anomaly of allowing one who is a beneficiary under the will both to take the devises to him or her and to defeat the other portion of the trade-off. The election, when made is to take *under* the will. The beneficiary elects to subject his or her property to the dispositive scheme of the testator. If no election is made, the property of the beneficiary does not pass under the will, but the beneficiary will be deemed to have renounced his or her devises under the will which are inconsistent with retention of his or her own property.

• Forced elections arise in community property states when the testator attempts to devise either the entire interest in a community asset (or, in Arizona, more than one half of the aggregate community wealth) to a person other than the spouse. Most community property states declare that the surviving spouse is entitled to one half of each asset, outright and in kind; therefore, an election is forced if the testator manifests the clear intention to give the entire community interest to a third person. Arizona holds that the surviving spouse is adequately protected if he or she is given one half of the net value of the community. Arizona, therefore, would look to the total amount received by the surviving spouse before declaring that an election was forced.

All elections involve testate situations, i.e., there is a will. In the forced share situations, the surviving spouse is given the option to take a minimum share established by law. In the forced election situations, the surviving spouse is called upon to allow his or her separate or community property to pass in accordance with the testamentary scheme of the decedent.

The forced election has been used extensively in estate tax planning. Some of the tax importance has been reduced by changes made in 1981 legislation, including the unlimited marital deduction and higher unified credit.

The election may involve an attempt by the testator to dispose of property belonging to another person by devise to a third person or by the testator putting limitations upon the property belonging to the survivor, such as by insisting that the survivor's community one half be placed into an irrevocable trust (usually paired with the testator's half of the community for more efficient management of the whole).

If forced to an election, the surviving spouse may either take that which is provided by the will for him or her, allowing the survivor's property to pass in accordance with the testator's will, or retain the survivor's property and relinquish all inconsistent claims under the will. The issue thus becomes "What are inconsistent claims?"

Courts often indulge in the presumption that the testator intended to dispose only of the portion of the property which he or she owned, i.e., his or her community half if the asset is community property. A bequest of "my automobile" is often construed as "my interest in our automobile". A bequest of "one half of my estate to my brother, the other half to my wife" may be construed to give the brother one fourth of the community property since the decedent had the right to dispose of only half of the community.

If this presumption is not raised or if the language of the will is too clearly indicative of an unmistakable intention to dispose of property which was not entirely his or her own, then an election is forced.

C. INDIVIDUAL STATES

ARIZONA

Arizona has adopted, with some modifications, the Uniform Probate Code. Arizona and Wisconsin reduce the significance between separate and community property upon death by providing the same intestate distribution scheme, regardless of character of the property. Of course, not all differences could be eliminated; the distinction remains important because the survivor's half of the community is not subject to the decedent's will.

The adoption of the same distribution scheme for community and separate property has eliminated in intestate estates the need in Arizona to adopt a statute creating and dealing with quasi-community property (as in California) at death. Arizona does have such a statute which applies in divorce situations.

Ariz.Rev.Stat. § 14–2102 provides that both the decedent's separate property and his or her half of the community shall pass to the surviving spouse if there are no surviving issue of the decedent who are not issue of the surviving spouse (i.e., step-children of the survivor). If there are step-children, the surviving spouse receives one half of the decedent's separate property in addition to the survivor's half of the community; the step-children take the remainder (i.e., one half of the separate property and the decedent's half of the community).

CALIFORNIA

1. Intestacy Statutes, Community and Separate:

California extensively revised and renumbered its probate code, effective for decedents dying on or after January 1, 1985. **Calif.Prob.Code § 6401** provides that the intestate share of a surviving spouse consists of the following elements:

a. The decedent's half of community property, as defined in **Calif.Prob.Code § 28**; and

b. The decedent's half of quasi-community property, as defined in **Calif.Prob.Code § 66**; and

c. A portion of the decedent's separate property which varies depending upon the relationship of other surviving kindred of the decedent (who are the takers of the balance of the decedent's estate under **Calif.Prob.Code § 6402**):

1. If two or more children survive (or leave issue who survive) the decedent, the spouse inherits one-third of the decedent's separate property;

2. If one child, or any parent or descendant of a parent (brother, sister, nephew, niece etc.) survives the decedent, the spouse inherits one-half of the decedent's separate property;

3. If no issue, parent nor issue of a parent survives the decedent, the spouse inherits the decedent's entire separate property.

2. Quasi-Community Property:

California introduced the concept of "quasi-community property". The need arose from the common situation in which persons retired after working in a separate property state and moved to California. In the separate property state in which a deceased wage-earner owned the family wealth, the widow or widower would have had a right to take a forced share or elect against a will which did not make a minimum provision for her or him. A similar right to take against the will does not exist in California. No wealth was produced while the couple was married and domiciled in California. Rents, issues and profits from separate property are not community property under

California law. Thus, the widow or widower of a retired immigrant to California lost both of the alternative protections, forced share upon death or community property. To rectify that situation, the legislature created a new character of property, "quasi-community property" and decreed that it would descend, upon intestacy, in the same manner as community property.

Calif.Prob.Code § **28** expressly converts into California community property for purposes of the California Probate Code "community property, or a substantially equivalent type of marital property under the laws of the place where the acquiring spouse was domiciled at the time of the acquisition." Thus Texas or Louisiana community property (including the income from separate property while married and domiciled in Texas or Louisiana) becomes California community property when a spouse dies domiciled in California.

Calif.Prob.Code § **66** defines quasi-community property:

As used in this code, "quasi-community property" means the following property, other than community property as defined in Section 28:

(a) All personal property wherever situated, and all [California] real property . . . acquired by the decedent while domiciled elsewhere which would have been the community property of the decedent and the surviving spouse if the decedent had been domiciled in [California] at the time of its acquisition.

(b) All personal property wherever situated, and all [California] real property . . . acquired in exchange for real or personal property, wherever situated, which would have been the community property of the decedent and the surviving spouse if the decedent had been domiciled in this state at the time the property so exchanged was acquired.

3. Ancestral Property:

"Ancestral property" doctrines of intestacy attempt to keep property in the blood line in which it originated rather than allowing it to pass to "in-laws" or other strangers to the blood of the ancestor from whom it descended. California has a unique intestacy provision which partially responds to that impulse:

Calif.Prob.Code § 6402.5 provides special intestacy rules for the disposition of certain former property (separate, community and quasi-community) of a predeceased spouse if the surviving spouse dies after 1984 without (another) spouse or issue surviving. The provision deals with separate property since it is limited to one who dies without a surviving spouse. The historical source of the property is that it came to the present decedent from a spouse who died within a certain period (15 years for realty, 5 years for personalty). The property passes to certain relatives (issue, parents or issue of parents) of the predeceased spouse if they exist.

IDAHO

Idaho's version of the Uniform Probate Code allows a surviving spouse to take all of the community property and all of the separate property of the decedent if it has a value of less than $50,000. Above that amount, the spouse is entitled to one half of the separate property of the decedent; the issue of the decedent take the other half. If there are no issue, the separate property is divided one half to the spouse and one half to the parents of the decedent. If there are neither issue nor parents, the surviving spouse is entitled to all of the separate property of the decedent.

Idaho grants a surviving spouse the right to take a forced share of the quasi-community property in the augmented estate by Idaho Code §§ 15–2–202 and 15–2–203. Quasi-community property is described and distributed in language almost identical to California, by **Idaho Code § 15–2–201:**

(a) Upon death of a married person domiciled in this state, one half (½) of the quasi-community property shall belong to the surviving spouse and the other one half (½) of such property shall be subject to the testamentary disposition of the decedent and, if not devised by the decedent, goes to the surviving spouse.

(b) Quasi-community property is all personal property, wherever situated, and all [Idaho] real property . . . acquired by the decedent while domiciled elsewhere and which

would have been the community property of
the decedent and the surviving spouse had the
decedent been domiciled in [Idaho] at the time
of its acquisition plus all personal property,
wherever situated, and all [Idaho] real property . . . acquired in exchange for real or
personal property, wherever situated, which
would have been the community property of
the decedent and the surviving spouse if the
decedent had been domiciled in [Idaho] at the
time the property so exchanged was acquired,
provided that real property does not and personal property does include leasehold interests
in real property, provided that quasi-community property shall include real property situated in another state and owned by a domiciliary
of [Idaho] if the laws of such state permit
descent and distribution of such property to be
governed by the laws of [Idaho].

(c) All quasi-community property is subject
to the debts of decedent.

LOUISIANA

Louisiana's civil law heritage shows strongly in
the provisions for administration and distribution
of a decedent's estate. A stronger sense of ancestral property pervades the intestacy provisions.

Legitimate descendants receive both the community and separate property of the decedent, but the
community portion is subject to usufruct (roughly
similar to a life estate) by the surviving spouse.

If there are no legitimate descendants of the decedent, the spouse receives (in addition to the survivor's one half of the community) one half of the decedent's half (i.e., an additional quarter of the total community property). The balance (i.e., the final quarter) goes to such of the father and mother of the decedent who survives the decedent; if both parents are dead, that final quarter of the community also passes to the surviving spouse.

The analogy of the common law forced share is found in the right of the surviving spouse to claim (but not to receive automatically) a "marital portion" (defined below) "[w]hen a spouse dies rich in comparison with the surviving spouse" in the terminology of La.Stat.Ann.—Civ.Code art. 2432. Legacies to and payments due to the surviving spouse are deducted from the marital portion. If there are children of the decedent, the marital portion of the spouse is limited to usufruct. The quantum of the marital portion is set out in **La.Stat.Ann.—Civ.Code art. 2434:**

The marital portion is one-fourth of the succession in ownership if the deceased died without children, the same fraction in usufruct for life if he is survived by three or fewer children, and a child's share in such usufruct if he is survived by more than three children.

A periodic allowance for the maintenance of the surviving spouse is also allowable, but it is dependent upon the right to, and subtracted from, the marital portion as finally fixed.

The property of a decedent who is survived by legitimate descendants is therefore subject to two types of usufructs in favor of the surviving spouse: First, the spouse is entitled to the usufruct in the community property as a matter of right. Second, on a basis of comparative need, the spouse may apply for the usufruct of the marital portion, from which any periodic allowance will be subtracted.

Louisiana grants the "legitime", a civil law forced portion of a decedent's estate (augmented by certain lifetime transfers), to legitimate issue of the decedent (or, in the absence of issue, to the parents of the decedent). There is no common law equivalent to the legitime; the common law permits the total intentional exclusion of issue and has demonstrated a trend to increase the share of a surviving spouse.

NEVADA

Nevada's intestacy statutes are similar to California in giving both halves of the community to the surviving spouse and dividing the separate property between the surviving spouse and issue of the decedent. If there is one child, the division is half and half; if there are children, the children receive two thirds and the widow or widower receives one third of the separate property.

If the decedent is not survived by any descendants, the separate property is divided one half to the surviving spouse and one half to the parents equally, or to the survivor of them, or, if neither survives the intestate, to their descendants by right of representation. If no member of the immediate family (i.e., no parent, sibling nor nephew or niece) survives the decedent, the surviving spouse receives all of the separate property.

Nevada also has limited provisions dealing with attempts to bring ancestral property, already inherited by a childless spouse, back into the blood line of the predecessors. As with the California statutes, a tortured definition of "heirs" is necessary to prevent circularity. Consider the following example:

EXAMPLE: H, the husband of a childless couple dies intestate, possessing only community property. Under Nevada law, W, the widow, is entitled to the entire community estate, one half because it is her own property and one half because she is the "heir" (taker under intestacy law) of her husband, H. When W subsequently dies, also childless and intestate, who is entitled to her estate?

The text of the ancestral property statutes is as follows:

Nev.Rev.Stat. 134.200: Whenever any husband dies intestate, leaving heirs, and if the wife dies intestate subsequently to her husband, without heirs, leaving property, her estate shall vest in the heirs of her husband, subject to expenses of administration and payment of legal debts against the estate.

134.210: Whenever any wife dies intestate without issue, leaving heirs, and if the husband dies intestate subsequently to his wife, without heirs, leaving property, his estate shall vest in the heirs of the wife, subject to expenses of administration and payment of legal debts against the estate.

Nev.Rev.Stat. 134.200 seems to say that W's estate will vest in W. Obviously, it is necessary to interpret the language in Nev.Rev.Stat. 134.200 and 134.210 to create an artificial group of heirs, rather than the heirs themselves. The artificial group which seems to have been sought is "those persons who would have been the intestate takers of the first to die of the married couple, determined at the time and place of the death of the first to die as if the order of death of the married couple had been reversed."

NEW MEXICO

N.Mex.Stat.1978 § 45–2–102 gives the decedent's half of community property to the surviving spouse. New Mexico has added to its form of the Uniform Probate Code additional language in N.Mex.Stat.1978 § 45–2–804 that the surviving spouse's half of the community property belongs to him or her.

Separate property is divided one fourth to the widow or widower and three fourths to the surviving descendants. If there are no surviving descendants, N.Mex.Stat.1978 § 45–2–102 gives the entire separate property of the decedent to his or her surviving spouse.

All of the community property is subject to the payment of community debts; **N.Mex.Stat.1978 § 45–2–804** provides:

B. Upon the death of either spouse, the entire community property is subject to the payment of community debts. The deceased spouse's separate debts and funeral expenses and the charge and expenses of administration are to be satisfied first from his separate property excluding property held in joint tenancy. Should such property be insufficient, then the deceased spouse's undivided one-half interest in the community property shall be liable.

TEXAS

Texas is closer to Louisiana than the other community property states in making intestate provisions which prefer issue of the decedent over the surviving spouse. The decedent's half of the community passes to his issue who survive him, by right of representation. Similarly, the intestacy provision for separate property if the decedent is survived by both spouse and issue gives the spouse one third of the personalty and a life estate in one third of the realty; the balance of the estate passes to the issue.

If the decedent dies without issue surviving him or her, then the spouse receives all of the community property, all of the separate property personalty and at least one half of the separate realty in fee. The other half of the separate property realty passes to the "immediate family" (the parents equally, or the survivor of them, and, if both are dead, to their issue by right of representation). If there are no members of this immediate family, then the spouse takes the final half of the separate realty. The spouse thus is the heir who receives all realty and personalty, separate and community, if no issue nor immediate family survive the intestate.

Texas has originated two concepts which affect the passage of property at death (in addition to lifetime implications)—the independent executor and the homestead.

The independent executor concept emphasized the non-intervention of the probate court after the qualification of the personal representative. Additionally, **Vernon's Ann.Tex.Stat. Probate Code § 155** provides:

When a husband or wife dies intestate and the community property passes to the survivor, no administration thereon, community or otherwise, shall be necessary.

The concept of the "homestead" and exempt personal property originated in Texas. Although designed primarily to protect a modest farm or family home and certain minimum amounts of clothing, furnishings and working equipment from execution of creditors, the protection to the family members has been extended after death of a spouse or parent. The extension was logical because otherwise death would terminate protection given to family members. The exemption from creditors has also been applied to be an exemption from the testate distribution by the decedent. Thus in Texas, as in many jurisdictions, the homestead and the exempt property can be claimed by the spouse or the children of the decedent in preference to most creditors. A family allowance is also capable of being ordered paid, as a preferred item, from the decedent's estate.

WASHINGTON

Washington subjects both halves of the community property to probate administration when either spouse dies. This allows a continuing control of community debts and payment from the probate estate. **Rev.Code Wash.Ann. 11.02.070** provides that upon the death of a decedent, "a one-half share of the community property shall be confirmed to the surviving spouse". The balance of that section, however, makes clear that it is a net one half of the community after the "payment of obligations and debts of the community, the award in lieu of homestead, the allowance for family support, and any other matter for which the community property would be responsible or liable if the decedent were living."

The surviving spouse in addition to having his or her half of the community property confirmed in him or her, receives the decedent's half of the community property by intestacy. The separate property intestate succession set out in Rev.Code Wash.Ann. 11.04.015 gives the surviving spouse one half if the decedent was survived by issue (who, of course, take the other half of the separate property). If the decedent is not survived by issue, the spouse takes three fourths of the separate property and the immediate family (parents if both are alive, surviving parent if one is alive, or issue of the parents by right of representation if neither parent survives the decedent) takes the other fourth. If there are no issue nor parent nor issue of a parent, the surviving spouse takes all of the separate property as well as all of the community property.

Rev.Code Wash.Ann. 11.04.095 provides a special rule for certain types of ancestral property: If a widow or widower who received all or substantially all of the property of his or her previously deceased spouse (during the joint lifetime or at the death of the first spouse to die) dies without a will or heirs so that property would otherwise escheat, the property of the second to die passes by intestacy to the issue of the first to die (i.e., the step-issue of the second to die) who survive the second to die.

Although during the continuation of the community, Washington separate property is not liable for community debts and Washington community property is not liable for separate debts, different rules apply as to timely filed creditors' claims in the probate estate. The community debts are paid from the total community, producing a net community; separate claims against the decedent are then asserted against his or her half of the community.

Washington created a unique type of testamentary contract by Rev.Code Wash.Ann. 26.16.120 which authorizes a married couple to make a contract which, among other things, disposes of the community property upon the death of the first of them. This survivorship contract does not have to be executed with the formalities of a will. It is a contract, which is not unilaterally terminable or revocable (as joint tenancy or a will, respectively, would be).

WISCONSIN

Wisconsin revised its probate administration and intestate and testate succession laws, effective January 1, 1986, the same time that it became a community property state. UMPA does not have comparable provisions.

The intestate share of a surviving spouse of a Wisconsin domiciliary who dies after 1985 consists of the following:

1. The deceased spouse's entire estate if no issue survive or if the surviving issue are all issue of the decedent and the surviving spouse; or

2. Half of the deceased spouse's property other than marital property and other than deferred marital property (defined below) if there are any

surviving issue who are not also issue of the surviving spouse.

Wisconsin law permits each spouse to will his or her portion of each item of marital property and his or her nonmarital (i.e., individual and unclassified) property, subject to the surviving spouse's elective rights.

Only the decedent's half of marital property is subject to probate administration. Survivorship marital property, like joint tenancy, belongs by operation of law to the survivor; therefore, it is not subject to administration nor does it pass by will.

Wis.Stat. 1985–86 § 766.58(3)(f) permits spouses to enter a marital property agreement containing provisions which act as a will substitute and transfer property without probate administration:

Providing that upon the death of either spouse any of either or both spouses' property, including after-acquired property, passes without probate to a designated person, trust or other entity by nontestamentary disposition. If a marital property agreement provides for the nontestamentary disposition of property, without probate, at the death of the 2nd spouse, at any time after the death of the first spouse the surviving spouse may amend the marital property agreement with regard to property to be disposed of at his or her death unless the marital property agreement expressly provides otherwise and except to the extent

property is held in a trust expressly established under the marital property agreement.

Because Wisconsin has been a community property state only since 1986, most property of Wisconsin spouses is not marital property. To afford surviving spouses some economic protection, an elective right (rather than an automatic property interest under UMPA) is provided to a surviving spouse. The surviving spouse may elect to receive up to 50% of certain nonmarital property called "deferred marital property" in the deceased spouse's probate estate. Deferred marital property is property acquired during marriage that would have been marital property had the marital property law applied when the property was acquired.

In addition to the right to elect deferred marital property, a surviving spouse may elect to receive up to 50% of the value of the "augmented marital property estate". The augmented marital property estate (a concept borrowed from the Uniform Probate Code) consists of certain nonprobate transfers on or after April 4, 1984, (the date on which the Governor signed the law) of deferred marital property to third parties, including certain trusts, joint tenancies and life insurance. The amount elected by the surviving spouse is reduced by amounts transferred by the decedent to the surviving spouse. The surviving spouse is eligible to collect the amount remaining after the reduction from the transferees of the deferred marital property. See Wis.Stat. 1985–86 §§ 861.03 to 861.17.

PART V

SPECIAL PROBLEMS

CHAPTER 11

PERIPHERAL MARRIAGES

A. OVERVIEW

1. General Outline

The community property system assumes the existence of a valid marriage between the parties. If the marriage is not valid, good faith of the parties may justify some amelioration. In cases where one or both of the parties did not enter a marriage in good faith, general principles of law might protect the parties in their dealings with each other.

2. Valid Marriages

Each state recognizes the validity of marriages solemnized in accordance with its own internal law. Additionally, each state recognizes marriages validly performed and solemnized in accordance with the law of another state, so long as that marriage does not violate public policy of the recognizing state. For example, common law marriages are recognized in Idaho and Texas; once such an informal marriage is established in either of those states, the other states will also regard the marriage as valid. On the other hand, acceptance of homosexual marriages, valid in Colorado, is not so widespread.

3. Good Faith Marriages, Putative Spouses

A ceremonial marriage, seemingly valid, could be subject to a fatal defect. The purported marriage may be void because of bigamy, incest or insanity or it may be voidable because of minority, improper formality or other reason. The judicial procedure by which the marriage is declared invalid is the annulment.

Traditionally, an annulment operates as if the marriage never came into being, but there has been a tendency to soften this approach. The divorce, on the other hand, treats the marriage as having existed between the dates of the wedding and the divorce decree. Whether or not a marriage existed affects the creation of community property, the legitimacy of children and the duty of spousal support among other things. There has been a tendency to blend some of the attributes of the divorce into annulment actions. The treatment of putative spouses fits into, but actually predates, that trend.

A putative spouse is an innocent member of a voidable or void marriage who in good faith thought there was a valid marriage. One or both members of a defective marriage may be putative spouses. The putative spouse rule gives to the good faith member of the putative marriage the same community property benefits which he or she would have obtained if the marriage had been valid. If both parties acted in good faith, the putative spouse doctrine treats them as if they were indeed husband and wife. While common law spouses *are* the members of a valid marriage in states which recognize such marriages (and, under conflict of laws rules, in states which recognize the recognition by another state), putative spouses are *treated as if* they had been legally married.

The putative spouse doctrine is derived from the civil law. Both Louisiana and Texas adopted the principle directly from the civil law; California and Wisconsin also recognize the doctrine. Although not all of the community property states accept the putative spouse doctrine, some non-community property states have indicated a willingness to apply the doctrine.

Good faith is required; the putative spouse doctrine protects "innocent" spouses. Good faith is an honest and reasonable belief that the marriage is valid at the time that the marriage is contracted. American jurisdictions also require that the good faith must continue. Once an innocent spouse knows of the defect of the marriage (and probably, at the earlier point when an innocent spouse has information which would put him or her on inquiry), the beneficial attributes of the putative status stop.

For our purpose, the effect of putative spouse status is to create for that spouse a type of property, sometimes called quasi-marital property, which is treated as if it were community property. Other applications concern the right of a putative spouse to be treated as a spouse for governmental benefits, such as worker's compensation, social security, for private contracts and trusts such as retirement benefits and for probate purposes, including the rights to family allowance, exempt property, homestead, the right to take against the will as a post-testamentary spouse, the right to take under intestacy provisions and (as a matter of interpretation) the right to take under a will in which the beneficiary is described as "my spouse". Other effects of the putative spouse status, including legitimacy of children and right to alimony, are not further treated.

EXAMPLE: H–1 is granted an interlocutory divorce from W–1. Before the divorce becomes final, H–1 purportedly marries W–2. Later, the final decree is entered and W–1 marries H–2. The purported marriage of H–1 to W–2 is bigamous and void. All parties involved could believe that the H–1 and W–1 divorce was complete and H–1's marriage to W–2 valid. Nevertheless, the marriage is void and H–1 remained married to W–1 until the final decree of divorce was entered. H–1 and W–2 are putative spouses of each other until they, individually, receive knowledge of the defect or facts which cause them to be put on inquiry about the defect. When the divorce was subsequently validly entered, it did not retroactively make H–1's second marriage valid. In Idaho and Texas, the common law marriage doctrine could validate the otherwise-invalid second marriage as soon as the first marriage is terminated. The remarriage of W–1 is valid, but estoppel doctrines will not validate H–1's remarriage.

A person could purport to enter into the marital relationship with more than the authorized number of members of the opposite sex. For example, H marries W–1 and then purports to marry W–2 and W–3 while W–1 is living and undivorced. The attempted marriages to W–2 and W–3 are void. If they entered into the attempted marriage in good faith, W–2 and W–3 are putative spouses of H. How should the earnings of H during these three marriages be divided? An examination of court approaches to that problem is set out below, in Part B of this chapter.

4. Meretricious Relationships

If the parties make no good faith attempt to enter into a formal marriage, they are generally not entitled to any of the attributes of a marriage, including the creation of community property. What the census bureau refers to as "persons of opposite sexes sharing living quarters" (POSSLQ), the common law calls a "meretricious" (from the Latin noun, "meretrix", a prostitute) relationship. Louisiana uses the term "concubinage".

Population studies indicate an increasing number of meretricious relationships despite a rigidly disapproving stance by the law. In many jurisdictions, criminal statutes prohibit such cohabitation. Courts generally refuse to enforce contracts which are predicated upon the delivery or exchange of sexual favors. Attempts to obtain the value of services or a share in property accumulated on the basis of performance of the spouse's role have generally been unsuccessful. The courts, by refusing such claims, have allowed the title to property to remain as it was created by the parties; no attempt is made to measure the good faith of the possessor or record title holder.

Persons who are not married to each other are not prevented, however, from entering into legal arrangements that are permitted in the absence of the sexual relationship. Thus, theories of equity, unjust enrichment, contract, trust, partnership, quasi-partnership and joint venture have permitted division of property in some cases. These theories are considered in more detail below.

5. Rights of Creditors During the Relationship

Most cases dealing with the property rights of unmarried couples who live together arise after the termination of the relationship. What is the status of the property during the relationship? How much property can be reached by a creditor of one of the parties?

The theory chosen by a putative or meretricious spouse may indicate the timing of the ownership. Should the creditor be allowed the same choice? Possible theories and their effect upon timing and creditors' rights are as follows:

● Louisiana's acceptance of the putative spouse, in effect, validates the marriage for almost all purposes. It would seem to follow that creditors could reach the "community" assets as if the marriage were valid.

● Equitable divisions, quantum meruit and payments for rehabilitation seem to arise at the time they are decreed by the court; if so, the claimant in the litigation would have no interest in the property until his or her rights were determined by the court. The creditors of each party would only be able to reach such interests as that party possessed at the time that attachment or garnishment was sought.

● A partnership theory, even an unequal partnership, subjects all of the assets of the "partnership" to the claims of creditors.

● Tenancy in common would permit unequal ownership in accordance with the contribution of each. In both tenancy in common and joint tenancy, only the interest of the particular party can be reached by his or her creditors.

B. DETAIL

1. Division Among Multiple "Spouses"

Ordinarily, there are only two claimants to quasi-marital property: The two purported spouses involved in an annulment action or two competing spouses of the same person after he or she dies. More claimants are possible: A marital adventurer can leave a trail of supposed spouses. At death, the attempt to dispose of the estate to a third party may compete with the demands of two (or more) purported spouses of the deceased bigamist. How is the estate to be divided?

The putative spouse doctrine assumes equal fractions between two claimants. Greater flexibility is available under the alternative theories: Payment for services or reimbursement for contribution of money or property can be in proportion to the total contribution of the two (or more) parties. Partnerships and tenancies in common permit unequal ownership.

Some results seem paradoxical when contrasted to valid marriages and community property doctrines: When an unequal division of property is made, one of the meretricious spouses receives more than one half and therefore more than if there were a valid marriage. A meretricious or putative, but not a real, spouse may seek compensation on a quasi-contract theory.

If there are three claimants in a putative spouse situation, is each entitled to a third? No cases have so divided the property. Instead, there has been a tendency to give one half to one (preferred) claimant and allow the others (usually two) to divide or fight over the other half. Louisiana, when the husband was not in good faith, gives one half each to the lawful wife and the putative wife. In a decedent's estate this is more practical, but the price of the husband's fault falls upon those who would be entitled to his succession. On the other hand, when the husband acted in good faith, he received the first half, leaving the two wives to receive one half each of the remaining half. This is more practical for situations in which the husband is still living. California, on the other hand, gave the first half to the putative wife in Sousa v. Freitas, 10 Cal.App.3d 660, 89 Cal.Rptr. 485 (1970).

Problems can also arise in connection with the question of what property is subject to division upon discovery of a putative spouse situation. For example, consider H who marries W–1, ineffectively divorces her and marries W–2, who is therefore the putative spouse because H's defective divorce made their marriage bigamous and void. If H is employed, the quasi-marital property for division is his salary. Assuming that H is not separated from W–1 in a way that would make his earnings separate property, W–1 is entitled to her community portion. W–2, if in good faith, is also entitled to her community portion. The principle of not killing the goose-that-lays-golden-eggs suggests that H should be left with something to make continued effort by him worthwhile.

Further complications arise if all three of the parties are employed: Is W–2 entitled to a share of W–1's income? Is W–1 entitled to a share of W–2's income? Is H entitled to a part of each of their earnings? If H earns less than either W–1 or W–2, does his good faith entitle him to a share of each of the earnings? Few cases have dealt with these problems.

2. Alternate Theories of Recovery

There are a number of theories of general law by which a person can seek to obtain or recover property from a person with whom a not-quite-marriage was entered. If there was good faith, (and, to the extent ignorance of any defect continues), these theories are available in addition to the quasi-marital property claim of a putative spouse.

If there was not good faith, one does not, by cohabitation alone, acquire rights in the accumulations of the other, unless one of the following theories can be utilized. As to any party who did not enter into the relationship in a good faith belief that there was no defect, these theories represent the only means of recovery:

a. Contract: Parties may contract between themselves so long as the consideration is not illegal, e.g., unlawful cohabitation. The contract can relate to a period of time or to one, a series or all of the property items acquired during their relationship.

b. Implied Contract: A person who has contributed services in the mutual home may claim compensation for keeping house, caring for their children, serving as hostess etc. The verbal skills of lawyers are strained as they itemize the services performed in a joint abode in an attempt both to show the benefit to the other party and to avoid unlawful consideration. Claims for long periods of service are generally cut short by statutes of limitation, so that only the final two, three, four or six years of service can serve as the basis for a claim. The stumbling block to a claim for the value of household services arises when the court requires that the claimant show the intention of the parties was that compensation be paid for the services. An alternative to the implied contract is a quasi-contract theory which does not require the expression of assent necessary in an implied contract.

c. Partnership: Another means of seeking compensation for services is to allege the existence of a partnership between the cohabitants. Formal agreements which seek a sharing of the collective wealth accumulated during the relationship often use this form. The partnership can be equal or unequal and can duplicate many of the features of community property. Generally, courts uphold such agreements if a business (or a ranch or farm) is involved and there is adequate proof of the partnership agreement. Occasionally, a court embraces approximately the same principles, but calls the combination a "joint venture" rather than a partnership. A pooling of earnings of both parties during the relationship tends to demonstrate the existence, and possibly the terms, of a partnership or joint venture. Although the pooling requirement operates only when both parties have income, rather large discrepancies in the contributions can be equalized by the pooling.

d. Form of Title: None of the community property states authorizes the tenancy by the entirety which is dependent upon the existence of a valid marriage. All of the community property states except Louisiana permit joint tenancies, and all of the states permit tenancies in common (or "in indivision"). Although the form of title is less important in civil law countries and it can be shown to fail to reflect the ownership of property, the form of title is a good protection of the interest of a person in an unmarried relationship. This principle, however, encourages craft and selfishness in a relationship which calls for honesty, openness and selflessness. Possession of non-registered items follows the same principles.

If the parties have contributed equally in money or goods to the purchase of property, either joint tenancy or an equal tenancy in common will accurately reflect their ownership. If, however, the contributions by the parties are unequal, only a tenancy in common in the same proportions as the contributions will prevent a gift or unjust enrichment.

e. Unjust Enrichment: Although courts are reluctant to compensate for goods or services contributed in a voluntary arrangement between parties, overbearing on the part of one person may prod the court into protecting the other. The contribution of money or goods is more likely to invoke response than the contribution of labor. Normally, there must also be a discrepancy between the position of the parties either because of the strength of the position of the person in possession of (or having title to) the property or because of the weakness (mental, educational or psychological) of the other party. The unjust enrichment claim may be rectified by the means of a constructive trust.

f. Constructive Trust: If by fraud upon or mistake of one alleged spouse, the title to property was acquired (either directly or by use of funds belonging to that spouse) by the other alleged spouse, so that unjust enrichment occurs, a constructive trust may be declared to exist by the court. The trust is deemed to be held for the benefit of the "true" owner.

g. Resulting Trust: When one party supplies the purchase price, title is taken in the name of a second party and no gift is intended, a resulting trust arises. The title is held for the benefit of the true owner.

h. General Equitable Principles: The courts of equity have long exercised powers to correct legal imbalances. The increasing number of non-marital relationships produces greater demands upon the systems of law and equity for correction of inequalities. In Marvin v. Marvin, 122 Cal.App.3d 871, 176 Cal.Rptr. 555 (1981), the trial court awarded $104,000 for "rehabilitation" on general equitable principles to the meretricious companion of a financially-successful movie actor; the intermediate court of appeals reversed the trial court, holding that there was no justification for the award in the record. The "rehabilitation" concept was based upon divorce law; the parties had not been married; therefore, divorce principles could not be applied by the court in its discretion.

C. INDIVIDUAL STATES

ARIZONA

Arizona acknowledged the putative spouse doctrine in Stevens v. Anderson, 75 Ariz. 331, 256 P.2d 712 (1953), but does not appear to have applied it at the appellate level. Meretricious spouses have been permitted to seek recovery on theories of partnership or contract, at least for the value of capital contributed or labor improving land.

CALIFORNIA

California generally recognizes the concept of the putative spouse and awards to such a spouse (at least when there are no other spouses) the community share of a true spouse. Although the same term, "putative", is used, California is more niggardly than Louisiana in accepting a putative marriage as the equivalent of a valid, formal marriage. Thus, good faith does not always earn all the rights of a spouse in California. For example, a putative spouse was not allowed the intestate share of a true spouse in one unreversed intermediate appellate court decision.

The share of a putative spouse was called, in older California cases, "quasi-community property" in recognition of the non-existence of a marriage. The term, "quasi-community", has subsequently been used to indicate property which would have been community had the couple been domiciled in California at the time that it was acquired; "quasi-marital" has been used to describe the status which arises in a putative spouse situation.

California includes in its legislation specific provision for division of so-called quasi-marital property in the annulment action. **Calif.Civ.Code § 4452** provides:

Whenever a determination is made that a marriage is void or voidable and the court finds that either party or both parties believed in good faith that the marriage was valid, the court shall declare the party or parties to have the status of a putative spouse, and, if the division of property is in issue, shall divide . . . that property acquired during the

union which would have been community
property or quasi-community property if the
union had not been void or voidable. The
property shall be termed "quasi-marital property". If the court expressly reserves jurisdiction, it may make the property division at a
time subsequent to the judgment. . . .

IDAHO

Idaho provides by statute that marriage arises
upon the combination of consent of the parties and
either a solemnization *or* a mutual assumption of
marital rights, duties or obligations, Idaho Code
§ 32–201. The alternative to solemnization is an
acknowledgment that a "common law" (i.e., non-
ceremonial) marriage is accepted in Idaho.

In addition to the common law validation of
what might otherwise be putative marriages, Idaho
has permitted recovery by a putative wife in a
constructive fraud action against the man to whom
she believed she was married.

LOUISIANA

Louisiana draws a sharp line, based upon the
good faith of the members of a non-marriage: Putative spouses are given almost all of the rights of
a true spouse. On the other hand, the female in
concubinage is allowed neither to retain gifts made
to her nor claim recovery for services on an express or implied contract. A proportionate recov-

ery is allowed in business ventures if they are not founded in concubinage.

Louisiana has codified the putative spouse doctrine which it adopted from the civil law. **La.Stat.Ann.—Civ.Code art.** 117 and 118 provide as follows:

Article 117: The marriage, which has been declared null, produces nevertheless its civil effects as it relates to the parties and their children, if it has been contracted in good faith.

Article 118: If only one of the parties acted in good faith, the marriage produces its civil effects only in his or her favor, and in favor of the children born of the marriage.

No authority was found concerning the subject matter of this chapter in the states of Nevada and New Mexico.

TEXAS

Texas recognizes common law marriages when three elements are established:

1. An agreement to become husband and wife;

2. Cohabitation pursuant to that agreement; and

3. Holding out of each other to the public as husband and wife.

In addition to the common law marriage, Texas recognizes the good faith putative spouse. A putative spouse is entitled to one half of the product of the joint efforts acquired while believing in good faith that a marriage exists, but the courts have not been consistent as to the terminology. Some cases have declared the share to be community while others have stated the shares to be the separate property of each party, i.e., that a putative status will not support a community of property.

Meretricious spouses have not been viewed with favor, but have been allowed to enforce agreements for partnerships or joint ventures when there have been contributions of labor or capital.

WASHINGTON

Washington has allowed claims by meretricious and putative spouses on the basis of an implied partnership when it can be shown that an agreement to operate a business for profit can be implied from the facts and circumstances of the case, Estate of Thornton, 81 Wash.2d 72, 499 P.2d 864 (1972).

The meretricious spouse in Washington is impeded in seeking to prove that the ownership is not identical with the form of title. Creasman v. Boyle, 31 Wash.2d 345, 196 P.2d 835 (1948) stated the presumption, as a matter of law, that the parties intended to dispose of property exactly as they did dispose of it, i.e., the form of title was intended. This presumption combines with the dead man statute to create a heavy burden of proof. *Creasman v. Boyle* has been criticized and distinguished, but remains as a part of Washington jurisprudence.

Washington is in the forefront in applying its divorce and annulment statute directly (not by analogy) to a putative spouse situation. Warden v. Warden, 36 Wash.App. 693, 676 P.2d 1037 (1984) held that the statutory provisions for the disposition of property upon divorce, separation or annulment applied to property "acquired by a man and a woman who have lived together and established a relationship which is tantamount to a marital family except for a legal marriage."

WISCONSIN

In 1922, Wisconsin allowed recovery on an implied contract theory in a putative wife situation. The "widow" believed in good faith that she was validly married while the purported "husband" knew that the marriage was invalid. See Estate of Fox, 178 Wis. 369, 190 N.W. 90 (1922).

In 1987, the Wisconsin Supreme Court held that unmarried cohabitants may raise claims based upon unjust enrichment following the termination of their relationship where one party attempts to retain an unreasonable amount of the property acquired through the efforts of both. See the companion cases (pun noted) of Watts v. Watts, 137 Wis.2d 506, 405 N.W.2d 303 (1987) and Lawlis v. Thompson, 137 Wis.2d 490, 405 N.W.2d 317 (1987).

CHAPTER 12

FEDERAL PROBLEMS

A. FEDERAL SUPREMACY

1. Overview of the Federal System

The United States has a federal system which contemplates a full body of state laws in each state and a superimposed network of federal laws. The federal laws are generally not all encompassing, but envision fuller interpretation by use of the various state laws. For example, bankruptcy is federal law, but state law determines which property is not subject to execution. Most of the fields with which this nutshell is concerned—property interests, creditors' rights, divorce and probate administration—are almost entirely a matter of state law with very little federal intrusion.

Whenever federal law and state law conflict, the federal law (if constitutional) is given priority under the "supremacy clause", Constitution of the United States, article VI, clause 2.

If a state law is considered destructive of the spirit and purpose of federal legislation, the federal legislature or courts can reject local law. For example, Free v. Bland, 369 U.S. 663, 82 S.Ct. 1089, 8 L.Ed.2d 180 (1962) asserted federal supremacy in the form of ownership of United States Series E and F Savings Bonds. The "or" form of ownership established a survivorship between the parties (similar to joint tenancy) as a matter of federal law; Texas provisions purporting to declare the bonds to be community property (without a survivorship feature) were required to yield.

An approach to constitutional interaction of federal and state laws is as follows:

a. Is the federal law constitutional? What power granted to the federal government authorizes the statute? Is the statute prohibited by any constitutional provision? Few federal statutes are deemed to be in excess of the constitutional power to enact laws which are necessary and proper to carry out the enumerated federal powers. There is a remote possibility that a statute might be deemed to attempt to take property without due process and therefore violate the 5th Amendment to the Constitution of the United States.

b. Does the federal statute purport to preempt the field or does it defer to state law? Federal laws may preempt a field, but they do not necessarily do so. There seems to be a growing tendency to read the intention to preempt into federal legislation.

c. Does the state law do major damage to clear and substantial federal interests? Inconvenience to the federal law has been extreme in some situations such as Poe v. Seaborn, 282 U.S. 101, 51 S.Ct. 58, 75 L.Ed. 239 (1930) which required federal taxation laws to accept the legal consequences which flowed from the community property system. Modifications of the federal tax laws including the income tax joint return, gift tax split gift and gift and estate tax marital deductions were necessary in order to eliminate the advantage otherwise available only in community property states. It appears that major damage to federal interests is more easily found in current cases.

2. Federal Preemption

Wissner v. Wissner, 338 U.S. 655, 70 S.Ct. 398, 94 L.Ed. 424 (1950) is the doctrinal ancestor of current cases dealing with the interaction of community property laws and federal programs. In that case, National Service Life Insurance upon the life of a deceased California domiciliary serviceman was not subjected to the community property laws of California. The portions of the federal act which were deemed to show a congressional intention to preempt the field were statements that the insured "shall have the right to designate" and change the beneficiary at all times and that payments of proceeds "shall be exempt from the claims of creditors, and shall not be liable to attachment, levy or seizure by or under any legal or equitable process whatever, either before or after receipt by the beneficiary."

Hisquierdo v. Hisquierdo, 439 U.S. 572, 99 S.Ct. 802, 59 L.Ed.2d 1 (1979); and McCarty v. McCarty, 453 U.S. 210, 101 S.Ct. 2728, 69 L.Ed.2d 589 (1981) are recent decisions of the Supreme Court of the United States concerning the application of state community property laws to federal retirement plans.

Hisquierdo dealt with the federal Railroad Retirement Act (which, in the words of the court, "resembles both a private pension program and a social welfare plan"). The Supreme Court held that the benefits resulting from employment during marriage while domiciled in California by a worker covered by that federal act are not community property subject to division upon divorce.

McCarty held that federal military retirement benefits could not be characterized as community property because the valid federal retirement plan objectives would be injured. The court in that case quoted *Hisquierdo* for tests which appear to be stretched by the application made of them.

Hisquierdo summarized the federal preemption doctrine, as enforced by the supremacy clause, as follows: The subjects of domestic relations and probate administration belong to the laws of the individual states rather than to the laws of the federal government. State laws must do major damage to clear and substantial federal interests before the supremacy clause of the federal constitution will override the state law. The tests applied are whether the asserted right conflicts with the express terms of federal law and whether its consequences sufficiently injure the objectives of the federal program to require nonrecognition. *Hisquierdo* classified as a critical term a prohibition against attachment or anticipation of a specified beneficiary's interest.

The McCarty decision was reversed by a federal statute, the Federal Uniformed Services Former Spouse's Protection Act (with its lisping acronym, FUSFSPA), 10 U.S.C.A. § 1408, which removed the federal preemption found to exist in McCarty and permitted states to apply their own laws in determining whether military retired pay is divisible as a marital asset.

The possibility of federal preemption remains in other areas.

B. STATE CONSTITUTIONAL PROVISIONS

1. Overview: Federal and State Constitutions

Areas in which community property problems tend to arise under the Constitution of the United States include the following:

•Supremacy clause problems which usually concern federal, as opposed to state, legislation or court decisions. These problems have been dealt with in the preceding part of this chapter.

•Fourteenth Amendment problems involving either the "due process" or the "equal protection" provisions of the Constitution of the United States applied to state, as opposed to federal, legislation and decisions.

•Privileges and immunities problems which arise primarily between domiciliaries and non-domiciliaries of the state. See Part C of this chapter, below.

Each of the community property states also has its own constitution. The problem areas under state constitutions are as follows:

● Identical clauses, in which the state constitution contains language identical to the federal constitution. The duplication of the language of the federal due process, equal protection or privileges and immunities clause serves a purpose: A state court decision based upon both the state and federal constitution is less capable of being reversed by the United States Supreme Court because there is an independent state law ground which is the basis of the decision. The federal court therefore could reverse the state court only if the state court decision fell under the supremacy clause.

● Definition of separate property clauses in state constitutions can be the basis of declaring a community property statute unconstitutional on its face or as applied.

● Equal rights, regardless of sex, provisions have been added or proposed in a number of states. New Mexico has added such a provision to its constitution. By application of the equal protection provision of the federal constitution, Suter v. Suter, 97 Idaho 461, 546 P.2d 1169 (1976) declared unconstitutional a sex-based distinction in the provision for the character of property acquired while a couple is separated. Earlier, Reed v. Reed, 404 U.S. 71, 92 S.Ct. 251, 30 L.Ed.2d 225 (1971) had invalidated an Idaho statute which preferred males in appointment of administrators of decedents' estates.

• Retroactive applications of substantive rule changes have been particularly suspect in California statutes and decisions.

2. State Constitutional Definitions of Separate Property

California, Nevada and Texas have state constitutional provisions which define the separate property of the wife or both spouses and, by inference, therefore define community property. The constitutional provisions have served as a limitation upon actions by the legislature in making and amending community property laws.

The remaining community property states do not have comparable authorizations in their constitutions; their statutes are therefore not objectionable because of potential conflict with the constitutional definition.

At one time, the text of the three state constitutional provisions was identical; subsequent amendments have changed the wording of all three constitutions. Even when the wording was identical, however, different interpretations arose.

The major difference in interpretation of the constitutional provision concerns whether the rents, issues and profits received during the marriage from separate property should be community (as they were under the Spanish and Mexican systems of community property) or separate property. Texas held in Arnold v. Leonard, 114 Tex. 535, 273 S.W. 799 (1925) that such income is community; California held that such income was separate in George v. Ransom, 15 Cal. 322, 76 Am.Dec. 490 (1860). Nevada indicated by dictum in Lake v. Lake, 18 Nev. 361, 382–84, 4 P. 711, 722–23 (1884) that it follows the California approach. Both Texas and California held unconstitutional statutes which attempted to transmute rents, issues and profits received during marriage from separate property; their disagreement was in the character which such income should be.

California based its decision upon the "fixed meaning in the common law" of the term "separate property". Ownership in the wife was deemed inconsistent with the husband having the power of management and control of the rents, issues and profits. Texas, on the other hand, viewed the omission of the term "rents, issues and profits" from the definition of separate property as an indication that they were not included within that definition. The Texas court went on to say that the legislature could neither enlarge nor diminish the wife's separate property because of the constitutional definition; therefore, a statute was unconstitutional if it attempted to make separate property out of the rents, issues and profits received during marriage from separate property.

Commentators generally agree that the California court incorrectly used common law analysis in reaching its result and that Texas was true to historical tradition. It is not likely that the California rule will be reversed, however. As we have seen, five of the nine community property states follow the California rule as to such income and only Idaho, Louisiana and Wisconsin follow the Texas example.

3. Retroactive Changes in Community Property Laws

a. Retroactivity: There is an initial ambiguity in defining "retroactivity" in the application of changes in community property laws.

A statute has an effective date which is determined either as a general rule applying to all statutes or to that particular statute by its own terms (for example, "emergency legislation" for an earlier effective date or a deferred effective date to allow adjustments to be made).

The effective date of a statute can be prospective as to some operative event, but retroactive as to some other operative event. For example, a statute which becomes effective after a couple is married is, in a sense, retroactive. A new law might affect titles obtained prior to the enactment date. There might be another operative event—incurring of a debt, making of a will, filing of a divorce action—which occurs before the legislation is passed. The type of legislative change made—presumption as to character, ability to donate, devise or manage or change in the rights of third parties—may dictate what operative event should serve as the line between retroactive and prospective operation.

Constitutional questions are sometimes avoided by presuming, as a rule of construction or property law that retroactive application is not intended. This approach seeks to determine whether the legislature intended the statute to operate prospectively or retroactively. The intention may be express, implied or inferred. If, after considering all pertinent factors, the court is unable to determine the legislative intent, the statute will be presumed to operate prospectively and not retroactively.

b. Vested Rights: Often, the inquiry revolves around a determination of what is a "vested right". Older cases tended to commence their logic with the proposition that the interest being changed was or was not a "right" and was either "vested" or a mere expectancy. Modernly, greater analysis is directed to determining whether the interest being examined is a "right" and how vested it is.

Amendments which seek to change in any manner the vested rights of the spouses between themselves cause an enlargement of the interest of one spouse at the expense of the other spouse. Therefore, as to property already acquired, one spouse is deprived of a potentially vested property right. If the deprivation is without due process or without compensation or denies one party the equal protection of the laws, the legislation has been applied in an unconstitutional manner. It is also remotely possible that the legislation could be treated as impairing the obligation of the marriage contract.

Constitutional objections are sometimes avoided by deciding that the interest is not a vested right. The attribute of the community property law which is beng changed (such as the ability to make gifts of community property without the consent of the other spouse or the management and control of community property) can be declared to be merely an "incident" to a right rather than a right itself. For example, if the rights of the spouses in community property are declared to be equal and vested, but the husband has management and control, then the rhetoric of equality is used to demonstrate that management and control is not a property right. Since it is not a property right, it cannot be vested. In effect, this approach declares that the incident itself is not constitutionally protected.

In some cases, the operative event is clearly defined: The change of domicile to a community property state and the date of death of the decedent are usually clear. Thus, the right of an heir-apparent to inherit is a mere expectancy while the predecessor in interest is living; the right of an heir to take under intestacy rules becomes a vested interest upon the predecessor's death.

c. **Disadvantages of Prospective-Only Application:** If a compelling social policy (such as equality between sexes) is the basis of a change (such as termination of the husband-only management and control), prospective-only application delays implementation and uniformity of the changes.

Another difficulty with prospective-only legislation is that a new class of community property is created with each legislative change. The administrative difficulties increase. Couples, who already had difficulty in tracing and proving contributions when separate and community property were mixed, would have the task of separating two or more different types of community property. The old law applies to property owned at the time of the change; the new law applies to property acquired afterward.

d. California Retroactivity: In California, Spreckels v. Spreckels, 116 Cal. 339, 48 P. 228 (1897), imposed a constitutional prohibition upon retroactive changes. An 1891 legislative amendment which required a wife's consent to gifts by the husband of community property was held constitutionally inapplicable to property acquired before the effective date. The rationale was that each spouse had certain vested rights in community property, and it was beyond the power of the legislature to deprive a spouse of his or her vested right without due process. California developed a considerable body of law in analysis of the question whether amendments to the community property law can be applied retroactively.

The other community property states have tended to find amendments to the community property law to be constitutional, even if applied retroactively. The Pennsylvania Supreme Court, however, held the Pennsylvania Community Property Act of 1947 unconstitutional in Willcox v. Penn Mutual Life Insurance Company, 357 Pa. 581, 55 A.2d 521 (1947) in part because of a violation of the due process clause in attempting retroactive application. The deprivation of property without due process consisted of the attempt by the legislature to define as community property the income and profits from separate property owned before the effective date of the act. The same case held the entire act unconstitutional because of vagueness and uncertainty.

e. Modern Shift in Emphasis: Modernly, the constitutional question shifts from asking "Is there any impairment of a vested right?" to "How much of an impairment of how important a right is made for how important a reason?" The emphasis, for constitutional purposes is upon the "due" of "due process". Is the change under consideration sufficiently necessary to the public welfare to justify the impairment?

In determining the value of the change, the factors to be considered include "the significance of the state interest served by the law, the importance of the retroactive application of the law to the effectuation of that interest, the extent of reliance upon the former law, the legitimacy of that reliance, the extent of actions taken on the basis of that reliance, and the extent to which the retroactive application of the new law would disrupt those actions", Marriage of Bouquet, 16 Cal.3d 583, 592, 128 Cal.Rptr. 427, 432, 546 P.2d 1371, 1376 (1976).

4. Texas Due Course

Texas has interpreted its constitution as imposing limits upon the extent to which a divorce court can assign the separate real property of one spouse to the other spouse upon divorce. In Eggemeyer v. Eggemeyer, 554 S.W.2d 137 (Tex.1977), the Texas Supreme Court prohibited such a transfer on the basis that it was contrary to two constitutional provisions—the definition of a wife's separate property in Texas Constitution, Article XVI, § 15 and to the "due course" provision of Texas Constitution, Article I, § 19. The "due course" provision is almost identical to the "due process" provisions of the federal and other state constitutions. The due course provision was deemed to require not only procedural, but also substantive, due course.

The majority opinion in *Eggemeyer* is revolutionary in applying the due course ("due process" in other jurisdictions) substantive provisions to prevent the taking of property upon divorce from one spouse and awarding it to the other spouse. The language of that opinion applies as much to personal property as to real property and as much to one half of the community as to the separate property of each spouse.

The *Eggemeyer* approach could be applied to declare unconstitutional most provisions for the division of property upon divorce, since such provisions tend to divide property "equitably" between the parties to the marriage without rigid conformity to previous ownership.

Eggemeyer could be viewed as an attempt to create consistency between divorce and other areas where community property is divided. The probate court is required to divide community property equally and is not authorized (except in homesteads and family allowances) to assign the property of one spouse to the other spouse. Creditors generally cannot reach more than the debtor's interest, in the absence of fraud. Nevertheless, divorce courts have traditionally divided property or assigned property nominally owned by one party to the other party.

It does not appear, however, that *Eggemeyer* will be so applied or expanded. Even in Texas, the due course argument of the majority opinion has been largely ignored. See pages 327–328.

C. CONFLICT OF LAWS

1. Choice of Law

The federal system permits diversity so that each state can decide whether it will have a community property system and what attributes that community property system will have. A price of the federal system is that the laws of various states can "conflict", i.e., reach opposing conclusions depending upon which system of law is chosen. To resolve conflicts of laws, courts seek to use one or more contacts; the method of "choice of law" is often to seek the jurisdiction with the most significant contacts with the subject matter of the litigation. Among the significant contacts are the forum, domicile, location of realty and place where a tort occurred.

a. Forum: The "forum" is the jurisdiction which contains the court in which a lawsuit is filed.

A state could declare that it intends to apply its own law to all situations regardless of the domicile and location of the parties and persons who come before it. In addition to constitutional and jurisdictional problems, this would make the applicable law almost entirely the choice of the plaintiff, since the choice of forum is made by the plaintiff.

The easiest law for the forum court to apply is its own law. In many instances, a choice of law problem is ignored because the existence of a contradictory system is not called to the attention of the court. For example, a couple who possess community property are divorced in a non-community property state; the divorce court might ignore community property problems because the parties and their attorneys fail to point out the problems. Similarly, the presumption that the law of another jurisdiction is the same as the law of the forum puts the burden of proving the different law upon the person who asserts its existence.

The total law of the forum includes both its internal law and choice of law provisions; therefore it is not precise to say that the forum court is applying its own law *or* the law of another state. The internal law of another state may be applied through the choice of laws law of the forum.

b. Domicile: Domicile is the legal status of citizenship and residency which results from a combination of physical presence and the intention to remain (or not to leave). Each person has one domicile at a time, but the domicile can be changed. The traditional doctrine for a married couple was that the husband's domicile is the domicile of the married couple, unless the wife was justified in establishing a separate domicile for herself. Thus, generally, "their" domicile was "his" domicile.

Domicile is the most important criterion in determining the application of community property law:

• The validity of the marriage itself is tested by the law of the place where it is executed, but the domicile of the parties may nevertheless declare the marriage invalid if the marriage is contrary to a strong policy of the domicile.

• Definitions of community property laws are based upon the domicile of the parties at the time that property is acquired.

• If the community is terminated by divorce, the domicile of the parties is the proper jurisdiction for the divorce action.

• If the community is terminated by death, the domicile of the decedent is the proper jurisdiction as to *personalty* to administer the probate estate, to judge the validity and effect of any will and to apply its intestacy rules.

• Jurisdiction over a defendant is usually most easily obtained at the defendant's domicile. Thus, the defendant's domicile is frequently the forum also.

c. **Situs:** Realty, the classic immovable, is generally governed by the law of its location ("situs" for those who prefer a Latin flavor to their law English). Thus, ancillary probate administrations are necessary in the estate of a decedent who dies owning property in states other than the domiciliary state. The choice of laws law of the situs state, like the choice of laws law of the forum, may look to the domiciliary state law in order to determine the character of property.

d. **Place Where Tort Committed:** The choice of law rule for torts generally looks to the law at the place where the tort was committed, the lex loci delicti. Thus, if community property state domiciliaries are tortiously injured in a non-community property state, the law of the place of the tort appears to be the proper law to apply. A number of conflicts of laws could arise. For example, if the community property domiciliary rules make the non-injured spouse a necessary party to the tort action and the non-community property site of the accident requires only the injured spouse, is the non-injured spouse a necessary party to the action?

2. Immigration to a Community Property State

a. Multistate Problems: There are a number of ways in which the laws of more than one state may be involved in deciding which law to apply to determine the character of property: Married couples move to, from or between community property states, own property or become involved in a tort in a state other than the state of domicile.

There is seldom community property unless and until a married couple has both married and become domiciled in a community property state. Just as there is no community prior to marriage, there is no community without domicile. Minor exceptions do exist: A wedding gift to a couple about to be married can be community property; a couple can marry with the plan to establish a new domicile in a community property state.

b. The Population Shift: The "sun belt" states of the United States have a climate which appears to be more attractive than colder portions of the United States. Many of the sun belt states (Arizona, California, Louisiana, Nevada, New Mexico and Texas) are community property states. The flow of married couples into community property states is therefore not an isolated phenomenon. The number of persons who retire and immigrate to Arizona, California or New Mexico is considerable.

Upon the death of the principal wage earner (typically the husband) of a married couple, the different approaches of community and non-community property states can leave a gap in coverage into which the immigrant surviving spouse falls: Separate property states use statutory substitutes for dower; these dower substitutes are based upon property owned by a domiciliary decedent at death (or disposed of in a manner which is deemed to be a will-substitute). Community property states, on the other hand, focus upon the accumulation of property during the marital period and while domiciled in the community property state. Thus, a married couple from a separate property state who immigrate to a community property state have neither the common law dower substitute (because the decedent was not domiciled in the separate property state at the time of death) nor community property (because they were not domiciled in the community property state at the time that the property was accumulated).

c. **Privileges and Immunities Problems:** The first attempt by California to treat immigrants the same as natives was held unconstitutional. In Estate of Thornton, 1 Cal.2d 1, 33 P.2d 1 (1934), a California statute attempted to include within the definition of community property any property acquired by couples while married even though not domiciled in California. The event causing the change of character of the property from what would have generally been separate property to community property was the entry by the couple into California and (probably) the change of domicile to California. The majority of the California Supreme Court held that, in addition to being a deprivation of property without due process, the provision denied immigrants the privileges and immunities of California domiciliaries.

d. Quasi-Community Property: In response to the immigrant problem while attempting to avoid the unconstitutionality fate of the *Thornton* case, California enacted a statute defining quasi-community property. Wisconsin and UMPA use the concept as a major transitional provision for domiciliaries who were married and owned property on the effective date of the community property law. Quasi-community property, although carved from separate property, was treated as if it were community property. The technique was applied first to probate situations and then to divorce situations.

Wisconsin uses the concept of "deferred marital property" (which is known as "property which would have been marital property if acquired after the determination date" in UMPA) for its form of quasi-community property in death situation. UMPA applies its provision at both death and divorce.

Quasi-community property statutes apply to divorce actions in Arizona, California and Texas and to probate administrations in California, Idaho and Wisconsin. The text of some of these statutes is set out on pages 319, 322, 350–351 and 352–353.

In death situations, the quasi-community property concept is applied only to the decedent's property which would have been community property. The surviving spouse's property is not treated as quasi-community property.

Addison v. Addison, 62 Cal.2d 558, 43 Cal.Rptr. 97, 399 P.2d 897 (1965) upheld the application of California's quasi-community property statute to the divorce situation. The *Thornton* case was distinguished on the ground that the statute with which it dealt attempted to alter property rights because and by virtue of the married couple entering California, while the new law applied after the parties both established a California domicile and filed for divorce.

3. Emigration from Community Property States

A change of domicile does not change the character (community or separate) of property previously acquired by a married couple. While some of the community property states have attempted to adjust for the immigrants from separate property states, practically never is a similar adjustment made by the separate property states to accommodate community property immigrants.

Community property remains community property when a married couple changes its domicile to a separate property state. The problem of adapting a separate property system to community property is similar to converting meters into inches without using fractions or decimals: The result is only approximate. Thus, the typical, and most correct, separate property state treatment of existing community property is to consider it as a form of the common law tenancy in common, giving equal shares to each party. This eliminates some of the attributes of community property such as the management and control, just as whole number usage eliminates fractions or decimals in a metric conversion.

The "Uniform Disposition of Community Property Rights at Death Act" has been enacted by Colorado, Hawaii, Kentucky, Michigan and Oregon. At the individual lawyer level, there is a danger that the lawyer will ignore community property aspects of a case. An attorney who does not pursue zealously the client's right to community property may face both professional discipline and malpractice claims.

The community property states have enough differences between themselves that it may be as necessary to distinguish the state of origin of the community property (e.g., Texas as opposed to California community property) as it is necessary to distinguish acquisition periods (e.g., "pre-1927" v. "post-1927" California community property) when statutes or other law changes apply only prospectively.[1]

1. Bet you thought that there were no footnotes in this nutshell!*

* There's even a footnote to the footnote!

*

INDEX

References are to Pages

HUMOR

IDAHO

†